James Gilbert Riggs.

A STUDY OF
PROSE FICTION

BY

BLISS PERRY

BOSTON AND NEW YORK
HOUGHTON, MIFFLIN AND COMPANY
The Riverside Press, Cambridge
1903

To

THE PRINCETON MEN WHO USED TO LISTEN
AMIABLY TO THESE DISCOURSES

PREFACE

THE aim of this little book is to discuss the outlines of the art of fiction. In writing it I have followed more or less closely the notes prepared, a few years ago, for a course of lectures on Prose Fiction at Princeton University. These lectures were repeated with several classes, and many teachers who have had occasion to examine the syllabus of the lectures, and the topical work assigned in connection with them, have asked me to print a book that would be adapted to effective use in the classroom. I have confidence in the general method of fiction study which is here outlined, although the kindly coöperation of my former pupils may have then given the study a certain ardor which the book will fail to impart.

It happened that the author wrote fiction, after a fashion, before attempting to lecture upon it, and he is now conscious that the academic point of view has in turn been modified by the impressions gained during his editorship of "The Atlantic Monthly." Whether the professional examination of many thousands of manuscript stories is calculated to exalt one's standards of the art of fiction may possibly be questioned.　But this editorial experience, supplementing the other methods of approach to the subject, may be thought to contribute something of practical value to the present study of the novelist's work.　It is as if an enthusiast for art, after serving first as painter's apprentice and then as lecturer on painting, had been forced to act as hanging committee for an exhibition, and now, with a zeal for his subject which survives every disillusionment, were to mount a chair in the picture gallery and preach to all comers!　For it is not to be denied that there is more or less sermonizing in this book.　The homiletic habit lurks deep in the New Englander as in the Scotchman, and many a Yankee who can claim few other

points of resemblance to Robert Louis Stevenson is like him at least in this, that he
" would rise from the dead to preach."

It should be stated distinctly that the present volume makes no attempt to trace the
history of the English novel. That task has
been adequately performed by several excellent handbooks, which are easily accessible.
Most of my illustrations of the various aspects
of the art in question are drawn, however,
from English and American stories. While
I have not overlooked, I trust, the work of
the more significant contemporary writers, I
have made no attempt to decorate these
pages with references to the " novel of the
year." On the contrary, wherever an allusion to the writings of masters like Scott and
Thackeray and Hawthorne would serve the
purpose, I have given myself the pleasure of
such illustration, knowing that their books
will continue to be read long after the novels
of the year have faded out of memory.

It is to be hoped that this discussion of
the pleasant art of story-writing will not

weigh too heavily upon the reader's conscience. If he likes, he may avoid the Appendix. But the "painful" reader, who is
after all the pride of the classroom and the literary club, and who deserves one of the best
seats by the family library-table, will, I hope,
find in the Appendix much that will prove
interesting and useful. The review questions
upon Scott's "Ivanhoe" are reprinted there
with the courteous permission of Messrs. Longmans, Green & Company, the publishers of
my annotated edition of that novel. A portion of the opening chapter on The Study of
Fiction has already appeared in print in the
eleventh volume of the Proceedings of the
Modern Language Association of America.
The chapter on The Short Story was printed
in "The Atlantic" for August, 1902.

BLISS PERRY.

CAMBRIDGE, 1902.

CONTENTS

A STUDY OF PROSE FICTION

CHAPTER I

THE STUDY OF FICTION

"There are few ways in which people can be better employed than in reading a good novel. (I do not say that they should do nothing else.)" BENJAMIN JOWETT, *Life and Letters.*

IN beginning any study, it is well to take a preliminary survey of the field, and to note the general character of the questions that are likely to arise as one advances. When the chosen field of study is one of the arts, it is obvious that the student's curiosity may be aroused by various aspects of the art under consideration. He may find himself interested primarily in the artist, or chiefly attracted by the work of art itself, or concerned with the attitude of the public which takes pleasure in that particular form of art. In the study of prose fiction, for instance, one person may

Nature of the problems involved.

discover that his chief curiosity is about certain novelists who have been eminent practi-
tioners in their profession. Another person
may care little for the personal traits of writers of fiction, but be greatly interested in
novels; and a third may find much to reward
his endeavor in noting the various characteristics of the fiction-reading public. The general nature of the problems arising in the
study of fiction is thus indicated, sufficiently
for our present purpose, in saying that they
deal with literary artists, with specific works
of art, and with the public, great or small,
to which the art of fiction makes a particular
appeal.

It confers a certain dignity upon
the study of fiction to remember
how universal is the human appe-
tite for fiction of some sort. In one of the
most delightful of Thackeray's " Roundabout
Papers," " On a Lazy Idle Boy " who leaned
on the parapet of the old bridge at Chur,
quite lost in a novel, Thackeray comments
upon " the appetite for novels extending to
the end of the world ; far away in the frozen
deep, the sailors reading them to one another
during the endless night; far away under

The universal
appetite for
fiction.

the Syrian stars, the solemn sheikhs and eld-
ers hearkening to the poet as he recites his
tales; far away in the Indian camps, where
the soldiers listen to ———'s tales or ———'s,
after the hot day's march; far away in little
Chur yonder, where the lazy boy pores over
the fond volume, and drinks it in with all his
eyes; — the demand being what we know it
is, the merchant must supply it, as he will
supply saddles and pale ale for Bombay or
Calcutta." The universality of the liking
for fiction is equaled only by the variety of
tastes that are gratified by fiction reading.
Some of the most intellectual men have confessed their preference for the most unintel-
lectual stories, and very ignorant and stupid
people are constantly — and in a most praiseworthy fashion! — endeavoring to assimilate
the lofty thought and profound emotion with
which the great masterpieces of fiction are
charged. Tastes are altered as we pass from
youth to middle age and old age; they
change with every vital experience; they
grow delicate or coarse in accordance with
the meat upon which they are fed. But the
desire for " the story " outlasts childhood and
savagery. It is a part of the spiritual hun-

ger of the most highly developed individuals
and races; and it is impossible to foresee the
time when fiction shall cease to be an important part of the world's literary production.
" The demand being what we know it is, the
merchant must supply it."

Variety of
motives for
fiction
reading.
Not only is this desire for fiction
an appetite common to humankind,
but it is also to be noted that the
particular motives which lead persons to read
books of fiction are strangely varied. Many
people like to read novels having to do with
subjects in which they already have some
special interest. As boys with a turn for
history will easily learn to read Scott, or
a scientifically minded youngster will take
naturally to Jules Verne, so an adult's fondness for adventure, travel, the study of
manners, for sociology, theology, or ethics
will often prescribe the sort of novels he will
read. There are other people who select
stories that will carry them as far as possible
from their ordinary pursuits and habits of
thought. Fiction of this character, chosen
for its power to afford distraction or even
dissipation to an overwrought mind, unquestionably serves a useful purpose, though it

need scarcely be said that an exclusive reliance upon trivial and sensational stories as furnishing mental relaxation is an indication of poverty of intellectual resources. From the point of view of the boy who sells novels on the train, "a good book" is the book that most easily absorbs the attention of the traveler, and there is much to be said for the train-boy's standard of criticism. Again, many of our choices, in the selection of fiction, turn upon the more or less unconscious desire to enlarge the range of our experience. Like Pomona in "Rudder Grange," we can first wash the dishes and then follow the adventures of the English aristocracy; we can journey to the California of 1849 with Bret Harte, to a hill camp in India with Mr. Kipling, to Paris or the French provinces with Balzac. We can thus live vicariously the sort of life we might have lived if we had been differently circumstanced. We seek in novels a compensation for the dullness and monotony of actual life, or contrariwise, finding actuality too strenuous and stimulating, we take refuge in the quiet sanctuary opened to us by art. I recall a mining expert who had just come East, after a horse-

back journey of several thousand miles
through the most inaccessible and dangerous
mining camps of the Rocky Mountains.   He
wanted something to read, and his friend, a
professor of chemistry, whose life was passed
in his laboratory and lodgings, recommended
to him a thrilling tale by Ouida, in which
he himself had been reveling.   But the
mining expert declared the book too exciting,
and settled down for a whole day's tranquil
happiness with Mrs. Gaskell's " Cranford " !
Smallest of all the classes of fiction readers,
and yet the most thoroughly appreciative of
excellence, is that group who approach a
novel without any preoccupation, who ask
only that it shall be a beautiful and noble
work of art.   Guy de Maupassant has expressed this thought in a frequently quoted
passage from the preface to " Pierre et Jean."
Yet it can scarcely be read too often.   " The
public is composed of numerous groups who
say to us [novelists] : ' Console me, amuse
me, — make me sad, — make me sentimental,
— make me dream, — make me laugh, —
make me tremble, — make me weep, — make
me think.'   But there are some chosen spirits who demand of the artist : ' Make for

me something *fine*, in the form which suits you best, following your own temperament.' "

Remembering this infinite variety of motive in choosing works of fiction, it becomes easier to avoid dogmatism. It is quite impossible to draw up a list of " the best novels " for any particular person. The variations in human nature and æsthetic discipline are too great. And yet criticism has a function here which should not be overlooked. It should be able to pronounce upon the objective qualities of any book : to say what it contains, and to pass judgment upon the excellence of the form in which those contents are clothed. When we repeat the old maxim, " De gustibus non disputandum est," we should not stretch the maxim beyond the very obvious truth which it expresses. Tastes are purely subjective matters, and arguments about them, though interesting enough, are futile except as evidences of personal temperament and training. But the objects of taste, nevertheless, have certain positive qualities which may profitably be analyzed and discussed. One reader may prefer Trollope's " Framley Parsonage " to Hawthorne's " Scarlet Letter,"

Dogmatism to be avoided.

and another reader's preference be precisely
the reverse. It may be useless to discuss
these preferences, but surely criticism can
pronounce upon the characteristics of the two
books.   It can show their radical difference in structure and style. It can point out
the excellences and limitations of each of
the two stories.   Discussions of this sort are
often illuminating and valuable; they are
not to be dismissed as the expression of mere
personal whim.   A man may prefer chocolate
to coffee as his breakfast beverage ; he knows
which he likes best, and it may not be worth
while to dispute with him about his taste.
But his physician, knowing the chemical pro-
perties of the two beverages and their relative effect upon the patient's digestive system, can probably tell him which drink is
the more nourishing or stimulating for him.
The physician's explanation of the positive
qualities of chocolate and coffee may be compared to the judgment of a competent critic
upon the constituent elements of a book.
After the physician has delivered his opinion,
it is still possible for his patient to say, " But
I like coffee best and shall continue to drink
it ; " and after the critics have declared a

book to be commonplace or degrading it may
be read even more than before. If the physician and the critic are blessed with a philosophical disposition they will now shrug
their shoulders and murmur, " De gustibus
non disputandum est." They have done
their part, and further discussion is useless.

We touch here upon another of *The study
of fiction
as related
to the en-
joyment of
it.*
the fundamental differences between fiction readers. There are
lovers of all the arts who wish to
keep their enjoyment of a beautiful object
quite separate from an analysis of the elements that enter into that enjoyment, who
prefer to be ignorant of the technical means
by which the pleasurable end is secured.
There are connoisseurs of music and painting
who profess to be guided by their personal
impressions of the sonata or the landscape
piece, without reference to any knowledge of
the mathematics of music or of the laws of
perspective. A good deal may be said for
this happy impressionistic fashion of gathering pleasure, and it has no stouter adherents
than among novel readers. A very large
proportion of the readers of a story take no
interest whatever in the technical side of the

novelist's craft; they are interested simply
in the results. They may possibly listen
while Stevenson or Mr. Henry James discourses upon the difficulties and triumphs of
the novelist's art, but they are chiefly concerned with the practical quest for another
good story. The Anglo-Saxon, particularly,
is not inclined to treat æsthetic questions
with much concern. He doubts whether the
serious amateur study of an art increases
one's enjoyment of that art. It is precisely
here that this book may part company with
some readers who have cared to follow its
opening pages.

For our discussion will proceed upon the
tacit assumption that the study of fiction
does increase one's enjoyment of it; that
as the traveler who has studied architecture most carefully will get the most pleasure out of a cathedral, so the thorough
student of literary art will receive most enjoyment from the masterpieces which that
art has produced. Upon the practical application of this theory of the relation of
technical knowledge to enjoyment, some common sense must of course be exercised. The
novel which survives the test of searching

analysis, of classroom dissection, — if you like, — and gives any pleasure at the last, must be a good novel to begin with. If the doll is stuffed with sawdust, it is better not to poke into its insides. But if the novel be the work of a master — if it be " Henry Esmond " or " Adam Bede " or " Ivanhoe " — there need be no fear of lessening the student's pleasure. He will soon learn to discover the conventional tricks, the commonplace devices of the hack-writer; the books of the great writers will seem no whit less wonderful than before. Knowledge and feeling must indeed be kept in their due relations. To know is good. To feel is better, when it is a question of appropriating the form and meaning of a work of art. Analysis must be subordinated to synthesis; the details must be forgotten in the cumulative impression given by the work as a whole. Yet the synthetic, comprehensive, sympathetic view of a masterpiece of fiction is not so likely to reveal itself to the casual reader as it is to the careful student of the means by which the supreme ends of literature are attained.

Methods of fiction study. What method of fiction study is it wisest to follow? In school and college, much will depend upon the size and proficiency of the classes, the extent to which the lecture system is adopted, the library facilities, the temperament and the training of the individual teacher. The independent student, or the member of a reading circle or club, must be governed more or less by special circumstances. And yet there are certain general modes of study between which a choice should be made at the outset.

Historical. For instance, the English novel may be treated historically. Its origins and the main tendencies of its development are not difficult to trace. One may plan a course of fiction reading which shall follow the sequence of history. He will find excellent handbooks to guide him. The advantages of following the historical method in studying any phase of a national literature are too obvious to be denied, and yet, as far as fiction is concerned, this method is not without its drawbacks. Very few libraries contain much material of an earlier date than the middle of the eighteenth century, or represent more than a handful of novelists from that time to the generation of Scott. The minor fiction of any epoch is often more truly representative than the work of its greater names. But even were the material at hand, the temptation in dealing with half forgotten or wholly forgotten authors is to content one's self with secondhand opinions about them, and it is precisely this indolent fashion of passing along a received opinion which has done much to bring the study of English literature into disrepute. The reader must get the book into his hand if he is to receive much benefit from the opinion of the critic or historian. Of course every student of English fiction ought to know something of the lines of its progress in the past — say as much as the little books of Professor Raleigh [1] or Professor Cross [2] will help him to acquire — but it is doubtful whether anything more than the mastery of such a general sketch can successfully be attempted

[1] *The English Novel.* By Walter Raleigh. New York : Charles Scribner's Sons, 1894.
[2] *The Development of the English Novel.* By Wilbur L. Cross. New York : The Macmillan Company, 1899.

under ordinary conditions. In the case of advanced students who have proper library facilities, the investigation of the historical development of fiction is too interesting to be likely to be neglected.

Criticism of contemporary fiction. Again, the criticism of contemporary fiction has been found to be attractive and stimulating, both in the academic class-room and the literary club. Such a course of study traverses the immense field of latter-day fiction, and selects for analysis and judgment striking examples of this and that literary tendency. From the standpoint of pedagogy, much may be said for this method. It requires little or no special preparation on the part of the student; he may be assumed to have a certain interest in the book of the hour. It puts the teacher on a level with the class, forcing him to see more truly and to express himself more clearly than they, upon books that have not yet won a permanent place in literature, and consequently have not become the object of conventional and hackneyed criticism. Nevertheless the method has its dangers. It may tempt the teacher to popularize in the bad sense, to try to say

clever things about the novel which happens
to be the latest fashion, to recognize, in
making a choice among current fiction, the
market valuation and thus to impress the
market-value standard upon the very persons who most need to be taught the falli-
bility of that standard. It certainly tempts
the student to criticise — that is, to perform
the most delicate of mental operations — before he is in possession of any canons of
criticism. It is always easy to mistake literary gossip for literary culture, and a course
of reading which gives prominence to contemporary books and living authors is likely
to result in a loss of true literary perspective. Good style did not begin with Stevenson, and good plots are much older than Dr.
Conan Doyle.

While every method has no doubt *The study of prose fiction as an art.*
its own advantages and disadvan-
tages, the method least open to
objection is that which, assuming that prose
fiction is an art, devotes itself to the exposition of the principles of that art. It takes
for granted that there is a " body of doctrine " concerning fiction, as there is concerning painting or architecture or music,

and that the artistic principles involved are no more incapable of formulation than are the laws of the art of poetry, as expressed in treatises upon Poetics from Aristotle's day to our own. They are indeed largely the same principles, as might be expected in the case of two sister arts. A student cannot begin the study of prose fiction more profitably than by endeavoring to grasp the relations between this art and the art of narrative poetry. Quite aside from the task of tracing historically the process by which the prose romance grew out of the epic, there are rich fields for investigation in connection with such topics as the material common to the two arts, the qualities shared by the novelist and poet, and the similarity of much of their craftsmanship in the sphere of formal expression. This suggests a study of their differences in the selection of material, their varying attitude toward their material, and the diverging requirements of effective expression in the two media of prose and verse. Then the affiliations of fiction with the drama must be made clear, through a study of such questions as the general similarity in construction of the novel and the play, and

the advantages and disadvantages of sub-
stituting the novelist's indirect methods of
narration and description for the direct representation of action by means of the stage.
Here the student may work out, in a comparatively new territory, the familiar principle of Lessing, and assure himself that the
real field of the novelist is forever separated
from that of the dramatist by the nature of
the artistic media which the two men em-
ploy.   The student may well be asked, also,
to estimate the bearing upon fiction of the
modern scientific movement, remembering
Lanier's remark about the novel being the
meeting ground of poetry and science, and
endeavoring to ascertain whether upon the
whole fiction has gained or lost by its contact
with the scientific spirit.   After such a clearing of the ground as has been suggested, it
is natural to pass to a detailed study of the
content of fiction, a study, that is, of character, plot, and setting, in themselves and as
interrelated.   Selecting for classroom material some novels that have stood the test of
time, methods of character delineation must
be observed; stationary and developing characters compared; the relation of main and

subordinate characters noted. The nature
of tragic and comic collisions must be analyzed ; the infinitely varied ways of tangling
and untangling the skein of plot reduced to
some classification that can be grasped by
the student. The circumstances or events
enveloping the action of the story — whether
it be set in some focal point of history or
merely keyed to a quiet landscape — must
be accurately perceived. Setting and plot
and character, whether analyzed separately
or grasped in their artistic relations to one
another, must further be discussed in connection with the personality of the fiction-
writer. Yet pupils should be taught to look
for the mark of personality, not in gossip
about a novelist's hour of rising and favorite
breakfast and favorite books, but rather in
connection with the creative processes upon
which the stamp of personality is really set.
The outward facts of an author's life, the
traits of his character, the history of his
opinions are significant to us only in so
far as they have moulded his imagination.
Finally, we must study the way in which
differences in the nature of material and differences in personality have resulted in the

development of the varying forms of fiction.
These forms are capable of infinite modification.   Each writer's thoughts, dreams, convictions, must be put into words.   His mastery of expression is the final element that
determines his rank as an artist, and there
is thus suggested to the student an endlessly
curious investigation of matters of technique
and style.

After some such equipment as is here
briefly indicated, the student may profitably
pass to the criticism of contemporary authors, if he pleases, or to some phase of the
history of the novel.   No one need depre-
ciate either of those methods of study, but
nevertheless the most important thing to be
learned about fiction at the outset is the
knowledge of what fiction normally is; a
sense of what it can do and what it cannot
do ; a recognition of the fact that in the
most insignificant short story may be seen
the play of laws as old as art itself ; that
Aristotle and Lessing, in short, wrote with
one eye on Mr. Kipling and Mr. Hardy.

As in the case of every other
fine art, the student of prose fic- Content
tion finds himself occupied with and form
in fiction.

questions concerning content and form, and
their relations to each other.   Back of every
art product there is a conception, vaguely or
definitely present in the artist's mind.   Upon
the character of this conception or content
depends the significance of the work of art;
its formal beauty depends upon the artist's
skill to express his thought or feeling in the
terms of the particular medium which he has
chosen.   Content and form are therefore
most intimately related in the artist's personality.   He can express nothing through
the concrete medium of his particular art —
whether it be a pigment or clay or a harmony of musical sounds or a succession of
words — unless it has first passed through
the lens of his own nature.   It is always
difficult, and in a certain sense unnatural, to
make a sharp separation between the elements of content and of form.   The artist
himself rarely attempts it.   He "thinks in
color" or feels in terms of musical sound.
The finer the work of art, the more indis-
solubly are the elements fused through the
personality of the artist.   And yet it is often
of the greatest value to the student to attempt this separate analysis, — to distinguish

what has gone into the work of art from the external form in which it is clothed, — and in prose fiction form and content are more easily separable than in poetry or music or even painting.

No one will deny the importance *The subject-* of the subject-matter with which *matter of* prose fiction deals. Its field is hu- *fiction.* man life itself ; the experience of the race, under countless conditions of existence. Fiction-writers have put into their stories a mass of observations, thoughts, and feelings concerning humankind. The significance of these records depends largely upon the sincerity, the truthfulness, of the writers. Some of them have been chiefly occupied with rendering the external truth of fact. Others, like the great romancers, have cared only for the higher truth which is revealed to and conveyed by the imagination. But however varied the scope of the fiction-writer's activity, they all have something to say about life. A chapter of first-rate fiction arrests the attention at every turn. It provokes interest, awakens curiosity, challenges comparison with one's own experience, and even while it is energizing the imagination, concentrates it. Poetry touches us at a higher level, it is true, provided it touches us at all. Poetry is a finer art than fiction, but for that very reason there are many readers who cannot come under the domination of poetry. They have no natural ear for its music, and at twenty or twenty-two they find themselves or think themselves too old to learn the notes. The appeal of prose fiction is more universal: it captivates the man who cares mainly for facts, as well as the girl whose heart is set on fancies. Its scope is so vast, it is so varied in its different provinces, its potency to attract and to impress is so indubitable, that the reader who makes no response to it, whose powers may not be developed by means of it, must be insufferably dull. Furthermore, prose fiction is, even more than music, the great modern art. By means of it we are brought into contact with modern ideas, with the tumultuous, insistent life of the present. And this, for good or evil, is our life; the life which we must somehow live, and about which we are conscious of an unappeasable curiosity.

Yet the educational value of fiction consists not merely in its content, in the significance of the
ideas which it conveys to the mind, but also
to a considerable extent in the form in which
those ideas are clothed. In the best fiction
that form is singularly perfect. The study
of expression as such, the cultivation of the
feeling for style, is inseparably associated
with a well selected course in fiction. The
special treatises in narration and description,
for instance, which many teachers of rhetoric are now using, draw their readiest and
aptest illustrations from the novelists. The
range of expression, the force and beauty
with which ideas are uttered by the masters
of English fiction, is unquestionable. It is
hard to see how any one can come away
from a close study of Thackeray or Hawthorne without a new appreciation of form,
a standard of workmanship; without learning once for all that imagination and passion may coëxist with a sense of proportion,
with purity of feeling, with artistic reserve.
These last are what we agree to call the
classic qualities. We send boys to Greek
and Latin literature in the hope that they

*The ques-
tion of
form.*

will catch something of their secret, but if
boys cannot or will not read Greek and
Latin, they need not necessarily be unfamiliar with works composed in the classic
spirit. In a time like ours, when everybody
writes " well enough," and few try to write
perfectly, it is no small thing that students
may be taught through fiction to perceive
the presence of style, the stamp of distinction. That sound Latinist and accomplished
musician, Henry Nettleship, once wrote to a
friend a passage about Wagner which is not
without its bearing upon literature. " Wagner tries to make music do what it cannot
do without degrading itself — namely, paint
out in very loud colors certain definite feelings as they arise before the composer. The
older musicians seem to me to aim rather at
suggesting feeling than at actually exhibiting it, as it were, in the flesh. I think much
of Wagner would vitiate my taste, *but perhaps my head is too full of the older music*
to take in strains to which my nerves are not
attuned." Professor Nettleship may have
been right or wrong about Wagner, but is
there a better service which the teacher of
fiction can render a pupil, or the solitary

student of literature perform for himself, than to make his head so full of the noble cadences of Scott and Thackeray, Eliot and Hawthorne, that there shall be no room there for what has been succinctly described as " the neurotic, the erotic, and the Tommy-rotic," and all the other contemporary varieties of meretricious and ignoble art ?

No one need seek in any novel an abstract and theoretical perfection. A novel universally significant in content and impeccable in form has never been produced. Some of the most stimulating and widely influential novels have been slovenly written; and some of the most charmingly composed stories have been barren of ethical and human significance. But it is the province of æsthetic criticism, none the less, to determine the extent to which these two elements enter into the novel under discussion, to make clear, if possible, the relation of the form or content of any work of fiction to the mind of the artist who produced it. If " there is nothing in the work of art except what some man has put there," it is interesting to the critic to understand not only what intention the

The novel as a field for æsthetic criticism.

man has put into his work but the form in
which that conception has been expressed.
To such criticism the novel presents a field
no less attractive than that of the other fine
arts.   The æsthetic critic regards prose criticism as one species of literary art.   He is
primarily interested in novels, not for the
useful information they may contain or the
ethical guidance they may furnish, but for
the æsthetic pleasure they impart.   His study
of fiction may lead him into history and biography, into grammar and rhetoric, perhaps
into ethics and sociology, but what he is
chiefly endeavoring to do is to ascertain
the laws that govern the artistic expression
of the phenomena of human life by means of
prose narration or description, as compared
with its expression through the media employed by the other arts.   Assuming, as we
have already said, that prose fiction is an art,
he proceeds to study its principles.   He tries
to formulate the group of facts and laws
which constitute the "body of doctrine"
concerning fiction.

The value of such a study lies
chiefy in the pleasure it yields, the
discipline it affords, to the student

The value
of this
study.

himself. The vast fiction-reading public is skeptical about the very existence of standards of judgment. "It is not that there is so little taste nowadays," said some one the other day, " there is so much taste, — most of it bad." But it is the scholar's business to take the world as he finds it and to make it a trifle better if he can. The public, lawless and inconstant, craving excitement at any price, journalized daily, neither knowing nor caring what the real aim and scope of the novel ought to be, has the casting vote, after all, upon great books and little books alike. From its ultimate verdict there is no appeal. But the ultimate verdict is made up very slowly and often contradicts the judgment of the hour. Meanwhile the scholar can quietly, persistently, assert the claims of excellence. From schools and colleges, from reading circles and clubs, from isolated and unregarded rooms whose walls are lined with books, come, to serve as leaven, people who know good work from bad and who know why they know it.

CHAPTER II

PROSE FICTION AND POETRY

"A novelist is on the border-line between poetry and prose, and novels should be as it were prose saturated with poetry."

LESLIE STEPHEN, *Daniel Defoe*.

"The great modern novelist is at once scientific and poetic : and here, it seems to me, in the novel, we have the meeting, the reconciliation, the kiss, of science and poetry."

SIDNEY LANIER, *The English Novel*.

THE quotation which has just been made from Sidney Lanier will serve to indicate the theme, not only of this chapter, but of the two following ones. In tracing the various relations of prose fiction, we must take account of its affinities with poetry, and with that specialized form of poetry, the drama. But we have also to reckon with science and with the influence of the modern scientific movement upon literary art. Let us begin by noting the affiliations of prose fiction with poetry.

Relations to the lyric.

Of the three great divisions into which poetry naturally falls, namely,

dramatic, lyric, and narrative, the first has so
much in common with prose fiction that their
lines of relationship will need to be discussed
in a separate chapter.   The province of lyric
poetry, on the other hand, is so distinctive
that its points of contact with prose fiction
can be easily defined.   The lyric is, beyond
any other form of poetical expression, the
vehicle of personal emotion.   The " lyric
cry " is the spontaneous overflow of the individual passion of the poet.   Its joy or pain
is egoistic.   It voices the poet's own heart, —
no matter how many other human hearts find
themselves beating in sympathy with his ut-
terance.   Now it is obvious that many novels
contain lyrical passages, — that is, episodes
of heightened personal feeling, transports of
happiness, anguish, or exaltation, which owe
their inspiration to the same causes as those
which produce, in the case of a poet, lyric
poetry.   There are certain novels, furthermore, which represent to a peculiar degree
the individual admirations and hatreds, the
ardent convictions and aspirations of their
authors.   Passages in the Brontë novels,
and whole books by George Sand, may thus
fairly be called lyrical.   But it is evident

enough that this highly emotionalized attitude, this intimate expression of purely personal feeling, is very far from being the
normal mood of the average fiction writer.

It is in the task of the narrative
or " epic " poet that we find a much
closer parallel to the work of the
artist in prose fiction. Both men have a
story to tell, and by comparing their methods
of workmanship one may learn a good deal
about the limitations and relative advantages
of prose and poetry as media for narration.
For the narrative poet, like the novelist, finds
much of his material ready to his hand, and
much more, no doubt, to be " invented," —
that is, selected and recombined from the
mass of unrelated memories and impressions
recorded in his mind. There is no better
way of tracing the inevitable remoulding of
narrative material by the poetic imagination
than to take one of the old stories of the
race and to see how poet and prose romancer
have in turn dealt with it. The prose romance is unquestionably a historic development from narrative poetry. Just as the
" Iliad " was formed out of hero sagas and ballads of unknown origin and antiquity, so the

Relations to narrative poetry.

Homeric poems, in turn, were broken up in early mediæval times into prose fictions like those of " Dares the Phrygian " and " Dictys the Cretan." The same process takes place with the post-classical romances of Alexander, the mediæval Arthurian romances, the stories of Charlemagne or the Cid. Verse passes over into prose ; prose in turn gets versified once more. The material, for the most part, is immeasurably old ; " 't is his at last who says it best." A study of these changing forms — of myth and legend as interpreted by different races and epochs and artists — throws much light upon the laws both of prose fiction and of poetry. It affects more or less directly our appreciation of contemporary literary art, for the universal sway of the mediæval prose romance — which itself sprang from a poetic imagination, and often out of actual embodiment in verse — prepared the way for the modern novel as we know it.

Yet those who possess neither the interest nor the facilities for the comparative study of mediæval literature can observe for themselves many of the correspondences and differences between

The common material of fiction and poetry.

prose fiction and poetry. Let us turn, for
example, to the material common to both
poet and novelist, the sources from which
they take the subject-matter of their art.
Novelist and poet alike are primarily interested in human life. They describe it as it
seems to have manifested itself in the irre-
vocable past, as it exists to-day, and as it
may be found in the imaginary, unknown
world of the future. They are interested in
all that surrounds human life and affects its
myriad operations. The external world, as
it is portrayed by the novelists and poets, is
chiefly a setting and framework for the more
complete exhibition of human characteristics.
The incidents which they narrate have for
their aim the portrayal of character in this
or that emergency and coil of actual circumstance, or else they are as it were the
mechanism — the gymnastic apparatus — by
which life might test and measure itself if it
pleased. Both novelist and poet, in a word,
care first of all for persons. The differences
of temperament and literary craftsmanship
which separated Tennyson and Thackeray,
for example, are relatively slight when compared with the common element of profound

curiosity with which these two writers observed men and women and reflected upon
the conditions of human society. Indeed,
the general distinction between men of letters, like Thackeray and Tennyson and
Carlyle, and men of science, like Tyndall,
Huxley, and Darwin, may be roughly indicated by saying that the former class are
mainly occupied with persons, and the latter
class with facts and laws.

The novelist and the poet, fur- Qualities
thermore, are alike in their habitual shared by
novelist and
mental operations. Both of them poet.
must, to compass any high artistic achievement, be thinkers. They must be able to
generalize from specific examples. But they
are not so likely as the historian, and surely
they are far less likely than the scientist, to
pass from particulars to a formulation of some
abstract general truth. They are more apt
to reason by analogy merely, to conclude
that because the real Lord Hertford did this
or that, the imaginary Marquis of Steyne,
some of whose traits were copied from Lord
Hertford's, would do it likewise. For artistic
ends, this sort of reasoning is no doubt
sufficient. The scientist and philosopher

may argue that because Lord Hertford was wicked all men are wicked. Thackeray will be content to assert or imply the concrete fact of the wickedness of the Marquis of Steyne, reasoning by the light of example cast by the real British lord who served as the " original " of the imaginary one.

Dealing with unknown quantities. But although the novelist and poet are likely to step out of their province and enter that of the philosopher and scientist in attempting to postulate general truths, it must not be imagined that they are limited to any hard-and-fast set of specific examples. Though they reason concretely rather than abstractly, they deal constantly with unknown quantities. They are forever asking themselves, and piquing the reader's curiosity by propounding to him, questions about the potential qualities of persons. How will this fictitious personage, more or less well known now to the reader, behave in these new circumstances? What will Ulysses do when he faces Penelope's suitors? Will Hamlet betray any excitement while his uncle watches the movements of the Player King? Will Rebecca yield to the Templar, and will Harry

Esmond marry Beatrice or Beatrice's mother? These are the questions — the immensely fascinating questions! — which poets and novelists propose to us. If we are sufficiently absorbed in the poem or tale, we may have our answers ready. The creator of the tale or poem is of course bound to have his answer ready too, and it will turn very largely upon his sense of the action possible to a given character under a given set of circumstances.

But the decision or deed of one personage affects all the others. It *With potential values.* brings, as a painter would say, a new set of " values " into the composition, just as a shaft of sunlight, thrown into a room, alters all the color scheme of the room. Or it may be more simple to say that the potential qualities of the personages of fiction, whether in prose or in verse, may be compared to the value of the various hands of cards in the game of whist. If diamonds are to be trumps, rather than hearts or spades or clubs, the value of every card in the pack is shifted accordingly, and a corresponding scheme of play must be instantly evolved. And if, in a novel or play, " hearts are trumps," if

Hamlet believes the Ghost, or Tito Melema resolves to feign ignorance of Baldassarre, all the relationships of the persons, all the turnings of the plot, are thereby affected. The power to evoke the reader's curiosity and sympathy for such potential actions and situations is an essential element in the skill of the imaginative artist.

Both use "artistic" in language.

The novelist and the poet have not only this common fund of interest in persons, and a similar fashion of making artistic use of the infinitely varied possibilities of human nature, but they are also working side by side in giving expression to their thoughts and feelings through language. Both are using what we rather indescriptively call " artistic " language, — that is, words chosen for their clearness, force, and beauty as vehicles for the communication of conceptions and emotions. Later nineteenth century fiction was particularly noticeable for the extent to which it availed itself of resources more commonly considered to belong to poetry alone. It cultivated " prose poetry," — words vaguely suggestive, instinct with emotional significance, and used in rhythmical combinations that give much of the æsthetic quality of verse.   Except in the hands of an artist like Poe, and indeed too often even with him, this use of poetic vocabulary and rhythm gives to prose fiction an over-ornamented, meretricious effect.   But when a master of language desires to produce at some crisis of his story an effect comparable to the vibrant, poignant impression which poetry imparts, what does he do ?   While holding firmly to the cadences of prose, he chooses his words, consciously or unconsciously, from the workshop of the poet.   Such wonderful lyric passages as Richard Feverel's first vision of Lucy by the river, the description of the Alps in " Beauchamp's Career," the Yarmouth storm in " David Copperfield," are examples of the intimate relationship of the language of heightened, impassioned prose to that of noble poetry.

The differences between the general functions of the poet and the novelist are no less suggestive. **Differences in selecting material.** Though they may draw from a common fund of observations upon human life, the poet is forced to make a much more narrow selection than the novelist. Since his task is the communication of emotion by means of verbal images, the poet may use only those images which affect us emotionally. Theoretically, a poem should contain nothing unpoetical, just as a piece of music should be free from discords. To assert this, however, is not to forbid the use in poetry of much material that seems at first view non-poetical, even if not actually unpoetical. The great poets, like the great musicians, are constantly surprising us by the beauty, the intensity of feeling, which can be suggested by the most unpromising material. But it is nevertheless more natural that we should be moved by the image of " a violet by a mossy stone " than by the image of a " little porringer." It is hackneyed criticism to remark that, if the poet just quoted had possessed a more unerring power of poetic choice from among the objects of common life which he celebrated in his verse, he would less often have made himself ridiculous.

But the novelist is bound by no
The novelist
has the larger such necessity to avoid the trivial
liberty.
and commonplace. He is not always, like the poet, occupied with the imme-

diate transmission of feeling. He may devote a whole chapter to mere topography.
He may chart the scene of his story, as
Stevenson did before he wrote " Treasure
Island," or as Blackmore made a map and
sketches of the Doone country before he
wrote his delightful romance. Like Balzac,
he may write page after page of description
of the external aspect of the house within
which the human drama is to be enacted ; or
like Flaubert, he may spend weeks of re-
search in order to investigate and describe
the precise details of a Carthaginian banquet
table. All this fidelity to fact, this careful
preparation of the stage scenery, may find its
justification in the added sense of reality, of
verisimilitude, conveyed by the story. But
whether or not always justified in actual
practice, this large freedom of the novelist
in the selection of material contrasts very
strongly with that compulsion which the poet
feels to make each line in itself a thing of
beauty. The novelist, in other words, is
always more likely than the poet to make a
generous use, in the practice of his art, of
the material furnished by his daily observation of men and things. One may imagine

the three men of letters, Longfellow, Hawthorne, and Mr. Howells, walking down a
street of Boston side by side. Out of the
multitude of objects which would meet their
eyes as possible raw material for literature,
it is likely that the poet would make the
most slender and scrupulous selection. The
romancer would probably exercise a wider
liberty of choice, and would retain in his
mental notebook many facts and impressions
which the poet would not find professionally
useful. But the last of the three, the novelist,
might conceivably make artistic use of every
sight and sound and odor of the street, finding a place for it somewhere or other in his
series of realistic pictures of contemporary
American life.

**The differ-
ence in
temperament.** There is a further difference in
the attitude of typical poets and
novelists toward their material.
The temperament of the prose writer is pro-
verbially cooler. He does not wait to invoke
the muses, nor does he ordinarily write under
that " fine frenzy " which often accompanies
the production of verse. The novelist, as
such, when compared with the poet, is more
of a quiet note-taker, a student of character

and manners and background. He is, as Henry Fielding loved to announce, "a historian of human nature." This temperamental and typical difference between the two artists, however, makes only the more noticeable those great lyric passages found here and there in the pages of masters of fiction, springing from the depths of emotion, and voiced with a nobility and beauty that we rightly associate with the poets alone. We may well believe that in the composition of such passages other novelists besides George Eliot have written under the overpowering impression which she described to Mr. Cross : —

> "She told me that in all that she considered her best writing there was a 'not herself' which took possession of her, and that she felt her own personality to be merely the instrument through which this spirit, as it were, was acting." Cross, *Life of George Eliot.*

The similarity already noticed between the tasks of the poet and the novelist, in that they both give expression through language to quickened moods of feeling, must not cause us to overlook the different requirements of expression in the two media of verse and prose. The

Verse and prose as differing media.

poet, thinking as he does in images, is bound
to use figurative language; thrilling as he
must be with emotion, that language naturally falls into rhythm; his instinct for
ordered beauty often leads him to the choice
of rhyme; and the nature of his imagination
compels him to the use of those words and
cadences whose very sound, through some
occult and unanalyzable associations and by
obscure imitative and suggestive potencies,
stir the deep, if vague, vibrations of the soul.
In these effects the writer of prose fiction
may, as we have seen, share to a certain extent. In proportion as his emotion rises in
intensity, his language will tend not only to
become tropical, but, like the language of the
impassioned orator, it will tend to fall into
periods of more or less regularly recurrent
stress. Yet this rhythmical effect, often to
be noted in powerful passages of prose fiction,
is very different from metrical effect; and
whenever — as notoriously in some of the
pathetic paragraphs of Dickens and the animal stories of Mr. Seton-Thompson — the
rhythm becomes the regular iambic beat of
English blank verse, the writer's intention
overreaches and defeats itself. With rhyme

the prose writer has of course nothing to do. Upon words of vague emotional connotation he sometimes does depend, in rendering certain actions of nature or moods of men, but, as we have already seen, " prose poetry " is at best dubious ground.   Most novelists fare better when, like Molière's enlightened hero, they speak prose, and know that they are speaking it.

It is not to be denied that the poet's use of metre, rhyme, and tone color will always give him technical resources beyond those of the prose writer. He has all the instruments that the prose writer possesses, and more besides, if one excepts the peculiar cadences, the distinctive melody and harmony that belong exclusively to prose.   It needs a very fine ear to perceive these as yet unanalyzed æsthetic values of "loosened speech," — the qualities that make a sentence of prose give pleasure through its sound alone.   It may be that we shall some day understand this better.   Future rhetoricians and metricists may be able to point out the tone values, the intricate and unrepeated harmonies of a page of Daudet, precisely as we now endeavor to analyze the expressional

The æsthetic values of prose.

values of a page of Racine. It is quite possible that they may assert that the prose writer was the rarer artist. But at present nothing is to be gained, and much has evidently been lost, by confusing the territories of prose and verse, and producing, under the name of " prose poetry " and the " poetic short story," a mass of nondescript gelatinous rhetoric which can be classified as neither flesh, fowl, nor good red herring.

There is still another way of approaching the subject of the relations of prose fiction to poetry. It is perhaps even more interesting than those considered hitherto, although, like them, its value consists rather in clarifying one's general perception of the variances in literary forms than in furnishing exact critical formulas. The method of approach is this : to select writers who have been both novelists and poets ; to study the different sides of their natures that have been expressed through the two arts ; and by this means to get light upon the character of the arts themselves. It is not difficult to see that George Eliot, for instance, betrayed through

Another method of approach.

the medium of such verse as "Jubal" and
"How Lisa loved the King" a yearning,
romantic vein of emotion which could find
no such natural channel of expression in her
realistic novels.   Thackeray's verse seems at
times to be an even more direct outpouring
of his own kindly, melancholy self than is to
be found in his fiction, in spite of the obvious fact that in his stories he is forever coming upon the stage himself to explain and
comment upon his characters.   The two
Walter Scotts, the poet and the novelist,
were quite different persons.   The novelist
was not merely the poet grown older, grown
tired of competing with Byron for the public favor ; he was a greater, saner, wiser
man, in closer touch with the enduring
realities of human nature.   But he had lost
something, too.   The rival arts of verse and
prose were fitted to be the medium of the
slowly changing outlook upon life which is
to be observed in passing from the younger
to the elder Walter Scott, and no one can
feel this without a new insight into the
essential nature of verse and prose as tools
for the literary artist.

The novel as "a criticism of life." There is a very familiar phrase of Matthew Arnold which applies to the modern novel even more aptly than to poetry. " Poetry," said that great .critic and admirable poet, " is a criticism of life." This remark has often indeed been understood in too narrow a sense. Arnold meant by criticism an interpretation, an appreciation of human life upon its ideal side, such an interpretation as Wordsworth or Dante or Goethe gives us. But the power to do this through the medium of verse is rare, and it has often happened that poets like Arnold, like his master Sainte-Beuve, like our own Mr. Howells, have gradually ceased to compose verse, and have turned their attention more and more to prose criticism. It is true that criticism as produced by such men is in itself literature; it may possess qualities of high and permanent worth. But such critics as these would probably be the first to admit that, compared with poetry of equally high relative position in its class, criticism is a second best. However stimulating it may be to the intelligence, however fortifying and tonic to the will, the natural instincts of the heart teach that poetry is somehow per-

forming a higher office than prose criticism.
It deals on the whole with nobler aspects of
things, and deals with them in a nobler way.
The same is true of the rivalry between the
novelist and the poet. Both may be seers,
but the novelist is compelled by the very
terms of his art to say what he sees, while
the poet sings it. And the singer is above
the sayer. Whether one is comparing the
differing gifts of a single writer like Victor
Hugo, who wrought such marvels in both
the arts — " Victor in Drama, Victor in Romance " — or comparing the typical poet
with the typical novelist, or studying the history of those prose romances and poems
which are a part of the intellectual heritage
of the race, it becomes clear that poetry is
the finer art. Yet the greatest triumphs of
prose fiction have been won by those books
in which the interpretation of life, the creative imagination, and the mastery of language have been akin to those revealed
by enduring poetry. Hence it is that the
student of prose fiction should constantly
observe, not the romancer alone, but also the
aims and methods of the poet and the
dramatist.

CHAPTER III

FICTION AND THE DRAMA

"It may fairly be claimed that humanity has, within the past hundred years, found a way of carrying a theatre in its pocket; and so long as humanity remains what it is, it will delight in taking out its pocket-stage and watching the antics of the actors, who are so like itself and yet so much more interesting. Perhaps that is, after all, the best answer to the question, 'What is a novel?' It is, or ought to be, a pocket-stage."

F. MARION CRAWFORD, *The Novel : What It Is.*

The terms "novel" and "drama" as here used.

WE have already noted some of the general relations between prose fiction and poetry, and have remarked that one of the chief poetic types, the drama, has such intimate affiliations with the novel as to deserve treatment in a special chapter. In commenting upon the similarities and differences of function that characterize these two literary forms, it will be more simple to use the term "novel" in a wide sense, as including the romance and short story, and the term "drama" as indicating plays written both in prose and in verse, but always as compositions intended for actual stage representation. The "closet drama" — the play that is not intended to be played — is an isolated though a very interesting literary species which does not fall within the range of the present chapter.

Using the "novel," then, as synonymous with narrative prose fiction, and the "drama" as meaning the acted play, we may begin

The object of both novel and drama: characters in action.

by observing that both novel and drama have for their object the exhibition of characters in action. How far a given personality can be made to reveal itself through visible action and audible words upon the stage must in each individual instance be decided by the dramatist. Mere physical "business" upon the boards, exits and entrances, crossing from left to right and back again, may not afford that kind of dramatic "action" which makes manifest the essential character of a stage personage. On the other hand, Hamlet's irresolution, his failure to act, is in itself a positive dramatic force; it may be reckoned upon like any other. The element of external action is indeed less necessary to the novel, because the author can describe mental attitudes instead of visualizing them for the eye of the spectator. He can sometimes rouse our intense curiosity and eagerness by the mere depiction of a psychological state, as Walter Pater has done in the case of Sebastian Storck and other personages of his "Imaginary Portraits." The fact that "nothing happens" in stories of this kind may be precisely what most interests us, because we are made to understand what it is that inhibits action. But the great majority of novels and plays represent human life in nothing more faithfully than in their insistence upon deeds. It is through action — tangible, visible action upon the stage, or, in the novel, action suggested by the medium of words — that the characters of the play and the novel are ordinarily revealed. In proportion as high art is attained in either medium of expression this action is marked by adequacy of motive, by conformity to the character, by progression and unity.

Similarities in construction. What is more, there are marked similarities in the general construction — the architecture, so to say — of the two literary forms which we are considering. Suppose we take up the separate portions of the drama, those "parts" and "moments" of its technical structure which have interested students of dramatic literature from the time of the Greek rhetoricians to our own. Each one of these various functions, performed by a definite portion of the play, has its parallel in the architectonics of prose fiction.

In both play and novel, for instance, it is the first task of the author to explain the characters and circumstances which are essential to an understanding of the plot. Upon his skill in so presenting his personages and their surroundings that they may be intelligently understood at the outset depends a large measure of his success. The first act of a play is thus spoken of as the act containing the "exposition." Like the overture of a musical composition, it indicates the nature of the whole. Now the opening chapters of a novel, or the first lines of a short story, have a precisely similar function to perform. It is true that in the novel the exposition may be far more deliberate. The play-wright has not a moment to lose after the curtain has once risen ; every moment of opening action

The exposition.

counts heavily for or against his chances of interesting the audience in the personages of the play. But Walter Scott and Thackeray and Dickens ramble along in chapter after chapter of pleasant prologues without appreciably advancing towards the real story which they have to tell, — so confident were these authors, no doubt, of their power to secure the attention of their readers, and so unerringly, in general, did they utilize all their apparently trivial descriptive and narrative details in instinctively forecasting the final cumulative effect of the tale.

Accurate presentation of detail. These details are not only more deliberately presented in the novel than would be possible in the play, but they are also more accurately presented. There is less for us to guess at. The novelist, in spite of all the suppressions which his art makes necessary, tells us more, and leaves us less often to our own inferences, than the play-wright. When the story-writer describes his heroine, we doubtless see her less distinctly than if the dramatist had sent her down the stage for our inspection, but whereas the dramatist is forced to let us infer what is in her mind by her appearance, her facial expression, gestures, words, and the attitude of other personages respecting her, the novelist can tell us precisely and at once what she is thinking about and what she is likely to do. But whatever may be the differences in technique, both novelist and dramatist are bent first of all upon introducing their characters.

Then comes, commonly in the middle or towards the end of the first act of the play, and not far
The "exciting" force or "moment."
from the beginning of a well constructed tale, what is called the " exciting (or " inciting ") force " or " moment." Something happens, and even though this happening may be apparently insignificant, it begins to affect the entire course of the plot. The Ghost appears to Hamlet; the witches confront Macbeth; Cassius talks with Brutus; the clash of interest begins; the lines of party or of faction, of individual ambition or resolve, are suddenly apparent. In the tale this " moment " — the little weight that turns the scale — is frequently quite undramatic and unimpressive, but it can usually be pointed out. In " Pendennis " it is where the major receives the letter from his

sister which tells about Arthur's infatuation
for Miss Fotheringay. In "The House of
the Seven Gables" it is the opening of the
shop after all the years of dust and silence.
In a romance of adventure, like Stevenson's
"Kidnapped," it is the orphan boy leaving
home at early dawn to seek his fortune up
and down the world.

The development. No sooner are the currents of
action fairly flowing, both in play
and in novel, than their speed and power per-
ceptibly increase. Throughout the second,
and into the third act of a five-act play, we
witness what Freytag called the "heighten-
ing;" that is, not merely quickened movement, but more passionate feeling, a closer
contact of personal forces, a more violent
collision of wills, a greater complication of
the various threads of the plot, the entanglement of a greater number of personages in
the intrigue or the achievement upon which
the play is based. In the novel this development is not necessarily, as upon the stage,
accompanied and indicated by a more rapid
and emphasized external action. It may proceed through the slow growth of character
alone, and only its silently accumulated re-

sults be in due time manifest. Dorothea
Casaubon in "Middlemarch" and Tess in
"Tess of the D'Urbervilles" pass through
such periods of almost unregarded preparation, of gradual ripening for the great crises
of their lives. Thus chapters describing
Dorothea's life after her marriage and Tess's
sojourn in Froom Vale belong to the "development" of the story, but are unexciting
enough in themselves. But the best novel,
surely, like the best play, is that in which
inner character and outward action are developed simultaneously; in which the growth
of mind and heart and will are expressed
through tangible and striking scenes. In
this respect "Vanity Fair" and "A Tale
of Two Cities" and "Adam Bede" and
"Pan Michael" — to choose stories of very
different types — accomplish what Shakespeare accomplished in "Macbeth." They allow us to watch the growth or the decay of
a soul even while we are fascinated by a
spectacle.

Near the middle of the typical
play — commonly in the third act **The climax.**
of a five-act drama — is what is variously
called the "highest point," the "turning

point," the "climax," or the "grand climax." It is the scene where the dramatic forces which are contending for the mastery are most evenly balanced. One cannot say whether the hero or the intriguer, the protagonist or the antagonist, will conquer. It is the point of greatest tension between the opposing powers. It is watched by the spectators with something of the feeling with which one sees a sky-rocket turn in its upward flight and begin its fall. This momentary equilibrium between the " rising " and the " falling " action of the play may not necessarily call forth the greatest excitement from spectators. That may be reserved for the catastrophe, which may be compared to the bursting of the sky-rocket as it nears the end of its downward flight. And yet the great climax scenes in Shakespeare, for instance, are stamped indelibly upon the memory : Macbeth at the banquet ; Lear in the hut ; Cæsar at the senate house ; Hamlet watching the play within the play.

The "tragic moment." In a tragedy the grand climax is usually immediately preceded or followed by what is called the " tragic moment," — the event which makes a tragic

outcome unavoidable and foredooms to failure every subsequent struggle of the hero
against his fate. The speech of Mark An-
tony, the killing of Polonius, the escape of
Fleance, are examples of the " tragic moment," and it will be seen how closely this is
associated with what the Greeks named the
" turn," — the beginning of the "falling
action."

It is not often that a novel pre- Climax in
sents such striking examples of the novel.
skillfully constructed climax. In the Spanish-
born picaresque romance, — so named because its hero is a *picaro*, a rogue, — and in
the modern romance of adventure, all that
is usually attempted is to invent a brisk succession of incidents and situations, designed
to capture the attention of the reader by any
device, rather than to conform rigidly to
those technical conventions upon which the
success of the play-wright is constantly dependent. In the novel of manners or the novel
of character, instead of a " grand climax "
there is likely to be a series of less noticeable
scenes which reveal or determine the personality of the men and women involved. There
could scarcely be a better illustration of the

difference in method, as between the drama and the novel, than that scene in George Eliot's " Middlemarch " where Lydgate, at the meeting of the directors of the hospital, is forced to declare his vote for either Farebrother or Tyke. It is a scene of thrilling psychological interest. A human soul is hanging in the balance ; but the situation is wholly lacking in dramatic impressiveness, judged from the point of view of the playwright. Yet in " Vanity Fair " the chapter which describes how Rawdon Crawley knocked down the Marquis of Steyne is very obviously the "grand climax " of the book. It marks the " highest point " in Becky's worldly fortunes, and her detection by her husband is the " turn " with which begins the long episode of her losing fight with society. In the stage version of " Vanity Fair " it is equally interesting to note the climactic quality of this scene. But it may be said in general that the novel has a far greater freedom of method than the play, as regards the use either of a grand climax or of a series of climaxes. So entirely lacking in dramaturgic possibilities is the plot of many a story that the climax is identified with the conclusion, and

one reads on with the simple desire to learn
" how it comes out," rather than to watch
— as upon the stage — the struggle of the
embodied forces upon which the outcome
depends.

We have already implied that
the " highest point " or " climax "   The " fall."
of a typical drama marks the division of the
two processes out of which the plot of a play
is made.   These processes are frequently described as the " complication " — the weaving
together of the various threads of interest
— and the " resolution " — the untangling
of the threads again.   " Tying " and " untying " are still simpler terms ; and the
French word for untying, the *dénoûment,* has
grown familiar to us, though it is often used
for what is technically known as the " catastrophe," rather than as descriptive of the entire
" falling action," of which the catastrophe
is only the final stage.   Freytag was one of
the first to point out that, in planning the
" fall " of a tragic drama, the play-wright
manages to maintain the interest of the spectators by striking scenic effects, by passages
of intense psychological interest, like Juliet's
monologue, or Lady Macbeth's sleep-walking

scene, or by making the hero struggle superbly against the " counterplayers." If the play be a comedy, he interposes new obstacles in the path of the lovers, or he removes these only to bring to view obstacles more formidable still.

The " final suspense." Both in comedy and in tragedy there is the " moment of final suspense," when the sinister or happy fortune presaged by the general nature of the " falling action " seems contradicted, or at least held in suspense, by some unforeseen occurrence, like Macbeth's triumphal announcement of the prophecy that he was not to be slain by any man born of woman, or the news that comes to Richard Third that the fleet of his rival, Richmond, has been destroyed by a storm.[1]

The catastrophe. And then comes swiftly the catastrophe, — the inexorable doom of tragedy, the " Bless you, my children ! " of conventional comedy, — the final allotment of fortune to the personages of the play. It must always seem reasonable, must appear to be of " the nature of things." However

[1] These illustrations are drawn from Freytag's *Technique of the Drama.*

much one may grieve over the pity and terror of it, it must be recognized as essentially,
though perhaps mysteriously, just. The visible catastrophe, like the death of Othello
or of Hamlet, is the outward symbol of what
has already taken place within the soul. It
embodies for sense-perception, as all art
must, the dramatist's thought; it sets the
seal of unity upon his completed work.

What parallel does prose fiction
offer to the dramatist's handling of The dénoû-
ment in
fiction.
the "resolution," the " untying," of
his plot ?   In the so-called " plot novel " the
parallel is very close indeed. The first half
of a detective story often occupies itself with
knotting as firmly as possible the threads of
the mystery; the second half is devoted to
a skillful untangling. When the hero or
heroine of fiction has once made a fatal
choice, the " fall " proceeds along precisely
the same lines as in the drama. The drama
has been defined as made up of impulse,
deed, and consequence, and in depicting the
" consequence " the novelist can adjust outward action to inward struggle as finely as
the dramatist. Indeed the tragic degenera-
tion of such a character as Tito Melema in

"Romola" can be expressed more sensitively
by the methods of narration and description
than by the relatively coarser effects necessary for visible representation upon the stage.
Novels as far apart in their aims and methods
of workmanship as Kingsley's "Hereward"
and Mrs. Humphry Ward's "Eleanor" have
in common this admirable adjustment of inner
mood to outward event. In psychological
romances like Hawthorne's "Marble Faun"
and "Scarlet Letter," the dénoûment takes
place in the heart and mind of the characters ; the author is so concerned with this,
his immediate purpose, that he frequently
becomes indifferent to the interests of external action. When Hawthorne's publishers
insisted upon his writing an additional chapter to the "Marble Faun," in order to tell
what became of the various personages of
the story, he good-naturedly complied ; but
it is evident that his task was perfunctory.
Indeed it may be said that in proportion as
the purely psychological interest predominates in a story it becomes less necessary to
arrange the external catastrophe with an eye
to dramatic effect. The great creators of
character in fiction have the art of making

us believe in the real existence of the men and women they portray. They throw a vivid light upon the few links of the endless chain of human existence and activity ; and though the story stops we have an irresistible impression that the men and women are continuing to live. Their personality so dominates the imagination that we refuse to think of them as merely pigeon-holed in some of the final-chapter categories, such as "happily married" or "dead." They are alive forevermore to the sympathetic imagination.

Rather curiously, the romance of mere adventure, like "The Three Musketeers," often treats the dé- *The dénoûment in romance.* noûment with singular unconcern. What interests us here is not so much the characters as the adventures which beset them upon the road, and when all the journeyings are ended it makes little difference in what room of the inn the personages find rest. It is the more normal type of fiction, where both character-interest and the interest of outward action are intimately joined, that affords in its dénoûments the closest parallels to the dénoûments of the conventional drama. It is closer to the realities of life than either the romance of pure psychology or the romance of pure adventure, for it conceives of the human mind and heart, not as something apart from external deeds, nor again of deeds as something intrinsically interesting, but rather of soul and deed together, inextricably joined.

The novel and the play as modes of reaching the public.

We have seen that the novel affords to the artist an opportunity to communicate, by means of narration and description, certain images which the dramatist can present in tangible, visible form. But the indirect method of presentation, by means of narration and description, is perfectly fitted to the gifts and circumstances of certain writers. Charlotte Brontë's ignorance of the world of action would probably have made it impossible for her to turn play-wright, but, apart from some obvious faults of unreality, it scarcely affected her achievement as a novelist. Authors with a far wider experience of life, like Cooper or Hawthorne, would have found their ignorance of the technique of the stage a formidable obstacle to communicating with the public through that medium.

Many writers, furthermore, shrink from the associations of the stage. Although there is far more pecuniary profit to the author from a successful play than from the average successful novel, and although in some countries, notably in France, the authorship of a play brings more instant personal recognition, play-writing demands a long and arduous period of apprenticeship. Even after years of familiarity with technical stagecraft, it is far more difficult to get a manuscript play accepted than it is to secure publication for a manuscript novel. Most authors choose, or are forced to follow, the easier path. If they really have something to say, they have the satisfaction of knowing that their novels bring them into touch with a more varied public than that which patronizes the theatre. The novel reaches thousands of isolated persons, as well as a community of pleasure seekers. Then, too, it calls forth, at least in its more powerful examples, a more sustained, uninterrupted emotional activity than is afforded by a play. Dramatic representations last but three or four hours at most; a great novel frequently dominates, possesses, the imagination of the reader for

many days. Not that the play is forgotten, but the book, after all, seems to come into a more enduring, permanent relation with its reader.

Besides these general and perhaps too theoretical differences between the novelist's and the dramatist's modes of addressing their public, there are certain definite and indisputable advantages which the novelist possesses. One is the power to convey mental phenomena with exactness. Although the dramatist, by the simple expedient of raising a curtain, can make us see the heroine as she sits in her chair, and cause us to apprehend her physical characteristics more clearly than any writer could convey them to us, the novelist has a great advantage when he wants to tell us what is passing in the heroine's mind. He is not forced, like the dramatist, to make us infer what she is thinking about; he is not left to the mercy of the actress's interpretation of his lines; he tells us precisely what the heroine thinks and feels. Furthermore, as the chapter on Setting will show, the novelist has it in his power to convey the effect of many natural phenomena, as for

Advantages of the novel as a medium.

instance the sea, far more perfectly through
words, than any stage carpenter and scene
painter and expert with electric lights can
possibly contrive to do. But the greatest
advantage of the novelist, no doubt, lies in
his liberty to introduce material which is not
strictly concerned, as every line of the dramatist's should be, with the exhibition of characters in action. He has some measure of the
poet's "unchartered freedom" to depict
beautiful objects, unconcerned with their immediate bearing upon the problem in hand.
He is by turns scientist, sociologist, explorer,
and historian, conveying all sorts of information about the world we live in, in its
infinite varieties of aspect and appeal. In
his own comment upon the personages and
action of his story, he usurps the function
of the ancient chorus, and turns philosopher.
He may forget his story, for the time being,
in these wise or profound or playful "asides"
to his readers. Yet though the laws of
purely objective art, both in drama and in
prose fiction, would deny him this privilege,
"he will still be prating," and in this very
weakness — as artistic theory would judge it
— of novelists like George Eliot and Thack-

eray, we discover one of the chief sources of
their actual power over the reader.

On the other hand, it may rightly
be claimed for stage representation
that it compasses certain results
that are out of the reach of narrative fiction.
Perhaps the most obvious of these advantages is the assistance which stage setting
affords to the imagination of the spectator.
Many readers lack the power of visualizing
the imaginary scenes depicted by the novelist, and hence they rarely or never feel
themselves in the presence of real persons or
surrounded by real circumstances. But the
modern play-wright is so varied in resource,
so fertile in mechanical expedients, that he
can create a stage setting of extraordinary
verisimilitude to the conditions demanded
by the particular play. A feeble, untrained,
unpictorial imagination thus finds itself as-
sisted in every scene. It is true that too
much help may often be given. The rude
sign-posts, " Athens " or " Rome," hung out
upon the stage of the Elizabethan theatre, as
the sole indication of a shift of scene, doubtless forced the audience to a free, playful
exercise of fancy which put them in accord

Compensating advantages of the stage.

with the dramatist's mood. They met him
half-way, and agreeing like children to play
a game with conventional symbols, entered
into it perhaps all the more heartily upon
that account, just as imaginary sugar lumps,
at a " make-believe " tea-party, often give
more pleasure than real ones. There is little doubt that the over-elaborate stage setting
of the present day sometimes dulls the imagination by giving it no exercise. But the
theatrical audience is a strangely composite
one, and the pictorial imagination of many
spectators needs all the help that can be
given to it. In the realistic setting that
represents a hotel office, a steamboat land-
ing, a telephone exchange, or a department
store, there is an appeal to the spectator's
knowledge and sympathy, a gratification of
his sense of recognition, which yield notable
satisfaction. The pleasure afforded by the
lavish mounting of many romantic plays is
of a higher type æsthetically. It is more
useful, too, in stimulating the imagination
of many spectators who would not and could
not respond to the detailed descriptions
drawn by the novelist. In this assistance
that it gives to the imagination of the tired

or uncultivated spectator the theatre bases
one of its most unquestioned claims to the
support of the public.

Individual moments.   Furthermore, it is undeniable
that the play-wright is able to em-
phasize individual moments of action with a
vividness and force quite beyond the reach
of the novelist. The often-quoted remark
about the acting of Edmund Kean, that it
was like " reading Shakespeare by flashes of
lightning," contains a truth applicable to
many varieties of dramatic art. Play-wright
and actor have it in their power to stamp a
single scene, line, attitude, ineffaceably upon
the memory. The " curse of Rome " in
" Richelieu," Mercutio's " a plague on both
your houses," Lady Macbeth's talking in her
sleep, all represent legitimate dramatic effects which for intensity, direct and immediate penetrating power, are beyond the scope
of the novelist.

The dramatization of novels.   It is easy to multiply these illustrations of the differences in
method which separate the art of
the novelist from that of the dramatist. A
more practical and instructive way of comparing the technique of the two arts, however, is to study the dramatization of novels.

It may well be doubted whether the recent popularity of such dramatizations has been beneficial either to the stage or to the novel, but it is easy for any student to draw useful comparisons between the two modes of presenting characters in action. Let him read " Vanity Fair," " The Scarlet Letter," " Dr. Jekyll and Mr. Hyde," " The Little Minister," " The Prisoner of Zenda," " The Christian," or " Tess of the D'Urbervilles," and watch, carefully and repeatedly, the plays that have been constructed from these stories. He will learn, better than any abstract analysis can possibly teach him, the inexorable conditions under which the play-wright is obliged to work, and the inevitable modifications which the play-wright is forced to make in the material supplied for him by the novelist. The chief lesson to be learned is this: that the novel and the play are not merely two different modes of communicating the same fact or truth. It is rather that the different modes result in the communication of a different fact. It is impossible that Thackeray's " Vanity Fair " should be presented upon the stage. Thackeray's " Vanity Fair " is a complex of personal impressions and convictions about life, trans-

mitted to us by a specific art of which
Thackeray was a master. A dramatized
" Vanity Fair " can no more transmit those
impressions than a novelized " Hamlet " can
give us Shakespeare's " Hamlet." The field
of the dramatist, in a word, is marked off
from that of the novelist by the nature of
the artistic medium which each man employs. Which medium is better depends
wholly upon the personality and the training of the artist, and the nature of the fact
or truth he wishes to convey to the public.
It is enough for our present purposes to remark that the two media differ as completely
as bronze and pigment, or marble and musical tone, and that the success of any artist
depends largely upon his instinctive or ac-
quired sense of the possibilities or limitations
of the material he chooses. As for the
dramatization of novels, it should never be
forgotten that a novel is typically as far
removed from a play as a bird is from a
fish ; and that any attempt to transform one
into the other is apt to result in a sort of
flying-fish, a betwixt-and-between thing, —
capable, indeed, of both swimming and flying, but good at neither.

CHAPTER IV

FICTION AND SCIENCE

" To ascertain and communicate facts is the object of science ;
to quicken our life into a higher consciousness through the feelings is the function of art.   But though knowing and feeling are
not identical, and a fact expressed in terms of feeling affects us
as other than the same fact expressed in terms of knowing, yet
our emotions rest on and are controlled by our knowledge. Whatever modifies our intellectual conceptions powerfully, in due time
affects art powerfully." DOWDEN, *Studies in Literature.*

BOTH the scientist and the artist
are constantly dealing with man,
and yet there is a striking contrast
between the characteristic ways in which the
scientist and the artist confront their human
material.   The scientist's interest in the human organism begins long before the dawn of
conscious life in the individual.   He studies
the laws of heredity, the influence of race,
family, and climate, as they affect the physical
and mental characteristics of the new human
being.   He follows the child's bodily growth
and intellectual development with the keenest scrutiny, finding here the key to many

Man as
material for
the scientist.

puzzling problems relating to the past history
and the future welfare of the race.   As the
child matures into manhood or womanhood,
every physical characteristic or social relation
of the individual becomes the object of the
scientist's closest study.   Experts in ethics
and economics, in sociology, law, government, in short in all the departments of social
and political science, make man the object
of their investigations and theories.   Furthermore, all the sciences dealing primarily
with things — such as chemistry, physics,
astronomy, geology — find their incentive
and their ultimate justification in the assistance they give to man in his ceaseless effort
to understand himself and his place in the
universe.   In a word, the aim of the scientist
is to know man as he is, in all his relations.

**Man as
material for
the artist.**   But how different is the function of the artist!   When he turns
to the human being in search of
material for his art, his chief endeavor is to
make something beautiful.   With this purpose the sculptor represents, with more or
less fidelity to actual fact, the outlines of the
human form.   The painter depicts the light
reflected from the human face and figure.

The poet translates the emotions of men and
women into conventional forms of beautifully ordered speech. The musician embodies man's inarticulate desires, his vaguest
dreams, in harmonies of sound. All these
artistic activities imply knowledge of men
and women ; but it is obvious that knowledge
is not with the artist, as it is with the scientist, an end in itself. It is only one element
in his chief task. That task is to create
some beautiful object. It is necessary to
keep this fundamental distinction clearly in
mind in endeavoring to estimate the nature
and extent of the influence of the modern
scientific movement upon the art of fiction.

It will be readily recognized that Fiction as
fiction, like every other depart- affected by physical
ment of human activity, has not science.
escaped the impact of that widespread and
deep interest in physical science which was
one of the most marked characteristics of the
nineteenth century. The influence of this
movement may be traced in almost every
field of literature. The constant reference
in Tennyson's later poetry to the doctrine of
evolution, and the application of the theory
of heredity in the problem-plays of Ibsen,

illustrate the scientific cast of modern literature quite as effectively as George Eliot's
masterly studies in environment, or the scientific romances of M. Jules Verne or Mr.
H. G. Wells. But it has happened more frequently in fiction than in other departments
of literary art that the writer has set himself
deliberately to the work of scientific or
pseudo-scientific demonstration, while avail-
ing himself ostensibly of the conventional
devices which are a part of the novelist's
stock in trade. The most famous, and upon
the whole the most influential, example of
fidelity to a method supposedly scientific has
been that of M. Zola. In his well known
essay entitled " Le Roman Expérimental," [1]
he has explained and defended the methods
which he has endeavored to follow in compos-
ing the novels of the Rougon-Macquart series.
The thesis of the essay can be summed up in
a few sentences.

"Le Roman Expérimen-tal."   M. Zola begins by pointing out
the difference between a science of
observation, like astronomy, and a
science based upon experiments, like chem-

---

[1] There is an English translation by B. M. Sherman.
London and New York: Cassell, 1893.

istry. The observer, he says, is only the
photographer of phenomena ; but the experimenter can alter the conditions, and, subject-
ing phenomena to these new conditions, can
prove or disprove some hypothesis. In similar fashion a novelist can " experiment "
upon a character, and study its behavior
under the particular conditions to which the
novelist chooses to subject it. Chemistry
and physics have now become exact sciences.
Physiology and psychology are likewise subject to fixed laws, since the " same determinism governs the stone in the road and the
brain of man." It is therefore the duty of
the novelist to apply the methods of the exact sciences to the intellectual and emotional
activities of mankind, and to replace the
romances of pure imagination by those of
observation and experiment. Idealistic writers
have had quite too much to say about the
unknown, about mysterious forces which
elude analysis. A writer ought to base his
work upon positive knowledge, upon the territory already conquered by science, and it is
only when he reaches the end of this territory, and is confronted with the unknown,
that he is free to exercise his intuition, his

a priori ideals.   Metaphysics must give place
to physiology.   " No doubt," says M. Zola
in closing, " the wrath of Ulysses and the
love of Dido will remain eternally beautiful portraitures ; but it is our duty to
analyze wrath and love, and to see precisely
how these passions perform their function in
the human organism.   Ours is a new point
of view ; it becomes experimental rather than
philosophical.   In a word, the experimental
method, in literature as in science, is in process of determining those natural phenomena,
individual and social, of which metaphysics
has given hitherto only irrational and supernatural explanations."

The weakness
in M. Zola's
argument.
Such, in brief outline, is the
argument of one of the most interesting and famous essays ever devoted to the art of fiction.   The weak points
in Zola's presentation of his case have
been indicated by M. Brunetière and many
other French critics.   Passing over entirely
Zola's assumption of a " determinism "
governing all phenomena, — an assumption
upon which his whole argument rests, and
which would find even fewer adherents
among men of science to-day than it did

twenty years ago, — there are at least two
fatal defects in his logic.   The first is that
in his use of the term " experiment " to describe the novelist's procedure towards his
characters, Zola is juggling with words.   No
novelist can possibly conduct an " experiment " with persons as a chemist does with
acids, or a physiologist with foods.   The novelist is either an " observer " pure and simple —
as far as his nature will allow — or else he
performs a purely imaginary " experiment "
in placing his personages in various supposi-
titious situations and telling us how they conduct themselves.   In other words, we have
to accept the novelist's statement of the
behavior of certain selected persons, in circumstances imagined by the novelist himself.
The " experiment," described with such solemnity, is a pure bit of " make-believe."

And secondly, M. Zola, who is **"A priori
a slashing and resourceful debater ideas."**
rather than a shrewd one, practically gives
away his case when he admits that in the
presence of the " unknown " there is an opportunity for one's " a priori ideas," for
" intuition," for the play of the artist's personality.   Zola and his opponents differ of

course as to the extent of the rôle which the
unknown plays in fiction ; but to admit its
presence at all is a serious halt in the triumphal march of his theory. What is still
more unfortunate for him, — since literary
theories are bound to depend, at last, upon
literary practice, — in M. Zola's own novels
there is a more astounding exhibition of "a
priori ideas," of a *parti pris*, of deliberate
ignoring of some facts and imaginative distortion of other facts, than in any other
romancer of his time. His "scientific"
principle, when carried into practice by himself, stands revealed as grossly unscientific.

The effects
of scientific
theory.

Whatever M. Zola's personal success as a debater or practitioner in
the field of fiction, there is no question as to the reality of the influence of the scientific temper upon the novelist's art. "True
it is that modern scientific study is inductive,
is experimental, is based upon comparison of
experiences. And true it is that the modern
scientific method has laid a heavy hand of compulsion upon the modern literary worker."[1]
This compulsion has varied in degree at dif-

[1] F. H. Stoddard, *The Evolution of the English Novel,*
p. 212. New York: The Macmillan Company, 1900.

ferent periods, but it may be traced in the
English novel ever since the seventeenth
century. " The works of the lesser writers
of the seventeenth century show the rise of
a new spirit, foreign to the times of Shakespeare, — a spirit of observation, of attention
to detail, of stress laid upon matter of fact,
of bold analysis of feelings and free argument upon institutions ; the microscope of
the men of the Restoration, as it were, laying
bare the details of daily objects, and super-
seding the telescope of the Elizabethans that
brought the heavens nearer earth. No one
word will finally describe it. In its relation
to knowledge it is the spirit of science ; to
literature it is the spirit of criticism ; and
science and criticism in England are the creations of the seventeenth century." [1] The
same tendency is to be observed in the fiction of the Continent, where it dominated
some of the most influential novels between
1870 and the close of the nineteenth century. Although few novelists would now
advocate it in the extreme and doctrinaire
form assumed for argumentative purposes by

[1] Walter Raleigh, *The English Novel*, p. 111. New
York: Scribner's.

M. Zola, it must everywhere be reckoned with.

What fiction has gained by it.
It is not to be questioned that fiction has gained, in more than one positive quality, from this saturation with the spirit that has entered so completely into the consciousness of modern society.

In range of interest.
For one thing, it has wonderfully broadened the range of the subject-matter of fiction. Science has taught us the significance of all facts. A thousand aspects of life and nature, which lay wholly outside the field of vision of the post-classical or mediæval romance, are full of interest and suggestiveness to the modern novel-writer. The moment that the writer and his reader share this conviction of the potential significance of objects or aspects of life hitherto regarded as trivial or meaningless, that moment the scope of possible subjects has broadened almost endlessly. To compare the field within which a mediæval romancer works professionally with the field open to Balzac, Zola, or Tolstoi, is to compare the number of objects visible to the naked eye with those visible to the observer possessed of a microscope.

Within this vastly widened field
of possible material the individual
details have been wrought out with a scrupulous and indeed microscopic care. The
exactness of observation which has everywhere resulted from the cultivation of the
physical sciences has changed the very texture of the modern novel. Dialect stories
furnish a convenient illustration. No novelist
would now care to put into the mouths of
negro characters the unheard-of sounds that
passed for negro dialect in the generation
of " Uncle Tom's Cabin." Many writers of
provincial dialect have given the most detailed and painstaking effort to the study of
phonetics. Compare the rustic dialect of
Thomas Hardy's characters, for instance, with
that spoken by Fielding's rustics. The difference is due to a century's progress in
recording impressions with scientific precision.

Instantaneous photography has
trained the eye of artist and public alike. To take the most familiar example, photography has taught us
that a running horse never extends all four
legs at once, in the way in which artists have

been wont to represent him. As soon as
the photograph has unerringly demonstrated
what is the actual position of the horse's
legs, the eye begins to analyze and readjust
its impressions in accordance with the newly
discovered fact. Frederic Remington's horses,
drawn after the revelations of instantaneous
photography, seem real to our generation;
the galloping horses in old pictures of British
hunting fields seem strangely unreal. It is
thus that science has taught us accurate and
analytic vision, and the training has been
instantly reflected in every form of art.
Whether a heightened beauty has always
resulted from this new treatment is to be
doubted. The æsthetic questions involved
are subtle and far-reaching. But the chief
point now to be noted is that our generation
has been taught to use its eyes in a new way.
The illustrated papers, for example, show us,
with the absolute fidelity of the camera, the
precise image of an athlete breasting the tape
at the end of a hundred-yard sprint. Whether
his face and form are as beautiful as we imagined, and whether the artist is justified in
representing him as he appears to the trained
rather than to the untrained observer, are

questions in which we have for the present
no concern. We have simply to note and remember the fact that artists and the public
are learning a new way of seeing things;
that in exactness of observation, in analytic
power, and in the power to generalize from
specific examples, the art of fiction has learned
a great deal from science.

Since fiction deals primarily with
man, the sciences that have particularly affected the art of fiction
are physiology and psychology. An undoubted advantage has come to the novelist
through the wider popular knowledge of the
physical man. The conscious realization of
the dignity and beauty of the human body,
reflected from so many departments of modern literature, has been nowhere more apparent than in fiction. The glorification
of "muscular Christianity" in the novels of
Charles Kingsley is a typical example. The
praise of bodily strength and endurance, the
frank pride in virility and courage, have
scarcely been depicted more superbly by Walt
Whitman himself than by the story-writers
of our time. The respect for the body, the
value set upon physical training and outdoor

Particular sciences: physiology.

sports, rests back very largely upon what science has taught us regarding the importance of these things. " The value and significance of flesh," which other poets besides Browning and Rossetti have endeavored to make clear, may be portrayed mystically, after the manner of poets, or realistically and in a manner more suited to prose; but in either case the science of physiology reinforces it, and affirms its claims to recognition.

Psychology. The progress of the science of psychology has unquestionably taught many novelists a better understanding of mental processes. Recent literature is full of examples of the transference of psychological theory to the pages of fiction, and though, as we shall notice shortly, this has not always resulted in a gain for fiction, it has given to the work of some writers a firmness and precision of analysis and phrase which would otherwise be impossible. One need not go to George Eliot and Mrs. Humphry Ward for examples. The admirable stories of Edith Wharton are essentially psychological both in theme and in workmanship. In passing from Professor William James's essays on psychology to Mr. Henry James's later studies in fiction, one is scarcely conscious of a change in the writer's attitude, though in clearness and workmanlike English the advantage frequently lies with the real critic of Mrs. Piper rather than with the creator of the imaginary Maud-Evelyn. Both pieces of work are studies in the psychology of spiritualism. The investigator has passed along to the fiction writer an almost endless list of possible material for stories, — material which never could have been utilized if it had not been for the professional labor of the psychologist.

Although the influence of the scientific movement has resulted in these obvious gains, both as to the scope and as to the technical methods of fiction, it is also possible to point out very serious disadvantages. The chief of these is the confusion of the distinction between science and art. The late W. J. Stillman, an accomplished critic and observer, wrote two papers on " The Decay of Art " and " The Revival of Art," [1] in which he argued with bitter force that the

Science as harming fiction: confusion between science and art.

---

[1] Reprinted in *The Old Rome and the New and other Essays*. Boston: Houghton, Mifflin and Company, 1898.

spirit of exact inquiry, the fidelity to nature
and to fact, are proving fatal to true artistic
production. " The shadow of science is the
eclipse of art. . . . Photography is the absolute negation of art. . . . The nearer to
nature, the farther from art." Such are
some of the characteristic sentences in his
brilliant attack upon that naturalistic temper
which just now is to be met on every hand.
Mr. Stillman believed that the glorification
of the natural sciences leads inevitably to
the extinction of the perception of the beautiful, that it antagonizes the development of
æsthetic feeling on the part of the public.
Nature should be the servant, not the master.
The " fundamental law is that in its sphere
art is supreme, and nature only its bricks and
mortar. So long as we confound fidelity to
nature with excellence in art, we ignore that
law." Many careful students of contemporary literature will, I believe, recognize the
validity of Mr. Stillman's criticism. The
immemorial heresy that art consists in imitation of nature has received strong support from a generation immensely interested
in the facts of nature.

But the greater the interest felt by artist and public in the facts, in "the human documents," the narrower is the sphere accorded to the imagination. If a careful study of a certain new field is a sufficient equipment for a novelist, why may not any patient observer turn out a masterpiece? Mr. Henry James's excellent advice to the young author, "You can never take too many notes," has been understood in so literal a sense that note-taking seems the end of the whole matter. "I have seventeen hundred pages of notes," M. Zola is reported to have said before the appearance of his novel "Lourdes." "My book is finished; all that I have to do is to write it." But books made after such a fashion usually afford ample warning of the danger of crushing the imagination under the sheer mass and weight of fact. If the human imagination cannot freely master its material, and remould fact in accordance with the demands of the higher, the spiritual truth, then the facts may prove worse than useless. It is well that the bee should bear honey to the hive, but if it tries to carry too much honey, it cannot use its wings.

Belittling of the imagination.

Materialistic tendencies. There are other special disadvantages which have resulted from the scientific depiction of physical fact. There has been, in much of the fiction produced under the immediate influence of the scientific spirit, a materialistic tendency. We have already noticed the philosophy of determinism that underlies the argument of M. Zola's famous essay. In his novels, as M. Brunetière and other critics have not failed to point out, there is constant evidence of the stress laid upon sensations rather than upon emotions, upon the body rather than upon the mind. This preoccupation with the concerns of the body has frequently resulted in grossness. Fiction has spread before us detailed descriptions of the human organism influenced by alcoholism, by opium, by many nameless forms of degeneracy and decay, and the tendency has been too often not merely towards grossness, but towards positively evil suggestion. Upon this point it is sufficient to quote the words of one of the most learned writers on æsthetic theory, Bernard Bosanquet : " The three anti-æsthetic tendencies of art, the scientific, the

moralistic, and the impure, are constantly
found in union." [1]

Turning from the depiction of A mechanical
physical facts to the analysis of psychology.
psychological processes, one may assert that
the extreme impulse given, in certain schools
of modern fiction, to the scrutiny of mental
states has resulted in a mechanical psychology.   The men and women of these stories
are mere puppets.   The authors simply pull
the wires, and the puppets dance as if gal-
vanized into a ghastly semblance of life.
The fondness for morbid states of mind has
kept pace with the unnatural interest in morbid conditions of the body.   Professor Josiah
Royce wrote not many years ago an extremely
acute study of the author of " Pilgrim's Progress," entitled " The Case of John Bunyan."
How many stories of Balzac or even of
Hawthorne might be called " The Case of
Mr. —— ! "   The real difficulty arises in the
temptation of the artist to assume that air
of scientific impartiality which in reality is
nothing other than unsympathetic.   From
being neutral, dispassionate, impartial, how
easy to become pitiless or contemptuous!

[1] Bosanquet, *History of Æsthetic*, p. 446.

Nor would it be difficult to point out that in
the excessive development of the psychological point of view, there is a tendency toward
over-cleverness which has robbed the art of
fiction of its simplicity and naturalness.
There are many pages in George Meredith
and in Henry James acute beyond belief,
subtle to the point of exciting our wondering .
admiration, and yet certainly oversubtle, perverse, and in the end pointless and ineffective. It is true enough that fiction, like
poetry, may normally undertake to criticise
life, but this criticism must not be refined to
the point of being refined away. How often
it fails to move either the reader's interest
or his sympathy! It transports us into the
laboratory, the dissecting room, the study,
but it fails to give us the image of palpitat-
ing, radiant life.

Has fiction gained or lost? On the whole it is difficult to
strike a general balance and say
whether fiction has gained or lost
by contact with science. The gains and
losses seem to me at least to be rather evenly
balanced. We are too close as yet to the
body of fiction produced since 1870 to be
aware of all its implications and indirect con-

sequences.   But there are few students of
the history of fiction who will be inclined to
regret that the scientific experiment has been
so thoroughly tried.   That experiment was
sure to come.   Unquestionably it has im-
paired the power and limited the imagination
of many a writer in our own time.   But it
has also taught some great lessons by which
our novelists of the future may profit if they
will.   These lessons are unmistakable, and
they go to the very root of the philosophy of
artistic creation.   In fiction, more clearly
than in any other field of modern literature,
may be traced the impact of the scientific
method upon the creative imagination.   And
these lessons will remain, however wide may
be the sway of the present reaction against
the scientific method, however sudden the
recoil into the field of mere adventure and
romance.   It should not be forgotten, also,
that the developments of the last thirty
years, the present reaction against them, and
whatever new influences the future may have
in store, are powerless to affect the great fiction produced in bygone generations under
the impulse of other forces.   One can always
go back to Sir Walter if he will.

CHAPTER V

THE CHARACTERS

" Nothing that Turgenieff had to say could be more interesting than his talk about his own work, his manner of writing.
What I have heard him tell of these things was worthy of the
beautiful results he produced; of the deep purpose, pervading
them all, to show us life itself. The germ of a story, with him,
was never an affair of plot — that was the last thing he thought
of : it was the representation of certain persons. The first form
in which a tale appeared to him was as the figure of an individual, or a combination of individuals, whom he wished to see in
action, being sure that such people must do something very
special and interesting. They stood before him definite, vivid,
and he wished to know, and to show, as much as possible of
their nature. The first thing was to make clear to himself what
he did know, to begin with ; and to this end, he wrote out a sort
of biography of each of his characters, and everything that they
had done and that had happened to them up to the opening of
the story. He had their *dossier*, as the French say, and as the
police has of that of every conspicuous criminal. With this material in his hand he was able to proceed ; the story all lay in
the question, What shall I make them do ? He always made
them do things that showed them completely ; but, as he said,
the defect of his manner and the reproach that was made him
was his want of ' architecture,' — in other words, of composition.
The great thing, of course, is to have architecture as well as
precious material, as Walter Scott had them, as Balzac had
them." HENRY JAMES, *Partial Portraits*.

**The novelist's
materials.** WITH this chapter we reach a
new phase of the discussion. We

have hitherto been studying the nature of
prose fiction, and its relation to other forms
of literature as well as to the general scientific
movement of the time. We have now to
consider the materials which the novelist
uses. The present chapter and the two following ones will be devoted to the essential
elements, the raw material, as it were, of the
story-writer's handicraft. We must then
trace in later chapters the modification of
this material due to the nature of the individual novelist and to those literary conventions and traditions which he shares in
common with his generation.

We are accustomed to say of any Characters,
work of fiction that it contains plot, and
setting.
three elements of potential interest,
namely, the characters, the plot, and the
setting or background. In other words, a
story-teller shows how certain persons do
certain things under certain circumstances,
and according to his purpose or the nature
of his particular book he emphasizes one
or the other or possibly all three of these
elements that are calculated to excite and
satisfy the curiosity of the reader.

The characters alone. Let us take, then, the first of these three elements and note the various methods in which story-writers have dealt with their characters. Where do they find them? How do they manage to make the characters clear to the readers of the book? These questions must be answered before we attempt to trace the relation of the characters to the plot, or the relation of both characters and plot to those enveloping circumstances and events which for convenience we have agreed to call the setting of the story.

The novelist's observation. First, then, from what sources does the novelist draw his characters? Either he observes them directly in the actual world, or hears or reads about them and thus appropriates the experience of other persons, or, finally, he may imagine his characters. As far as direct observation of character is concerned, it is obvious that any man's experience with various types or specimens of human character is necessarily limited, although the difference between various novelists in this regard must be singularly great. If one compares the variety of human types that fell under the eye of Fielding with the types with which Richardson was personally acquainted, the advantage would certainly lie on Fielding's side. Sir Walter Scott would certainly be at a disadvantage as compared with Mr. Kipling. Yet these illustrations will suggest the fact that a wide acquaintance with the different forms of human nature is by no means essential to the highest achievement in character-drawing. Novelists like Hawthorne and Charlotte Brontë, with the very narrowest experience and personal acquaintance, have often been able to observe and portray personal characteristics in a fashion that puts the ordinary globe-trotter to shame. The commercial traveler's superficial acquaintance with many men and many cities, affording as it does countless opportunities for the observation of varied traits of human character and action, may not after all be so valuable an equipment for story-writing as the limited and sustained and profound observation of some country minister who has watched men and women from the cradle to the grave.

But a great deal of the material **Indirect** of the novelist comes to him from **knowledge.** what he hears in his conversation with others

or reads in books.   The latter source of information is of course of peculiar value to
those story-writers who have occupied themselves primarily with history.   Dr. Conan
Doyle has remarked that before he wrote
" The White Company " he read three hundred books dealing with the fourteenth century, and the number of volumes read by
George Eliot in preparation for writing
" Romola " and " Daniel Deronda " is said
to have been far greater than this.

"Invention"
and imagina-
tion.

Yet it is clear that few novelists
of high rank ever transfer directly
to their pages the material which
has reached them at second-hand through
conversation or through books.   Nor is it so
common as we suppose to transfer directly to
the pages of the story the material furnished
by the writer's own observation.   In proportion as he is a genuine artist his imagination
plays an increasing rôle in remoulding memories of objects or persons.   We may be sure
that the novelist usually, if not always, desires
something a trifle different from what he has
actually seen or read.   The basis of his character-drawing will always rest to a certain
extent upon self-knowledge, upon his power

to place himself in the imaginary person's
situation and to determine the acts of the
imaginary person by what the author fancies
that he himself would do under those circumstances. The limitations in the range of
character-drawing are not all to be found,
therefore, in the necessarily restricted spheres
of direct observation and second-hand knowledge. A man's comprehension of the possibilities of human nature is also limited by his
knowledge of his own nature.

With these different types of The writer's
character in his mind, ready to be attitude to-
portrayed, what is the attitude of characters.
the writer towards his characters? Sometimes he seems to gaze upward at them in
frank admiration of their beauty and virtue.
Scott's attitude towards his young lady heroines, as has been frequently pointed out, is
one of undisguised worship. And many another romantic novelist has allowed himself
to drop on his knees and fold his hands and
look up at his heroines until he quite forgets
to draw them. Conversely, there are abundant examples in French fiction — the work
of Flaubert and Maupassant affording constant instances — of the author's looking

down upon his characters in an attitude not
merely of detachment but of apparent hos-
tility.   Flaubert regards the struggles of his
most famous heroine much as a biologist
studies the nerve reactions of some insect
pinned to his table for the purposes of experiment.

Friendly in-
terpretation.   There is, however, a happier
mean between these two extremes ;
namely, when the author seems to stand on
a level with his characters, looking them
frankly in the eyes, reading each weakness
clear, but studying them as it were with the
level gaze of friendship.   Every novelist has
his favorite characters ; that is, personages
whom he draws with exceptional sympathy
and fullness of detail, into whose mouths he
may put his own sentiments, whose hearts
seem to throb in unison with his own.   Very
often the novelist betrays in this way his unconscious sympathies.   M. Brunetière many
years ago, in a brilliant essay entitled " Le
personnage sympatique dans la Littérature," [1]
claimed that Shakespeare's Falstaff and Hamlet were examples of this kind of unconscious revelation of the more profound and

[1] *Revue des deux Mondes*, Oct. 15, 1882.

instinctive traits of the writer himself. It is likewise easy to believe, to take an even more familiar example, that Milton was unaware of the fact that he was making Satan the hero of "Paradise Lost."

Moral sympathy is necessary if the work in question is to exhibit *Moral sympathy.* any moral perspective. The artist's delineation should, of course, be impartial, and it is better, in the great majority of cases certainly, that his sympathy should be implicitly rather than explicitly expressed. But the sympathy should be there. The writer of great fiction not only recognizes the difference between good and evil, but he does not allow himself to speak of good and evil in the same tones. To quote Tolstoi on Maupassant, —

" I remember a celebrated painter once showing me a picture of his which represented a religious procession. It was wonderfully painted, but there was no indication of the artist's relation to his subject.

" ' Well, now, do you consider these ceremonies to be good, and that one ought to take part in them or no ? ' I inquired.

" The artist, with a show of condescension to my simplicity, explained that he knew nothing about that, and thought he had no need to know. His business was to depict life.

"'But, any way, you sympathize with all this?'

"'I cannot say so.'

"'Well, do you dislike these ceremonies?'

"'Neither the one or the other,' replied this modern, highly educated artist, with a smile of compassion at my stupidity. He represented life, without understanding its meaning, and unmoved by its aspect to love or dislike. So it was, one regrets to say, with Maupassant.''

Methods of delineating character: direct portrayal. With this material for character-drawing ready to his hand, and with these conscious and unconscious sympathies and antipathies to guide him in his work, how are his characters to be delineated? It is usual in commenting upon the task of the play-wright to make a distinction between direct and indirect methods of character portrayal. The same distinction holds good in fiction. The novelist must often content himself with exhibiting without comment, except so far as the requisite physical description is concerned, the personal appearance of his characters. He narrates their actions, reports their words, or by one of the immemorial conventions of the story-teller's craft, he tells us what is lurking in their thoughts.

But this direct delineation is by no means so frequent as that kind *The author's comment.* of character-drawing which is accompanied with some sort of comment designed to interpret and enforce some of the features of the story. Sometimes the author himself, as so frequently in the novels of Thackeray and George Eliot, takes the stage and explains or moralizes upon the behavior of his personages. Very often there are characters or groups of characters performing something of the function of the ancient Greek chorus in interpreting to the reader the bearing, the moral results, of the act which is taking place. It frequently happens that this character is the "sympathetic personage" whom M. Brunetière has described; that is, the character in deepest accord with the fundamental nature of the author himself. But it by no means happens that this interpreting personage is invariably the leading character of the story. More often it is one of the minor characters who from time to time by indirect comment reveals to the reader the essential nature of all that is happening.

What is called in the case of the play-wright indirect delineation of *Indirect delineation.*

character has also its correspondence in fiction. "I am no longer beautiful," said a famous French woman; "the sweepers no longer turn to look when I cross the street!" Something of the same effect is secured in the chapters of a story as upon the stage, by describing not the hero and the heroine, but the effect produced by them upon the other personages. Some of the most masterly touches in the closing chapters of "Vanity Fair" are devoted to the portrayal of the social and moral position of Rebecca Sharp, but Thackeray does not venture to do this directly. He simply shows how she is treated by the inhabitants of the little town of Pumpernickel. In the stage version of "Vanity Fair" these scenes are brought sharply home to the consciousness of many spectators who probably missed the point of Thackeray's delicate insinuations in the text of the story. The more subtle, the more psychological the particular work of fiction happens to be, the greater become the possibilities of this indirect method of character-delineation. Hawthorne's most effective descriptions of Judge Pyncheon in "The House of the Seven Gables" are not the passages where he describes the judge directly, extraordinarily vivid as these are; they are rather in those paragraphs where the effects produced by Judge Pyncheon's personality upon the transparent nature of Phœbe are made clear to the reader.

The illustration just used suggests a new distinction which we must draw; namely, the difference between the characters as delineated. Let us imagine that the personages of the story, whether drawn directly or indirectly, whether presented with or without comment, now stand before us. Let us suppose ourselves to look at them as quietly and completely as we should observe actors upon the stage. What is the most obvious difference between these people whom the novelist has drawn for us?

Characters as delineated.

One obvious distinction is that between simple and complex characters. Phœbe, in "The House of the Seven Gables," is a deliciously simple character, a nature of such flawless purity that it seems possible to comprehend her at a glance. She belongs to Goethe's Gretchen type, the sort of girl he loved, in his plays, to place in dramatic contrast with accomplished women

Simple and complex.

of the world. Sir Walter Scott's fighting
men are similar examples of perfectly simple
characters.   One understands them at a
glance, and however much one loves or hates
them upon deeper acquaintance, they never
confuse or delude the reader.   A single
fibre makes up the texture of their natures.

Dominant traits. But far more commonly the personages in the novel are complex.
Very often they have one trait which predominates over their others, — as selfishness
is the dominant motive in Becky Sharp, and
love for her husband the dominant motive of
Fielding's Amelia.   Sometimes it is difficult
to say of these complex characters what the
strongest element in their natures will prove
to be.   In " The Marble Faun " much of the
fascination of Miriam's character, especially
when thrown into contrast with Hilda's, turns
upon the extremely complex traits out of which
the character is woven.   The same is true of
Gwendolen in " Daniel Deronda," as compared with Dinah Morris in " Adam Bede."

Stationary and developing characters. Another distinction which plays
a constantly increasing rôle in mod-
ern fiction is that between the stationary and the developing characters.   Cer-

tain personages, and these not the least interesting and congenial to the reader, remain,
like Horatio in the play, constant quantities
to the last.   The vicissitudes of the action
do not affect them.   One is conscious that
whatever happens they will remain to the
end precisely what they were in the beginning, harmonious, evenly balanced characters,
from whose natures the waves of worldly circumstance and trial are thrown back spent
and baffled.   In the novel of adventure, and
particularly in those of the picaresque type,
there is little attempt at any portrayal of character development.   The pawn, the bishop,
the knight, remain to the end of the game
the same as in the beginning.   Mere pieces
on a chess board, they do not change their
nature with the progress of the story.   It is
generally true of the minor characters in the
fiction of the present day that the closing
chapters reveal them exactly as they were in
the beginning.   They are like trees upon the
bank of a river, by means of which one may
measure the swiftness of the stream itself.
But the main characters of the story may be
likened without exaggeration to the river
itself, constantly altering its course, accelerat-

ing or retarding its current, and never quite
the same from one moment to another. This
development of personality in the characters
of the novelist is one of the most subtle and
powerful modes of affecting the sympathy
and interest of the reader. Let us note
some of the ways in which this development
is accomplished.

In fiction, as in life, growth is
Struggle: con-
scious and usually the result of struggle. But
unconscious.
the struggle may be conscious or
unconscious, and may end in victory or in
defeat. There is something very fine about
the wholly unconscious fashion in which
Scott's characters perform their rôle in the
human comedy. There is little self-examina-
tion, no morbid analysis of motives. Most
of his finest personages are of the true
Horatio breed. They behave as if the particular things they do were the only things
possible for them to do and they were not
to trouble themselves about either the acts
or their consequences. The same is true of
many of the most attractive personages of
Dickens, Kingsley, and George Meredith.

Struggle end-
ing in victory George Eliot's novels, on the
or defeat.
other hand, are full of examples of

conscious moral struggle. The men and
women whom she depicts most fully are
constantly analyzing their motives or struggling forward towards some goal. In the
cases of Adam Bede and Daniel Deronda the
conscious moral efforts are successful. These
characters accomplish the aim which they
have established for themselves. The same
may be said for Henry Esmond, and for
Lord Kew in "The Newcomes." Few of
Thackeray's characters torture themselves in
self-analysis, in conscious moral questioning,
and yet the struggles of Esmond and of Lord
Kew are no less real on that account and no
less representative of human nature.

Some of the most famous ex-
amples of character-drawing in **Deterioration.**
modern fiction represent, however, not moral
victory but defeat. To watch a character
deteriorate, no matter how strongly it battles
against adversity of circumstance or inherent
weakness of nature, imparts to fiction the
tragedy of actual life. Lydgate in " Middlemarch " is a familiar example of this deterioration ; so is Anna Karenina in Tolstoi's
novel, and Tess of the D'Urbervilles in the
novel by Thomas Hardy. Both Thackeray

and George Eliot have given us masterly examples of character gradually deteriorating without any real effort to lift itself above the stream of circumstance. Tito Melema in "Romola" and Lord Mohun in "Henry Esmond," like Bartley Hubbard in Mr. Howells's "Modern Instance," steadily drift from bad to worse, and their downward progress is indicated with a precision, a truth, and a moral observation which make a profound impression upon the reader.

Development under special influences.
Very often, however, the characters of fiction are portrayed to us as developing not so much under the stress of conflict, but under the influence of such forces as prosperity, as in "John Halifax, Gentleman," or adversity, as in "Silas Lapham" and "Silas Marner." Or we watch the character alter as it approaches old age, as with Colonel Newcome, or submit to the force of a stronger personality, as in "Richard Feverel." We see it acting under the influence of religious impulse, as with Dinah Morris and David Grieve. We are asked to study the effect upon it of some theory of art or philosophy, as in Pater's "Imaginary Portraits" and Voltaire's "Can-

dide." In all these ways it will be observed
that the author of fiction has endeavored to
hold the mirror up to nature, to make his
book reflect something of the actuality of
moral experience which is the condition of
the growth or the retrogression in the lives
of real men or women.

However real the fictitious per- Character-
sonality may seem to the writer, he istic traits.
must depend upon certain artistic devices for
making the characteristic traits of his personage seem real to the reader. It was the cus-
tom of Scott to devote a page or two of
personal description to each character at the
time of its first introduction into the story.
After this preliminary description of the personal appearance and costume of the character, Scott seemed to trouble his head no more
about the matter. The personage was supposed to be portrayed once for all, and to be
visualized by the reader in the terms of that
presentation. It is more common, however,
to find these characterizing details, whether
of outward appearance or of inner nature,
presented gradually to the reader. Sometimes the characteristic trait in fiction corre-
sponds closely to the " gag " upon the stage,

that is, a trick of speech or action obviously used to identify the character. We grow familiar in " Romola " with Tessa's " baby face." Mr. Brooke in " Middlemarch " is forever saying, " I went into that a good deal at one time." In " David Copperfield " Barkis is always " willin'." These repeated idiosyncrasies of talk, or face, or dress, or manner undoubtedly help to accentuate the individuality of the character, but if too exclusive reliance is placed upon them it is easy to turn them, whether in a book or upon the stage, into caricatures.

Professional traits. It is extremely interesting to notice the delicate and sure touches with which masters of imaginative fiction have portrayed the characteristics of the various professions and occupations. In the Prologue to the " Canterbury Tales," for instance, one never wearies of admiring the simplicity of the soldier, the awkwardness of the sailor on horseback, the lawyer who seemed busier than he was, the doctor who had studied but little of the Bible, the merchant whose talk was of money-making.

Class traits. Class characteristics are also interesting to observe. In an English or Continental novel one is constantly called upon to take account of certain recognized class distinctions, upon which many of the relations of the characters are instantly seen to turn. " A *bourgeois* interior " has a distinct connotation in a French or German novel ; but to describe a similar American interior the word *bourgeois* would not suffice. The cash basis of classification of American society, — so far as it prevails, — while it frequently piques or rewards the professional interest of the literary artist, requires far more labor on his part than if he were to describe the upper, the middle, or the lower classes, removed from one another by the almost impassable barrier fixed by centuries of social tradition.

It is also interesting to note that individuals in fiction frequently take on certain typical traits due to the particular rôle which the individual is to play in the story. The débutante, the dowager, the " woman thirty years old," the " woman misunderstood," have a distinct function in certain stories, and this function affects more or less directly the behavior of the individuals who have been cast for that

Representatives of certain rôles.

particular rôle.   The same is true of the
persons who represent moral failures and
triumphs.   The drunkard, the gambler, the
miser, the philanthropist, have, as types, certain easily recognized traits, and these typical characteristics are not to be left out of
account in studying the character-drawing
of the persons to whom these traits belong.
The same is true of those personages to whom
are assigned definite rôles in the plot of the
story.   The villain, the lover, the intriguer,
the heroine, are parts suggesting definite
lines of character-drawing, and it is impossible to construct an individual character in
fiction without regard to the conventional
requirements of the rôle which the person is
asked to play.

National and sectional traits.   Furthermore, there are typical
national traits which are always to
be noted in addition to those lines
of difference which we have just discussed.
The Italian, the Frenchman, the Englishman,
when introduced into a novel, must show to
a greater or less extent the typical behavior
of the Italian, the Frenchman, or the Englishman.   In depicting national characteristics, sectional traits, too, play an important

part. In introducing an American into a
story few novelists are willing to satisfy
themselves by representing such a " typical
American" as is presented upon the Paris
or London stage. The novelist with a fine
sense of precision in character-drawing would
certainly wish to note those characteristics
that distinguish the Southerner from the
Northerner, the Hoosier from the Californian
or the Texan. Even within the boundaries
of a single section, as the history of New
England fiction so abundantly illustrates,
there is an immense variety of different
types.

It becomes essential, therefore,
that we should distinguish closely
between the individual and the
type. What is really meant by these two
words? And which should the artist aim to
delineate? We say in actual life that men
like Samuel Johnson or Abraham Lincoln possess individuality, — that is, that they have
certain sharply defined personal characteristics which readily and absolutely separate
them from all other individuals in the world.
In fiction, persons like Becky Sharp and
Colonel Newcome have precisely this same

individual characterization, and cannot for a moment be confused with other persons in other stories. As compared with these examples of individuals what do we mean by a type? The dictionaries suggest two lines of definition, both of which are of use to the student of fiction. According to the first, type means an *ideal representation* of a species or group, combining its essential characteristics. It is this sense of the word which dictionary makers have in mind in describing the type as the ideal hovering before the artist. But in the terms of another definition, type also means an *example* of a species or group combining its essential characteristics. When, therefore, we speak of types in fiction we sometimes mean that a person is portrayed as embodying more or less perfectly certain ideals which exist in the mind of the artist, and we also mean very frequently that the typical person is simply an excellent example of a well known species or group.

The type in natural history.

We shall find a convenient illustration in natural history. I remember hearing a famous naturalist say that the crow is a typical bird, —

that is, that, compared with the woodpecker, the hawk, the crane, the crow represents the normal form of the bird family. Naturalists speak, indeed, of the type genus, the type species, and the type specimen, meaning thereby a division that is especially characteristic of the larger group which it represents. And our distinction in fiction between the individual and the type would perhaps be more fully illustrated by the use of the terms " genus," " species," and " specimen." Genus, let us say, *corvus ;* species, *corvus Americanus ;* and specimen, some particular crow under observation, — for example, old " Silver-Spot," so agreeably described by Mr. Seton-Thompson. This distinction is a perfectly simple one. When we say that the fox terrier is intelligent, we mean that the type is intelligent. When I say that my fox terrier is intelligent, I have the individual in mind.

Let us see how all this bears on the question of character-drawing in fiction. We will suppose that the novelist wishes to introduce into his story the figure of Abraham Lincoln. It is obvious that he must represent Lincoln as

This distinction applied to fiction.

belonging to the family of man, the genus
American, the species Westerner, but that
all these generic and typical traits must be
further differentiated by delineating the qualities which distinguish the individual specimen, Abraham Lincoln, from other Western
American men.

Confusion of the type with the individual. But nothing is more frequent in
fiction than to find these two
things confused. How does it happen? First, through an attempt to describe
the individual by typical traits merely. If I
say that a tramp came to my back door this
morning and asked for some breakfast, and
that he had torn shoes, old clothes, a slouch-
ing gait, the face of a drinker, I do not identify him in the slightest. If I were to put
the police on his trail, armed with such a
description, it would fit fifty other tramps as
well as the one I have in mind. It is obvious
that to identify this particular individual I
must be able to describe some peculiarity of
person or costume which differentiates him
from others of his class, or at least to describe such a combination of qualities and
details as is not likely to be found in the
case of any other tramp.

Secondly, the type and the individual are often confused in character-drawing because the writer substitutes for the individual some moral abstraction. In the old moralities and miracle plays such characters as Good Fame, Virtuous Living, Tom Tosspot, Cuthbert Cutpurse, are nothing but signs of certain moral qualities, to be praised or reprehended according to the pleasure of the play-wright. Even the Elizabethan drama, in all its wealth of individual portraiture, is constantly presenting to us personages who are mere personifications of moral qualities, and Bunyan's masterly power of characterization does not prevent some readers from considering Mr. Worldly Wiseman and Mr. Faintheart to be moral images rather than men.

Moral abstractions.

Thirdly, the type is frequently confused with the individual because the artist gives a caricature rather than a portrait. In pictorial caricature, as we know, certain features are exaggerated until the individual is far removed from reality. Tweed and Croker, if we are to believe the caricaturists, are not real persons. They are simply embodiments of certain abstract and

Caricatures.

highly reprehensible moral qualities. It is easy to point out, in some of the very greatest fiction, examples of the fatal ease with which the writer can turn a portrait into a caricature. Sir Pitt Crawley's stinginess apparently tickled Thackeray's fancy so thoroughly that he could not resist the temptation to exaggerate it until it was so much out of drawing that it robbed the character of its actuality. As compared with Sir Pitt Crawley, Becky Sharp's portrait shows constant restraint and a steady sense of proportion. Those personages of Dickens whom we are wont to speak of as " Dickensy " characters are all too frequently caricatures rather than portraits. Certain traits are so magnified for purposes of identification or humor that we see not the real person but only the " gag," the trick, the turn of farce, which presents him to the audience. Children delight in this sort of thing, of course, but many older persons wonder, when they come to Dickens again, how all this false drawing could ever have given them pleasure.

The causes of confusion: lack of clear vision. It is more interesting, however, to inquire into the causes of this confusion. Why is it that the artist allows himself to substitute typical for individual traits and hence to lose the power of imparting a sense of actuality to his fictitious personages ? It is often true, no doubt, that the author fails to see clearly what he wants to express. He falls into abstract, typical delineation through mere irresolution or inattention, or it may be the overfondness for what he may like to call the " ideal," that is, for the abstract rather than for the concrete. To this latter predilection must be attributed the feebleness of a great deal of Romantic art. It accounts for the weakness of Scott's character-drawing of ladies in comparison with his masterly delineation of peasant girls.

Then, too, the prevalence of a fashionable artistic type is often found to overpower the artist's originality. The " Gibson girl," who is said to be due originally to the influence of a certain model in Mr. Gibson's early career as an artist, has continued not only to dominate most of Mr. Gibson's own drawings of women, but has been nothing less than an obsession, though a charming one, upon a whole school of American draughtsmen. In similar fash-

Prevalence of fashionable types.

ion, there was a sort of Richard Harding Davis heroine who used to make her periodical appearance in college stories. Indeed, college stories furnish an excellent example of the prevalence of a certain fashionable type and the consequent neglect of individual portraiture. In all the college stories which have appeared in the last dozen years how few sharply characterized individuals are to be found! It is far easier to describe the category under which a particular student belongs and to give the general traits of the " football man," the " sport," the " grind," than it is to portray the particular person who belongs to the category. In other words, most authors of college stories content themselves, as far as character-depiction is concerned, by describing the pigeon-hole rather than the man in the pigeon-hole.

Failure in expression. In the third place, although the fiction-writer may see the individual with perfect distinctness, either as actually present before him or in imaginative vision, he may nevertheless not be able to express what he sees. He draws the general characteristics of the type rather than the individual characteristics of the person because his vocab-

ulary is not sufficiently delicate and precise
for the task of portrayal. Here, again, college stories afford a useful illustration. It
is not to be supposed that the authors of
those stories see their fellows less distinctly,
nor that they perceive imaginative types with
less clearness of outline, simply because they
are dealing with young men and young women. The defect is chiefly to be attributed
to the lack of training in flexible and precise
expression.

But for one or another of these
three causes which have been briefly *Few individ-*
ual charac-
outlined, how few individual char- *ters created.*
acters have been created in fiction in the
last ten years! We have had certain types
drawn over and over again with wearisome
reiteration, but we have had few fictitious
personages who have given us the impression
of actuality. It must be remembered after
all that the type is, in the last analysis, only
a subjective abstraction, either in the reader's
mind or in the mind of the artist. The masters of fiction, surely, have generally con-
tented themselves with creating personages
and letting the type take care of itself. If
the personage be so drawn as to convey a

vivid sense of reality, his individual characteristics will be firmly outlined ; and if he gives
to the reader an impression of moral unity,
there is little doubt that he will in the true
sense contain the type.   For the type, so far
as it is of any artistic value, is implicit in the
individual.

Character-contrast. Before bringing to a close the
consideration of the delineation of
character, we should note that some of the
greatest triumphs in the portrayal of character
have been due to an effective sense of character-contrast.   The differences between members of the same family — as for instance
between Adam and Seth Bede, Rachel and
Beatrix Esmond, George and Henry War-
rington — have been utilized with consummate effect.   The same is true of those pairs
or trios of friends of which the history of
the drama and of the novel offers so many
brilliant examples.   Hamlet and Horatio,
Athos, Porthos and Aramis, Mulvaney, Ortheris and Learoyd, gain immensely in sa-
liency and picturesqueness of outline because
they are thrown into dramatic contrast with
those friends in whose presence we are wont
to watch them.

Character - grouping on a still *Character-grouping.* wider scale results from those mani- fold social, economical, and political rela- tions which place differently constituted indi- viduals in clearly marked lines of relation- ship. Master and servant, mistress and maid, lover and confidant, debtor and creditor, the dwellers on the farm or in the village, the representatives of a profession, the ad- venturers in some commercial or political enterprise, are linked together by bonds which give an opportunity for striking groups of characters. Indeed, in every story, as in every play, there is commonly some unifying principle, like a love affair, a crime, a journey, a business scheme, which instantly throws all the persons of the story into some sort of relationship with one an- other. Their attitude towards certain facts instantly ranks them, as by a kind of irre- sistible physical or moral gravitation. They are thrown into main groups or subordinate groups according to the part they play in the main plot or in the sub-plot of the tale. They work out their individual destiny in harmony or in contrast with the general destiny that presides over the fate of the personages in the narrative; they advance or retreat, compromise, surrender, or triumph as the judgment and the insight of the writer shall dictate. But in all the manifold and subtle relations into which the persons in the story are thrown, there is an opportunity for the most searching, the most spirited, the most brilliant methods of character-delineation. If, as Goethe said, a character is formed in the stream of the world, the characters in a novel form themselves into more and more plastic outlines as the stream of the story sweeps to its close.

Harmony of character and action. It is, therefore, quite impossible to conceive of characters in a novel without taking into consideration the actions in which those characters are involved. The two elements, character and action, should be harmoniously treated. There will always be in fiction, doubtless, examples of "plot-ridden" characters; that is, persons whose rôle in the story makes them do something which they would not naturally do. A high-minded girl is made to listen at the door simply because it is desirable that she should be aware of a conversation taking place between her father and

her lover. An honest man is made to commit a crime because a crime is essential to
the particular web of circumstances which
the author desires to weave. But these
instances of the violation of truth in character are usually punished by the sense of dis-
belief which the reader is quick to feel. It
is natural that we should demand in fiction,
as in life, that the character should be true
to itself, that under the given circumstances
it should exhibit consistent behavior.

What is more, we instinctively
demand in the characters that im- **Moral unity.**
press us by their individuality that moral
unity by virtue of which each character
shows evidence of what has happened to it in
the past. Just as each one of us is conscious
of his past, and is also conscious of the
possibilities of the future, and bears this
consciousness, although perhaps without real-
izing it, into every act of the present, so we
desire that the men and women described for
us in the pages of the novelist should give
this sense of the continuity, the unbroken
web of life. To enter a railroad station —
say at Buffalo — and see an east-bound express standing on the track, resplendent in

paint and gilt, and ready to pull out of the station, is to receive an impression of actuality and power. But one has a far higher sense of power if one watches at the station this same train coming in from the West, an hour late, with vestibule and roof and windows covered with snow and ice, in evidence of the storm through which the train has passed. We picture to ourselves the winter landscape over which it has been flying in its struggle against time. We know that before it reaches Albany or New York that lost hour must be made up, if engine and engineer can do it. The past and the future of the train unite in their impression on our consciousness, and impart a thrilling sensation of personal force. In the same way, our vision of men and women in the greatest books of fiction is not confined to the immediate moment when they are present to our view; we are more or less dimly conscious of the past and of the future of those characters and of all the moral potentialities of their lives.

CHAPTER VI

THE PLOT

" Let him [the fiction-writer] choose a motive, whether of character or of passion ; carefully construct his plot so that every incident is an illustration of the motive, and every property employed shall bear to it a near relation of congruity or contrast ; avoid a sub-plot, unless, as sometimes in Shakespeare, the sub-plot be a reversion or complement of the main intrigue ; . . . and allow neither himself in the narrative nor any character in the course of the dialogue, to utter one sentence that is not part and parcel of the business of the story. . . . And as the root of the whole matter, let him bear in mind that his novel is not a transcript of life, to be judged by its exactitude ; but a simplification of some side or point of life, to stand or fall by its significant simplicity." R. L. STEVENSON, *A Humble Remonstrance.*

IN discussing the affiliations of the novel with the play, in the third chapter of this book, I have had occasion to say something about the plot and its relation to the theme and to the characters of the play or the novel. The word means, as its etymology implies, a weaving together. Or, still more simply, we understand by plot that which happens to the characters, — the various ways in which the forces represented

What plot means.

by the different personages of the story are
made to harmonize or clash through external
action.

Sources of
plot.
In determining the nature and
the details of the action of a story,
it is obvious that the novelist may draw on
the same sources of knowledge which he
uses in the construction of the characters.
The plot may be suggested to him by his
own observation, by memories of what he
has heard or read, or through the pure gift
of inventiveness.   One can scarcely say that
there is marked superiority in any one of
these methods.   Many novelists, like Hawthorne, have been inclined to confess rue-
fully : " I have seen so little of the real
world, that I have nothing but thin air to
concoct my stories out of."   On the other
hand, the experience of writers like Dickens,
Thackeray, or Mr. Kipling has crowded their
memory with incidents and events admirably
adapted to furnish the raw material of countless plots.   Sometimes, no doubt, it is difficult to readjust such matter and make it
sufficiently plastic to give free play to the
imagination.   The stories that come to one
by inheritance through half forgotten memo-

ries of country-side legends and traditions, nar-
ratives which one dimly remembers from old
books or scraps of history and ballads, have
often proved more stimulating to the constructive imagination than any hints given
by actual experience. Just as Liszt wrote
his rhapsodies by utilizing hints and fragments of folk-lore and popular melodies, so
Thomas Hardy finds it easy in his " Wessex
Tales " to utilize the histories of decaying
families, stories of adventure of long ago,
strange tales that have been whispered by the
hearth-fire from immemorial times. " Truth
is stranger than fiction," and truth often
needs to be recast by a fictive imagination
before it is quite ready for the fiction-writer's
hand.

But this matter of plot gives lit- Often a mat-
tle difficulty to those born story- ter of instinct.
tellers who have the gift for conceiving characters in action. For these natural spinners
of the yarn, to whom invention is the most
easy, the most fascinating, the most capti-
vating of gifts, — for a Stevenson, a Scott,
a Dumas, — to block out the plot of a story
is a mere bagatelle. In Scott's own words,
he " took the easiest path across country,"

following merely his whim or his natural instinct; and one is bound to record the fact
that the novels written or planned by these
reckless, inveterate story-tellers afford quite
as much satisfaction to technical students of
plot-construction as do the more elaborate
plans and devices of those writers whose interest lies foremost in the creation of character, and with whom the element of action is
of secondary concern.

Plot in its
simplest form.
Plot in its simplest form may
concern itself with nothing more
than the progress of a single character and
its development and experiences at the different stages of its career.   Take, for instance, that admirable story by Hawthorne,
" Wakefield," which concerns itself with the
psychological analysis of the character of
an excellent gentleman to whom it occurred
one day that it would be a good plan not to
go home that night, and who consequently
sought lodgings in another street and stayed
away from home for twenty years.   Hawthorne makes real to us the whimsical, yet
singularly human and consistent motive that
actuated this strange character in his aston-
ishing performance ; and although the story

involves but a single personage, it would be difficult to point to any short story of equal length in which the reader feels greater interest.

Usually, however, the plot of a story involves at least two characters. They embody different

Dealing with two characters.

forces, different ways of facing and fighting the world of circumstance with which they are brought into collision. In "Silas Marner," for instance, the human problem involved is the influence of the love of a child on the lonely and embittered nature of a hermit. The action of the story is designed to bring these two forces together and to note the nature of their mutual reactions. The plot of Hawthorne's "Rappaccini's Daughter" involves the struggle between scientific curiosity and paternal love. These forces are embodied in the persons of the scientist and his daughter, and the plot is inevitably worked out by the natural laws of human character, "the truth of the human heart," under the peculiar circumstances which the author chooses to describe. And, to choose another short story of a different type, there is Mr. Kipling's "His Private Honour." In this story a young British lieutenant, in a moment of extreme irritation, strikes a private soldier. The act is one that calls for dismissal from the Queen's service. What is the officer to do? He cannot send money to the soldier — who happens to be the redoubtable Ortheris himself — nor can he apologize to him in private. Neither can he let matters drift. Ortheris, too, has his own code of pride and honor; he too is " a servant of the Queen;" but how is the insult to be atoned for? The way out of this apparently hopeless muddle is a beautifully simple one, after all. The lieutenant invites Ortheris to go shooting with him, and when they are alone, asks him to " take off his coat." " Thank you, sir ! " says Ortheris. The two men fight until Ortheris owns that he is beaten. Then the lieutenant apologizes for the original blow, and officer and private walk back to camp devoted friends. That fight is the moral salvation of Lieutenant Ouless. The plot of " His Private Honour " is, therefore, the narrative of the struggle between two kinds of pride, the pride of the officer and that of the enlisted man, and the solution comes through Mr. Kipling's power to make us realize the English love of fair play, the fundamental human equality which is common to both men despite the difference of their rank.

It is far easier, however, to throw the lines of a plot into swift com- Three characters. plication when there are at least three characters involved. The attitude of two of these characters towards the third may instantly be utilized to establish and carry forward new lines of action. In " The Knight's Tale " of Chaucer the two young men imprisoned in the tower catch their first glimpse of Emily, and this moment marks the first entanglement of the threads of the future plot. In Miss Wilkins's " New England Nun " there is an extremely skillful example of this kind of plot. The story opens with a picture of Louisa Ellis, an " old maid," sitting in her quiet room on a summer afternoon, and receiving an embarrassed visit from her betrothed lover, Joe Daggett. Their engagement has lasted fifteen years, while he has been absent in Australia seeking his fortune. Each has been faithful to the other, yet now that the wedding is only a week away, disorder and confusion seem entering

her cloistered life in place of peace and harmony.   She does not dare tell her lover how
much, after all, she dreads to marry him.
He, too, has become aware that their passion
is a thing of the past; he is conscious of a
love for Lily Dyer, a younger woman; but
he is as finely loyal to his old promise as
Louisa herself.   How does Miss Wilkins
cut the knot?   By making Louisa stroll
down the road one moonlight night and unwittingly overhear a conversation between
Joe and Lily, in which she learns that they
love each other, but that they both believe it
cruel and wrong for Joe to break his engagement with Louisa.   It is now easy and natural
for Louisa to release Joe, to see him married
to Lily Dyer, and happily, prayerfully, to
number her own days " like an uncloistered
nun."

The "three-
leaved
clover" re-
lationship.
It may be added that the essential elements of this three-cornered
game played by two men and one
woman, or two women and one man, here
handled by Miss Wilkins in one of its most
innocent and unsophisticated phases, present
to the fiction-writer, for purely technical reasons, a fascinating problem.   Such a three-

fold relationship inevitably involves the play
of strong passions, the elements of fear, of
jealousy, of danger, of surprise, of remorse;
and all of these are furnished, as it were, ready
to the novelist's hand by the theme itself.

As was pointed out in the chap- Complication
ter devoted to the drama, the of plot.
complication of the plot begins with the
introduction of new incidents or new personages, or with the introduction of new motives growing out of the relationships which
are made evident at the outset of the story.
In Hawthorne's "The House of the Seven
Gables" the opening of the shop marks the
beginning of the complication. In "The
Scarlet Letter" it is the entrance of Roger
Chillingworth. It is an interesting question
how far the complication of the plot may
be carried out without confusing or perplex-
ing the reader. Novelists of the Latin races
have commonly given evidence of a greater
instinct for unity, are more simple in the
constructive features of their work, than
those of the Teutonic races. The novels of
Dickens and Thackeray probably mark the
extreme limit of complexity, as regards
the number of personages introduced, the

variety of sub-plots, and the length of time
required for the main action of the story.
There are said to be seventy-five personages
in " Our Mutual Friend," and sixty in " Vanity Fair."   In " Middlemarch " there are
twenty-two persons whose portraits are painted
at full length.[1]   American fiction has apparently been more influenced of late by Continental than by English examples, and the
result has been a more marked simplicity in
construction.

Incident and situation.   In studying the complication of
the plot, it often becomes advan-
tageous to distinguish between incidents
which reveal the true nature of the characters and situations which determine character.   The difference in the thing is more
to be insisted upon than the differentiation
of names, and yet it is fair to characterize as
an " incident " any event which gives the
reader a clearer insight into the constitution
and motives of the personages in the story.   In
"The House of the Seven Gables " the elaborate scene at the breakfast-table has for its
sole aim the presentation of the character of

[1] C. F. Johnson, *Elements of Literary Criticism,* p. 89.
New York: Harpers.

Clifford, and the whole chapter is devoted to the revelation of the finer and more æsthetic traits of his worn, delicate nature. It is for this purpose only that the breakfast-table scene finds its justification. In " Henry Esmond," Harry's drive on the downs with Lord Mohun is the incident used to give a more complete exposition of character, as well as of the relationship gradually growing up between Harry and Rachel Esmond. It determines nothing. It simply informs us of what is going on, what must be reckoned with. On the other hand, to take another illustration from the same novel, the scene where Harry sees Beatrix descending the staircase, and also the one where Harry breaks his sword in the presence of the Pretender, or in " The House of the Seven Gables " again, in the scene where Judge Pyncheon demands entrance into the parlor and is refused, — these are situations which really determine character as well as reveal it. Esmond is a different man after those scenes have been depicted ; and Judge Pyncheon has himself been judged.

Perhaps enough has been said   Climax. in the third chapter to illustrate the similarity between the climax in the novel and the climax in the play. In both of these parallel forms of literature there is commonly some scene which marks the greatest tension, the keenest suspense, involved in the relation of the characters. The elopement of Stephen Guest and Maggie Tulliver, Gwendolen's awful moment of hesitation when Grandcourt is struggling in the water, will illustrate George Eliot's management of climax passages. In such passages the personal forces involved are for the instant in equilibrium. Thenceforward everything sweeps on to the dénoûment or catastrophe of the story. There is little difference between the novel and the play in the technical disposition of the series of incidents and situations which make up the " rising " and the " falling " action.

Catastrophe.   There is, however, a noticeable distinction in the technical handling of the catastrophe. The absolute necessity in the drama of externalizing upon the stage the forces knit together in the final struggle makes compulsory the actual exhibition of various events which the novelist would prefer to suggest merely. Indeed, it has come to be the favorite theory with a certain school of psychological novelists that, as life seldom presents any dramatic catastrophes, fiction had better avoid catastrophes too. In the novels of this sort nothing in particular occurs. At the close we miss the " God bless you, my children ! " and also the tragic allotment of disaster or disgrace. The characters live on, quite as if nothing had happened, and it is only the new insight into personality, the new descriptions of the natural world or of social forces, which the reader has as a reward for his pains.

All this turns, as a matter of course, upon the relation of the personages to the underlying theme. In the novel of character, as opposed to the novel of incident, the author is chiefly concerned with the solution of certain problems of emotion or of will. When he has worked these out to his satisfaction, his task is finished, and he becomes relatively indifferent to the final disposition of all the personages of the tale. It is well known that Hawthorne added the present closing chapter to " The Marble Faun " at the request of his publishers, and this fact suggests the irreconcilable difference between the point of view of the romancer absorbed in moral problems and of the reader who merely wants to know what happened "ever afterwards."

The plot-novel.   In the plot-novel, on the other hand, the inner truth of character may often be neglected or distorted, provided successive shocks of surprise and pleasure are cleverly arranged. The detective story, for instance, deals chiefly with the elements of curiosity and suspense. But the curiosity, while it must be stimulating, must not be carried to the extreme of perplexity, and the suspense must not be too long sustained. In proportion as the stress is laid upon adventure merely, as in the picaresque novel, there need be little if any complexity in the plot. The mere succession of incidents, like those in Stevenson's "St. Ives," is enough to hold the fascinated attention of the reader. The weakness, however, in many of the modern types of the novel of adventure, is not due to placing too much stress upon mere incident as an element, but to the fact that character-interest has become a negligible quantity. If the reader does not, for the time being, believe in the reality of those characters whose adventures he is asked to follow, he soon finds himself little concerned with the adventures. For, after all, as the history of the drama has shown so abundantly, that which perennially fascinates us in the human spectacle is the exhibition of character in action. Characters who do not act, and conversely the mere outward show and stir of movement not informed by any real intellectual or passional life, alike fail to move our interest, our hopes, or fears.

The question of suspense in the plot leads naturally to the element **Mystery and mystification.** of mystery. In any good story we are led to a normal interest both in what the characters will do under the stress of unsuspected circumstances and in the shape which events will take. But this expectation of " something evermore about to be," which lends interest to fiction as it does to life, must be distinguished from that element of mystery with which many novelists have loved to surround certain of their characters, and in which they have liked to hide the intricacies of their plots. It is in this sense that Miriam in " The Marble Faun " is a mysterious character, and that there is a " mystery " in most detective stories. While this element of mystery is

by no means essential to the interest of a
work of fiction, it is capable of the most
artistic handling. But when the mystery
becomes mystification, when both the personages in the story and the readers of the story
are deliberately fooled by the author, the
book commonly pays at last the penalty of
this deception. When we learn at the end
of Mrs. Radcliffe's "Mysteries of Udolpho"
that all the mysterious terrors which have
played such a potent rôle in the plot were the
result of a mechanical contrivance, it is impossible to reread the book with any of those
delightful thrills of horror which the impres-
sionable reader experienced upon the first
reading. But between this deliberate deception of the reader and the painful efforts of
some realistic novelist to place the reader in
possession of all the facts, there is an infinite
variety of possible methods. Perhaps the
critic cannot do more than say that that book
is likely to give the most pleasure to the reader
which presents, in accordance with the conventions and in the terms of art, the sense of
uncertainty, the blindfold striving, the constant awaiting of the revelation of the coming
moment, which play such an appreciable part
in life itself.

Closely allied with the element of mystery is that of accident, **Accident.** sometimes used as a complicating but more often as a resolving force. It is accident that weaves and unravels the plot of many a novel. The hero picks up a handkerchief, or steps on a lady's train, or unwittingly insults an unknown rival, or knocks at the wrong door of an inn, and upon these trivialities hangs, or seems to hang, his entire fortune. Similarly, when the climax of a story has been reached, there is often in fiction, as in the drama, some petty incident, apparently accidental but really hidden deep in the nature of things, which determines the catastrophe.

Indeed, it may be said that it matters little how frequently the **Retribution.** novelist complicates or simplifies his plot by the introduction of the element of accident, provided the accidents seem to be thus a part of the natural order of things. Richard the Lion-Hearted dies by a chance arrow, and yet what other fate would be so inevitable to an adventurous, reckless, wandering hero? Bill Sykes hangs himself with a noose of his own making, and yet Dickens seems to be a fellow-worker with Providence in designing such an appropriate and wholly pleasing end for such a villain. It is a temptation to the unskilled novelist to kill off his personages at a convenient time, to resort to all sorts of advantageous and unexpected devices to get rid of the superfluous figures in his story. But to link apparently accidental, external circumstances with inner laws of character and conduct, to make what happens to the characters a fit result of all which the characters have done or been in the past, gives an opportunity for the most profound insight into the moral structure of the world. When Judge Pyncheon tries by brute energy and with deadly hatred of purpose to force his way into the little parlor of the Pyncheon house, Hepzibah says to him, "God will not let you." The Judge replies, "We shall see." And we do see through the long hours of the ensuing night the terrible retribution which came instantly upon him. Yet Hawthorne takes pains to suggest that there may be a perfectly natural physical explanation of the sudden death of the Judge. Not the "visitation of God," as juries are wont to say when at their wits' end, but an inherited tendency to apoplexy,

joined with a moment of intense bodily and
mental excitement, is sufficient to account for
the Judge's death.   An even more familiar
example of extraordinary insight and truth
on the novelist's part is evinced in the Templar's death in "Ivanhoe." Here, too, a
natural explanation is at hand.   Ivanhoe has
appealed to "the judgment of God;" yet
the Templar dies, Scott tells us, through the
"violence of his own contending passions."
But the threads of the story are drawn together with so sure a hand that the reader
feels certain that this dread event is fated.
"'This is indeed the judgment of God,' said
the Grand Master, looking upwards — '*Fiat
voluntas tua.*'"

It is hard to say, indeed, just
what we mean by fate in discussing
the dénoûment or catastrophe of the **Fate in the modern novel.**
modern novel.   It is easy enough in com-
menting on the Greek drama to point out the
beginning and the end of the Nemesis action,
and the conventions of the Greek drama as
well as many of its moral implications have
descended to us almost unbroken.   Yet it is
hardly possible, in a world pervaded, like our
modern world, by Christian ethics and a Chris-

tian philosophy, that the old Greek theory of
the rôle which fate plays in human affairs
should still prevail. In one sense the world of
art, the world revealed to us by the imagination of the novelist or the poet, is a world
which is neither Christian nor pagan. Even
this imaginary world, however, can never be
unmoral unless it be at the same time unreal.
"Morality," said Mme. de Staël very finely,
"is in the nature of things." The laws of
human life itself, laws older than any pagan
or Christian interpretation or revelation of
them, assert that in any long view of life it
is well with the good and ill with the wicked.
It is true that in any stage of the world's
progress it is possible that the individual
artist may revert to an earlier, outworn type
of philosophy and faith. He may cherish a
pagan theory of the Christian world. Like
Thomas Hardy at the close of "Tess of the
D'Urbervilles," which is an admirable expression of a poignant, thoughtful, yet thoroughly pagan interpretation of life, he may
utter a cynical jest at the moral order of
this planet. Says Mr. Hardy, "Time, that
arch satirist, had had his joke out with
Tess."

This is consistent with the theme "Poetic justice." of the book, but it is inconsistent with the world in which Mr. Hardy is living and with the noblest teachings of the greatest masters of his art. In assigning "poetic justice" to the men and women of their stories, they have succeeded most truly when they have allotted the fates of their personages in accordance with what they have conceived to be the laws of Divine Justice. The profounder artists in the imaginary world of fiction, and the Providence, however named, who presides over the real world of nature and human life, are working on the same terms and expressing the same truth.

In following the main lines of action in a story, the student of Sub-plots. fiction will do well to observe the different ways in which the main and the subordinate plots are related. Often the subordinate plot is the mere reflection of the greater plot, as the love affair of Lorenzo and Jessica in "The Merchant of Venice" is the obvious replica of that of Portia and Bassanio. And where the theme of the novelist is philosophical or scientific, designed to show the presence in human affairs of certain lines of causation and certain modes of thinking and feeling, the lesser group of characters may often be used most skillfully to reflect, in different degrees, the main teaching of the book. Thomas Hardy's peasants furnish excellent examples of this philosophizing, as do the rustics of George Eliot. Frequently the sub-plot follows inevitably upon the main plot. If the story of "Silas Marner" turns upon the redemption of a lonely old man by a child, it becomes necessary to provide a child for the purpose, and this leads to the invention of Godfrey Cass's unfortunate marriage. Very often, however, the sub-plot is joined to the main plot in a purely artificial fashion. The minor characters are designed to give variety or relief, to supply a love interest or an element of comedy, or to pique one's historical interest concerning some great person who is made to appear for the moment upon the scene. Rose and Langham, although they are most attractively and carefully wrought figures, have nothing to do with the real plot of "Robert Elsmere."

Savonarola has no rôle to play in George Eliot's "Romola" except in so far as he is introduced to give advice to the heroine in the hour of her need, and to illustrate certain characteristic phases of fifteenth century Florence.

Something has already been said about the danger of plot-determined characters. Where the plot *Plot-determined characters.* requires a love episode the novelist is tempted to make a given man fall in love with a given woman "upon compulsion," even if the natures of the two persons, as well as the circumstances involved, protest against the alliance. There is no surer mark of the amateur in fiction than the fascination said to be exerted by certain characters who obviously have no fascination to exert. "Bright ideas" come to characters who could never by any stretch of the imagination conceive of a bright idea. We are assured of the sudden access of courage or devotion or folly in persons in whose temperaments and characters there is no room for these traits which it becomes necessary for the unfortunate author to discover and utilize.

Finally, the action of the story
Plot as re-
lated to set-
ting.
itself should be related not only to
the characters themselves, but to
those circumstances and events indirectly
involved in the tale, and furnishing as it
were the background and setting for it. The
plot of the " Tale of Two Cities," for instance, must do no violence to the supposed
characters of Dr. Manette and Sydney Car-
ton, but it must also be faithful as far as
possible to the spirit and the external facts
of the French Revolution itself. Indeed, in
the case of this particular book, it is well
known that Dickens's imagination began to
work on the period, upon the events and passions of that stormy time, rather than upon
the distinctive personages of the tale. He
carried around in his pocket, for months before he began to write the story, a copy of
Carlyle's " French Revolution," familiarizing
himself with the dramatic forces involved in
that extraordinary epoch. When he came
later to invent his personages and to assign
to them their appropriate rôles in the drama
which they were to play, he depicted both
characters and action in harmony with the
enveloping circumstances, with the fears, the

hopes, the anguish, the suspense of the Revolution itself. If, as we saw at the conclusion of the preceding chapter, it is necessary that the characters of a novel should be conceived in reference to the part they are to play in the plot, we must now recognize with equal clearness that the plot itself must stand in artistic relation to the setting.

CHAPTER VII

THE SETTING

"Either on that day or about that time I remember very distinctly his saying to me: 'There are, so far as I know, three ways, and three ways only, of writing a story. You may take a plot and fit characters to it, or you may take a character and choose incidents and situations to develop it, or lastly — you must bear with me while I try to make this clear' — (here he made a gesture with his hand as if he were trying to shape something and give it outline and form) — 'you may take a certain atmosphere and get action and persons to express and realize it. I'll give you an example — *The Merry Men*. There I began with the feeling of one of those islands on the west coast of Scotland, and I gradually developed the story to express the sentiment with which the coast affected me.'" *The Life and Letters of Robert Louis Stevenson*, by GRAHAM BALFOUR.

"It is the habit of my imagination to strive after as full a vision of the medium in which a character moves as of the character itself. The psychological causes which prompted me to give such details of Florentine life and history as I have given [in *Romola*] are precisely the same as those which determined me in giving the details of English village life in *Silas Marner* or the 'Dodson' life, out of which were developed the destinies of poor Tom and Maggie." GEORGE ELIOT, quoted in her *Life* by J. W. CROSS.

Meaning of the word. WHEN we read Victor Hugo's "Ninety-Three," Pierre Loti's "Iceland Fisherman," Tolstoi's "War and

Peace," or, to take a modern instance, Mr.
Frank Norris's "The Octopus," we are conscious of one strong element of interest
which lies outside of the sphere of character
or action.   This interest is provided by what
we will call, for lack of a more satisfactory
word, the setting.   Sometimes we shall use
this word as synonymous with *milieu*, — the
circumstances, namely, that surround and
condition the appearance of the characters.
Sometimes the setting of the novel corre-
sponds precisely to the scenic effects of the
stage, in that it gives a mere background for
the vivid presentation of the characters.   It
will thus be seen that in the setting, that
tertium quid which is neither characters nor
action, we have something corresponding to
what we should call " atmosphere " if we
were to speak in the terms of art, or " environment " if we were to use the terminology
of science.

The novelist secures the setting
of his stories precisely as he ob-
tains his characters and his plot ; that is,
by his observation, from his reading, and
from that function of the imagination which
recombines and invents, using the unassorted

Based upon what?

fragments of experience. Tolstoi's " War
and Peace " reproduces the author's memories
of the Crimean War. " Lorna Doone " is
an accurate presentation of Blackmore's study
of the Doone country. In Scott's Borderland
novels, as everybody knows, there is an
easily successful effort to suggest the atmosphere of his own country-side ; and together
with this Scott utilized all the materials furnished by his vast and miscellaneous reading
to construct the imaginative background for
his historical tales. But very few books
present to us, as far as the setting is concerned, a strictly veracious, unaltered transcript of life. The novel is rather what a
painter would call a composition from studies, and the studies are brought together
from strange and unrelated sources. Yet
even in the most Utopian of novels, where
writers have striven to invent a new world
of the future and to present their heroes and
heroines in an atmosphere wholly unfamiliar
to the contemporary reader, they have never
succeeded in getting very far away from the
earth we know. The greater triumphs of
fictive genius have commonly been in those
stories where the setting is that of the ordi-

nary field and stream and town, but where the imagination touches all this with a new transforming light.

The present passion for histor- Historical
ical novels makes the subject of setting.
historical setting one of unusual interest. If one compares the work of Scott with that of George Ebers, the novels of Kingsley and Bulwer Lytton with those of Mr. Stanley Weyman and Mr. Maurice Hewlett, one will be conscious of an immense gain in accuracy. The growth of historical knowledge has been constant. There has likewise been a steady increase of interest in antiquarian detail. The elaborate and painful efforts of the modern stage to secure historically correct costuming has unquestionably affected the consciences of our novelists. More than one of them has confessed the toil it has cost him to prepare himself to write a book involving precise knowledge of such matters as heraldry or the details of monastic life. Some of our writers have shown extraordinary zeal in " getting up " their subjects, and have been able, in spite of it, to mould their material with some freedom. Nevertheless, generally speaking, one may say that as the

standard of accuracy rises, the imagination, that other and indispensable end of the balance scales, goes down. The spirit of truth to fact, as we have seen in the chapter on science, has often been hostile to the spirit of imagination. Doubtless there never were such persons as Scott's Saracens or Cooper's Red Men, but fiction would be greatly the loser if Scott and Cooper had confined themselves to the basis of demonstrable fact. That mediæval world in which Scott's imagination moved so delightedly and with such incomparable vigor and variety had no existence outside of the pages of his novels. But "Ivanhoe" is no worse a book from the fact that such Saxons and Normans as move through its pages never wandered over actual English fields.

Local color. The modern spirit of precise observation, however, has unquestionably aided many novelists in giving to their books the atmosphere of a definite locality. When a writer places the scene of his stories in the Tennessee mountains, a Californian mining camp, upon a New England hillside, or a Louisiana bayou, we can usually depend now-a-days upon a certain fidelity to fact and

sensitiveness to local coloring. He has probably made an honest effort to realize in his
story the impression made upon him by the
landscape and the people of those quarters
of the world.

The same is true of those studies
of great human occupations which
have been so frequent in modern
fiction. English politics or English clerical
life thus affords an effective setting for Trollope's stories. Captain King chooses war, Mr.
Hamlin Garland farming, Mr. Richard Harding Davis cosmopolitan adventure, Charles
Dudley Warner the life of the unemployed
rich, Mr. Zangwill the life of the unemployed
poor, as the setting, the enveloping action
and circumstances of their stories. Prevalent social ideas, long-standing social institutions, afford similar backgrounds for the work
of the novelist. It thus becomes natural to
speak of Scott as the romancer of feudalism,
or of Mr. Howells as the novelist of American democracy under contemporary social
conditions. Other fiction-writers have used
socialism or patriotism or monasticism as furnishing the underlying framework for their
productions. In all these cases it will be

Occupations and institutions.

noted that the setting is something which lies back of the characters, and which may even be considered apart from them.

Landscape setting: Rousseau. Let us take one of the most striking instances which literature affords of the development of what was once a minor and accidental feature of the work of fiction into a recognized and immensely significant element of it, namely, the evolution of the use of landscape in fiction during the last century and a half. In Rousseau's " New Heloise " there was a new force at work which the readers of that singular romance were not slow to recognize. It was the part which nature herself played in the story. The mountain, the lake, the stream, were there not merely for adornment, but as an integral part of the story itself. All the literary children of Rousseau have followed him in this recognition of the potency of natural scenery as influencing the thoughts and sentiments of human personages. In the fiction of Chateaubriand and of Victor Hugo, of George Sand, of Balzac, of Maupassant, of Pierre Loti, there is everywhere to be traced that influence which was so apparent in the " New Heloise."

In England and America the in- Eighteenth
direct influence of Rousseau has century
instances:
been scarcely less significant. In Defoe.
the earlier part of the eighteenth century
there is almost no landscape setting worthy
of the name. Scarcely more than half a
dozen passages describing natural scenery in
the modern spirit will occur to the memory
of the reader of Defoe. One of the most
striking isolated instances of the effective use
of setting is that passage in Defoe's "Captain Singleton" which describes, in terms
that Robert Louis Stevenson might have en-
vied, a struggle with African wild beasts on
"one windy tempestuous night:" —

"During our encampment here we had several adventures with the ravenous creatures of that country; and
had not our fire been always kept burning, I question
much whether all our fence, though we strengthened it
afterwards with twelve or fourteen rows of stakes or
more, would have kept us secure. It was always in
the night that we had the disturbance of them, and
sometimes they came in such multitudes that we
thought all the lions and tigers and leopards and
wolves of Africa were come together to attack us. One
night, being clear moonshine, one of our men being
upon the watch, told us he verily believed he saw ten
thousand wild creatures of one sort or another pass by
our little camp; and as soon as ever they saw the fire

they sheered off, but were sure to howl or roar, or whatever it was, when they were past.

" The music of their voices was very far from being pleasant to us, and sometimes would be so very disturbing that we could not sleep for it; and often our sentinels would call us that were awake to come and look at them. It was one windy tempestuous night, after a very rainy day, that we were indeed all called up; for such innumerable numbers of devilish creatures came about us that our watch really thought they would attack us. They would not come on the side where the fire was; and though we thought ourselves secure everywhere else, yet we all got up, and took to our arms. The moon was near the full, but the air full of flying clouds, and a strange hurricane of wind to add to the terror of the night; when, looking on the back part of our camp, I thought I saw a creature within our fortification, and so indeed he was, except his haunches; for he had taken a running leap, I suppose, and with all his might had thrown himself clear over our palisadoes, except one strong pile, which stood higher than the rest, and which had caught hold of him, and by his weight he had hanged himself upon it, the spike of the pile running into his hinder-haunch or thigh, on the inside, and by that he hung growling and biting the wood for rage. I snatched up a lance from one of the negroes that stood just by me, and, running to him, struck it three or four times into him, and despatched him."

Mrs. Radcliffe. Fielding has some admirable paragraphs of out-door description, but ordinarily, even in Fielding's novels, it rains

only to delay the coach, and not to affect or
symbolize the sentiments of the passengers.
But with the rise of the romantic school at
the end of the century came an inrush of sentiment regarding natural scenery.   In such a
typical novel of this school as Anne Radcliffe's "Mysteries of Udolpho," hero and
heroine alike tremble into tears under the
slightest provocation of the landscape.   Here
are four representative passages : —

"It was one of Emily's earliest pleasures to ramble
among the scenes of nature; nor was it in the soft and
glowing landscape that she most delighted; she loved
more the wild wood-walks that skirted the mountain;
and still more the mountain's stupendous recesses,
where the silence and grandeur of solitude impressed
a sacred awe upon her heart, and lifted her thoughts
to the God of Heaven and Earth.   In scenes like these
she would often linger alone, wrapped in a melancholy
charm, till the last gleam of day faded from the west;
till the lonely sound of a sheep-bell, or the distant
barking of a watch-dog, was all that broke the stillness
of the evening.   Then the gloom of the woods; the
trembling of their leaves, at intervals, in the breeze;
the bat, flitting in the twilight; the cottage lights, now
seen, and now lost — were circumstances that awakened her mind into effort, and led to enthusiasm and
poetry."

.   .   .   .

"The dawn, which softened the scenery with its

peculiar gray tint, now dispersed, and Emily watched the progress of the day, first trembling on the tops of the highest cliffs, then touching them with splendid light, while their sides and the vale below were still wrapped in dewy mist. Meanwhile the sullen gray of the eastern clouds began to blush, then to redden, and then to glow with a thousand colors, till the golden light darted over all the air, touched the lower points of the mountain's brow, and glanced in long sloping beams upon the valley and its stream. All nature seemed to have awakened from death into life. The spirit of St. Aubert was renovated. His heart was full ; he wept, and his thoughts ascended to the great Creator."

.   .   .   .

"From Beaujeau the road had constantly ascended, conducting the travellers into the higher regions of the air, where immense glaciers exhibited their frozen horrors, and eternal snow whitened the summits of the mountains. They often paused to contemplate these stupendous scenes, and, seated on some wild cliff, where only the ilex or the larch could flourish, looked over dark forests of fir, and precipices where human foot had never wandered, into the glen — so deep, that the thunder of the torrent, which was seen to foam along the bottom, was scarcely heard to murmur. Over these crags rose others of stupendous height and fantastic shape ; some shooting into cones, others impending far over their base, in huge masses of granite, along whose broken ridges was often lodged a weight of snow, that, trembling even to the vibration of a sound, threatened to bear destruction in its course to the vale.

Around, on every side far as the eye could penetrate, were seen only forms of grandeur — the long perspective of mountain-tops, tinged with ethereal blue, or white with snow; valleys of ice and forests of gloomy fir. The serenity and clearness of the air in these high regions were particularly delightful to the travellers; it seemed to inspire them with a finer spirit, and diffused an indescribable complacency over their minds. They had no words to express the sublime emotions they felt. A solemn expression characterized the feelings of St. Aubert; tears often came to his eyes, and he frequently walked away from his companions."

.   .   .   .

"In the cool of the evening, the party embarked in Montoni's gondola, and rowed out upon the sea. The red glow of sunset still touched the waves, and lingered in the west, where the melancholy gleam seemed slowly expiring, while the dark blue of the upper ether began to twinkle with stars. Emily sat, given up to pensive and sweet emotions. The smoothness of the water over which she glided, its reflected images — a new heaven and trembling stars below the waves, with shadowy outlines of towers and porticoes — conspired with the stillness of the hour, interrupted only by the passing wave or the notes of distant music, to raise those emotions to enthusiasm. As she listened to the measured sound of the oars, and to the remote warblings that came in the breeze, her softened mind returned to the memory of St. Aubert, and to Valancourt, and tears stole to her eyes."

In the earlier decades of the nineteenth century this sort of Nineteenth century.

sentiment was left mainly to the poets. The
use of landscape as an aid in powerful emotional effects begins again, however, with
Dickens. It is noticeably rare in Thackeray,
although here and there in single phrases
and sentences he introduces the element of
landscape with singularly delicate effect.
But George Eliot, William Black, and Thomas
Hardy have written whole chapters, one may
almost say books, drenched with their feeling for the natural landscape against which
their fictitious personages are relieved. In
the stories of Ouida, and in some of the
sketches of Lafcadio Hearn, the landscape
sense runs riot. But if rightly subordinated
to the human element, as is almost always
the case in the novels of Turgenieff, or in
the stories of Mr. Kipling or Miss Jewett, it
becomes an element of extraordinary power
and charm.

Used for
vividness.
Sometimes the landscape seems
to be used for mere vividness, for
giving us a clearer vision of the characters
at some crisis of the story, or simply for
painting an attractive picture. Here are a
few sentences from James Lane Allen's
" The Choir Invisible " which are designed

apparently to do nothing more than give us
an intimate sense of the physical presence
of the things and the persons described.

"Near the door stood a walnut tree with widespread-
ing branches wearing the fresh plumes of late May,
plumes that hung down over the door and across the
windows, suffusing the interior with a soft twilight of
green and brown shadows. A shaft of sunbeams penetrating a crevice fell on the white neck of a yellow col-
lie that lay on the ground with his head on his paws,
his eyes fixed reproachfully on the heels of the horse
outside, his ears turned back towards his master. Beside him a box had been kicked over : tools and shoes
scattered. A faint line of blue smoke sagged from the
dying coals of the forge towards the door, creeping
across the anvil bright as if tipped with silver. And
in one of the darkest corners of the shop, near a bucket
of water in which floated a huge brown gourd, Peter
and John sat on a bench while the story of O'Bannon's
mischief-making was begun and finished. It was told
by Peter with much cordial rubbing of his elbows in
the palms of his hands and much light-hearted smooth-
ing of his apron over his knees. At times a cloud,
passing beneath the sun, threw the shop into heavier
shadow ; and then the schoolmaster's dark figure faded
into the tone of the sooty wall behind him and only his
face, with the contrast of its white linen collar below
and the bare discernible lights of his auburn hair above
— his face proud, resolute, astounded, pallid, suffering
— started out of the gloom like a portrait from an old
canvas."

Contrast. Sometimes this vividness of effect is secured by the familiar artistic principle of contrast. The physical weariness of the figure in Millet's picture of "The Sower" gains in poignancy because of the infinite peace of the evening landscape against which the figure is outlined. In similar fashion, in Mr. Hardy's "The Return of the Native," what a Rembrandt-like feeling for light and shade is in that gambling scene on the heath when the two men throw dice by the light of glow-worms! "The Choir Invisible" may be used for another illustration. The second chapter introduces Mrs. Falconer at work in her frontier garden, and these lines present the singular contrast between the woman and her surroundings : —

"From every direction the forest appeared to be rushing in upon that perilous little reef of a clearing — that unsheltered island of human life, newly displaying itself amid the ancient, blood-flecked, horror-haunted sea of woods. And shipwrecked on this island, tossed to it by one of the long tidal waves of history, there to remain in exile from the manners, the refinement, the ease, the society to which she had always been accustomed, this remarkable gentle-woman."

Harmony. The principle of artistic harmony is utilized at least as frequently as that of contrast.   The Wordsworthian shepherd seems to be, as Wordsworth indeed usually conceives him, a part of the very hills where his sheep are pastured.   Cooper's Indians and frontiersmen blend into his forest backgrounds with a harmony that is the result of true artistic instinct.   Let us take additional illustrations from " The Choir Invisible : " —

"And then more dreadful years and still sadder times ; as when one morning towards daybreak, by the edge of a darker forest draped with snow where the frozen dead lay thick, they found an officer's hat half filled with snow, and near by, her father fallen face downward."

Or this : —

"She quickly dropped her head again ; she shifted her position ; a band seemed to tighten around her throat ; until, in a voice hardly to be heard, she murmured falteringly : 'I have promised to marry Joseph.' He did not speak or move, but continued to stand leaning against the lintel of the doorway, looking down on her.   The color was fading from the west, leaving it ashen white.   And so standing in the dying radiance, he saw the long bright day of his young hope come to its close ; he drained to its dregs his cup of bitterness she had prepared for him ; learned his first lesson in the victory of little things over the larger purposes of life, over the nobler planning ; bit the dust of the heart's first defeat and tragedy."

Or again : —

"The next morning the parson, standing a white cold shepherd before his chilly wilderness flock, preached a sermon from the text: 'I shall go softly all my years.' While the heads of the rest were bowed during the last moments of prayer, she rose and slipped out. 'Yes,' she said to herself, gathering her veil closely about her face as she alighted at the door of her house and the withered leaves of November were whirled fiercely about her feet, 'I shall go softly all my years.'"

Influencing the characters. It will be observed that in these passages from Mr. Allen, as in countless similar passages from fiction-writers of our generation, the landscape setting actually influences the moods of his characters, and in this way plays no inconsiderable rôle in the evolution of the plot. M. Brunetière, in a well known critical essay, has brought M. Zola to task for pretending that the varying color in the water in the gutter on different mornings should influence the action of his hero, Coupeau. But the principle which is here illustrated in its extreme form is one that cannot be neglected in a study of present-day fiction. Let us choose a more sympathetic instance of the influence of landscape on character. It shall be from Mr. James Shorthouse's "Blanche, Lady Falaise:" —

"They came back down the steep path over the strewn and withered leaves. The rain clouds were sweeping from the valley across the sun, and the bareness and chill of winter was on the woods and on the blackened grass. A blank depression and presentiment settled down upon Blanche's spirit. It seemed to her as if she were walking in a troubled nightmare, amid difficulties which were absurd, yet from which she was utterly unable to extricate herself. It seemed to her, at least for the moment, that in all the illimitable universe, limitless as the sky and plain before them, there was truly ' no other girl ; ' that in some mysterious way, struggle as she might, contemptuous as she might outwardly seem, her fate was irrevocably bound up with his."

Here is a longer and most significant passage from the same story : —

"He threw away his half finished cigar, and placed himself by her side, and they walked up the woodland path that wound round the paddock. George Falaise stood looking at them for a moment as they moved up the path — but only for a moment. Then he turned away and moved towards the seat before the baywindow of the drawing-room — the same seat on which he had sat that first morning when Blanche had come out to him. There he sat down to finish his cigar.

"The winter sun, setting behind the oak woods on the other side of the paddock, cast a kind of false and cold halo over the place where he sat and over the front of the house. He felt deserted and neglected. He hated this man. The cold winter sky, clear and soft and delicate though it was, out of the cloud tissues

of which happy men might weave fairy colored wreaths,
seemed to him dun and chill.

.   .   .   .

"For about a quarter of an hour perhaps he had sat
there. The rhythm of the breeze through the sur-
rounding woods soothed him as did the narcotic influence of his cigar, when the setting sun, just sinking
behind the woods, cast a sudden glow of dying brilliancy over the place, and above, over his head, a golden
haze of glory spread itself, beneath the rain clouds and
the deep winter sky. He looked up suddenly, and
they were coming back. He rose, threw away the end
of his cigar, and went toward them.

"Damerle evidently had been talking well. Whatever he was he was no hypocrite. Whatever he felt
for the moment he really felt. The climate, physical
and mental, of Clyston St. Fay affected him, with an
intensity which it would not have exerted upon another
man less easily affected in other ways. George Falaise
even, who felt himself, so to speak, a stranger and a
pilgrim everywhere else; to whom this silent village,
this home where Blanche lived, was the only spot upon
earth, so far as he knew the earth, where he seemed
really to breathe — even he did not feel this excited
revulsion and contrast of feeling and enthusiasm.
Damerle had been speaking of high and sacred things
and of the work which lay before them, for the girl's
face was flushed, and her whole being and nature
seemed instinct with a strange happiness and beauty
which was not of earth. Never before, at any time,
and most surely never afterwards, did George Falaise
see her look like that, — the departing flash of sunset
around her, the set purpose of devotion, the glory of

unselfish love, the beauty which God gave to woman, all around her for a moment as they came up the path.

" The angry, disappointed, perturbed spirit left him at this sight. All self-seeking, all self even, was lost in delight. He felt, in spite of himself, a supreme stillness and calm, a sense of result, of something, long wished for, being gained. It is a great mystery why such things are; but to him, to whom so much had been given, had been added also the priceless gift of unselfish love. To what issue can love tend but to the happiness of the loved? The perfect vision that awaits love must surely be this. At this happy moment, as it seems to me, many of us might well envy him; yet at that moment the one thing in the wide universe that was denied him was the one thing upon which his heart was set.

" As they came up the path the sunset glow faded from the sky above, and what a moment before had been a glory of yellow light was now gray and dark. They went back into the house."

A more familiar illustration is in George Meredith's " Richard Feverel," where the great storm scene towards the close of the story develops a new sentiment in the hero and affects profoundly the dramatic situation. Mr. Thomas Hardy, in his pantheistic interpretation of nature, finds it still easier to emphasize the intimate relation of his characters with their natural surroundings, and over and over again in his novels he has made nature itself take a hand in the evolution of the plot.

> " Amid the oozing fatness and warm ferments of Froom Vale, at a season when the rush of juices could almost be heard below the hiss of fertilization, it was impossible that the most fanciful love should not grow passionate. The ready hearts existing there were impregnated by their surroundings."
>
> *Tess of the D' Urbervilles.*

Determining the incidents. It is even possible to assert that the setting not only affects the situations of the novelist, but that it frequently determines the nature of the incidents that are to take place. This is peculiarly true, of course, in the novels which deal primarily with some occupation or handicraft. But even in novels of adventure, the novelist is compelled by the very force of circumstances to keep close to mere adventure. In a book like " A Gentleman of France " one is tempted to think that anything may happen, but after all only those things may happen there which are pertinent to the road, the camp, or the court during the progress of a particular campaign. In other words, the writer of adventure, who is

apparently enjoying such unhampered freedom, is in reality working within closely
drawn lines of limitation ; he is bound by
the very terms of his implied contract with
his readers to supply them with adventure
and with little more.   We know pretty well,
therefore, what is going to happen.   It is in
novels like " A Nest of Nobles," or " Anna
Karénina," or " Adam Bede," or " The Choir
Invisible," that we cannot tell what will happen, because anything may happen.

Finally, it is the setting of a story   Giving unity
which often gives the deepest unity   to the book.
to the work as a whole.   The setting is used
to emphasize the fundamental idea of the
book, to accentuate the theme, to bring all
the characters of the story into proper perspective.   In a railway novel the scream of
the whistle may be heard in every chapter.
The characters of the story, from the president of a great system down to the humblest
employee, all stand in certain definite relations to " the road."   It is " the road " which
affects their feelings, their ambitions, their actions, and one need not have the anthropo-
morphic imagination of Zola to conceive of a
railway as a monster, either beneficent or ma-

lign, which dominates the individual fate of every personage in such a novel. But in truth it is Zola who has given to our generation the most impressive examples of this myth-making instinct, which gives institutions like the department store, occupations like mining or farming, great campaigns like the Franco-Prussian War, great cities like Rome and Paris, each a personality of its own. In such cases one may freely grant that the setting is distorted, thrown into unnatural proportions, and frequently depicted with a morbid imagination that recalls the worst obsessions of romanticism. Indeed, it is largely because of this element in his work that Zola has been called by many keen critics essentially romantic rather than realistic. But whatever the justice of this criticism, there is no denying that beyond most other novelists of our own day he has succeeded in making the setting of his novels reveal the essential unity of the book. That germinal idea which first stimulated the creative imagination of the author remains with the reader as a haunting impression long after the persons and the action of the tale have faded from the memory.

CHAPTER VIII

THE FICTION—WRITER

" Quelle que soit la formule, il n'y a jamais au fond des œuvres que ce que les hommes y mettent."

F. Brunetière, *Le Roman Naturaliste.*

"Every artist is a thinker, whether he knows it or not ; and ultimately no artist will be found greater as an artist than he was as a thinker." David Masson, *British Novelists.*

"There is one point at which the moral sense and the artistic sense lie very near together ; that is in the light of the very obvious truth that the deepest quality of a work of art will always be the quality of the mind of the producer. In proportion as that intelligence is fine will the novel, the picture, the statue partake of the substance of beauty and truth."

Henry James, *The Art of Fiction.*

WE are entering once more upon a new phase of our subject. In the last three chapters we have been studying the materials, whether of character or plot or setting, which are at the disposition of the literary artist. We are now to study the use made of these materials by individual men. What we have hitherto done may be likened to an investigation of the general relations of the art of painting, let us say, to the other arts ; then, applying a closer scrutiny, we have watched the various colors upon the palette of the painter, and have noted some of the technical processes by means of which these pigments are utilized. We have now to scrutinize the painter himself.

The man behind the work. For after all, the use of the materials of any art depends upon the man who employs them. The words of the great French critic, quoted as the first motto for this chapter, have been repeated in various forms by most of the writers who have thought deeply upon the expression of personality by means of art. It is conveyed in the famous formula " Art is a bit of nature seen through a temperament," as well as in the more technical definition of the writer on æsthetics, that the artist is " the middle term between content and expression." Yet this interest in the story-writer himself is a more or less modern factor in the development of fiction. As we recede towards mediæval times, the fascination of the story becomes increasingly dependent upon the tale itself rather than

upon the individuality of the teller; and it
is undeniable that the modern interest in
literary personality has its seamy side. Personal gossip about famous novelists has
often taken the place of real criticism. No
details of family history have been considered too sacred to be offered to the public.
In an age when a man is scarcely blamed for
selling his father's love-letters for hard cash,
it is not to be expected that the reading public will respect the reticences and reserves of
private life. And one is forced to admit
that an acquaintance with a fiction-writer's
real experience of men and things, a familiarity with the more marked phases of his
career, a knowledge of his friendships and
his politics, of the things he hated, of the
books he loved, is of great significance in
the interpretation of his literary work. One
can scarcely understand Balzac's novels without knowing something of Balzac himself;
and if, as Hawthorne has reminded us, the
details of an author's biography often hide
the man instead of revealing him, it is nevertheless true that even in Hawthorne's own
case a knowledge of his history affords one
of the readiest modes of penetrating to the

essential nature of his productions in literature.

The novelist's experience. The fiction-writer's use of the materials of his art is conditioned first by his experience.   Experience provides the starting point for the work of the constructive imagination ; it is a pier sunk into the solid earth from which the arch is sprung into the unknown.   Here is a man who professes to interpret life for us.   Well, what sort of life has he himself known ?   What kind of men and women has it been his lot to encounter in his journey through the world ?   Upon his answer to these questions depends very often his artistic verdict upon life itself ; that is, his handling of the elements of character and action in the fictional world of his stories.   It must be borne in mind, however, as we have seen in a previous chapter, that extensive experience with men and things is often not so important a factor as intensive experience.   " The Story of an African Farm " can be told, provided the writer has insight and imagination, by one who has never left the boundaries of the farm.   It is not the number of men and cities which the novelist has seen that counts

so much as do the eyes out of which he has
looked and the brain which has reflected
upon these observations. For experience at
best furnishes suggestions rather than complete details. Said George Eliot : —

"It is invariably the case that when people discover
certain points of coincidence in a fiction with facts that
happen to have come within their knowledge, they
believe themselves able to furnish a key to the whole.
That is amusing enough to the author, who knows
from what widely sundered portions of experience —
from what a combination of subtle, shadowy suggestions, with certain actual objects and events — his story
has been formed."

In another of her letters she wrote : —

"There is not a single portrait in 'Adam Bede,'
only the suggestions of experience wrought up into new
combinations."

Secondly, the fiction-writer's use *The novelist's*
of the materials of his craft turns *thought.*
upon his thought as well as upon his experience. That is an admirable passage in Professor Masson's book upon " British Novelists : " " Every artist is a thinker, whether
he knows it or not ; and ultimately no artist
will be found greater as an artist than he
was as a thinker." Sidney Lanier had this
distinction in mind when he said of Edgar

Allan Poe that Poe did not know enough to be a great poet.   He did not mean that a man rises in the capacity to produce poetry in accordance with the amount of information he possesses, but rather that one very real test of a poet's greatness is his power to coördinate the results of experience, to reflect upon the diverse phenomena of human life, and to construct, at least to some degree, a philosophical unity from the confused impressions which life offers.   Yet the artist's power of thought is but one of the elements by which his work is to be judged.   Dickens was surely not a thinker in the sense in which George Eliot was a thinker, nor was Dumas a thinker in the sense in which that word may be applied to Balzac.   There is here, as everywhere in the world of art, a variety of equipment and a difference of gifts.

Emotion. Thirdly, this difference is never more sharply marked than in the varying capacities of different writers for feeling and expressing emotion — emotion called forth by their experience of life and reflection upon its phenomena.   With a certain type of fiction-writers, as for instance Trollope, the capacity for emotion seems to be defective, though this does not prevent admirable work within certain limits. But there is no limitation which more sharply sets the bounds for a man's possible achievement. In other writers, of whom Dickens is the readiest example, we are constantly called upon to observe the evidence of overwrought emotion. Dickens is forever bidding us laugh or cry where Trollope simply asks us to look. Frequently, too, a work of fiction seems to owe its origin to the author's instinctive love or hatred for certain objects. There is where the novel and the eulogy on the one side, and the novel and the satire on the other, touch hands. Here is a striking illustration of hatred furnishing the artistic motive for an extraordinary masterpiece of fiction. Flaubert, writing of his "Madame Bovary," says to a correspondent : —

"They think me in love with the real, whereas I execrate it : it is out of hatred of it that I have undertaken this book. . . . Do you really believe that this mean reality, whose reproduction disgusts you, does not make my gorge rise as much as yours? If you knew me better, you would know that I hold the everyday life in detestation. Personally I have always kept myself as far away from it as I could. But

æsthetically I wanted this time, and only this time, to
exhaust it thoroughly.''

Imagination.

More significant still is the influence of the artist's imagination
upon his use of the materials of his art.   It is
a kind of resultant of his experience, thought,
and emotion.   Imagination, in the words of
the Century Dictionary, is '' The act or power
of presenting to consciousness objects other
than those directly and at that time produced
by the action of the senses.''   Without attempting any arbitrary classification, we may
note that the imagination of the novelist is
constantly dealing with two classes of what
we agree to call realities, and also with two
classes of what are commonly designated as
unrealities.

**Dealing with
realities.**

What do we mean by these
'' realities ''?   In the first place,
the imagination of the story-teller is con-
tinually at work in depicting things in the
physical world as they are.   The objects and
events upon which the light of the imagination is turned are brought home to the every-day consciousness of the matter-of-fact
reader.   Defoe does not meddle in the least
with '' things as they are; '' he contents

himself with painting exact, vivid pictures of them, without seeming to alter his facts by a hair's breadth. He achieves a triumph of the artistic imagination; but it is equally a triumph of that imagination when the artist portrays the work of those spiritual forces which are not to be apprehended by the physical senses. For in dealing with the mysteries of personality, with the profounder forces of the spiritual world, the imagination is penetrating to another and more veritable reality; not what Hawthorne called "the big, solid, tangible unrealities" of the actual world, but that world which is no less eternal for being unseen. I remember hearing a clever woman say of a man who reproached a certain novelist for lack of imagination: "Mr. A. forgets that imagination consists in seeing things as they are, and not as they are not."

As for "unrealities," there are two fields where the writer's imagination is called upon to display itself. **Dealing with unrealities.** There is first a mysterious borderland, a shadowy half-world, between the realm of unquestioned spiritual forces and the realm where the fear of superstition holds full sway.

The novelists of the " School of Terror," at
the end of the eighteenth century, reveled
to their hearts' desires in this ghostly atmosphere of apparitions, portents, spirits, witches,
and devils.   As mankind advances in intelligence and scientific knowledge, it is constantly reducing the territory of the unknown,
beating back this frontier of darkness and
evil.   Many of the phenomena, however,
which in one generation would be accredited
to demoniac possession, witchcraft, or the
mysterious influence of other personalities,
are in a later generation, as the history
of hypnotism and telepathy so abundantly
proves, capable of scientific demonstration.
Such subjects still offer a tempting field,
perhaps a field more tempting than ever to
the imagination of the fiction-writer; but the
theme itself becomes transferred, with the
advance of civilization, from the realm of
the unreal to the realm of the real.   And
finally, the imagination frequently exhibits
its power in dealing with a second variety
of the unreal, namely, the physical world
of things as they are *not*.   Nothing in the
work of Victor Hugo or of Dickens is more
impressive and masterful than the " pathetic

fallacy" by means of which they love to distort our vision of the physical world, and seem to make its external phenomena and its secret forces sympathize with the spirit and the fate of their human characters. Such passages do violence, indeed, to the demonstrable truth of fact, but they often succeed in interpreting a higher truth of spiritual emotion, — the " truth of the human heart," which Hawthorne thought it the function of the romancer to express.

These illustrations of the four fields in which the imagination displays itself will possibly throw **The "four stages of fiction."** some light upon Mr. Brander Matthews's frequently discussed theory concerning the four stages in the evolution of fiction. He has remarked with indisputable acuteness that the development of fiction has been from " the Impossible to the Improbable, thence to the Probable, and finally to the Inevitable." It is a convenient formula to bear in mind; but one must also remember that fiction displays a constant tendency towards reversion to primitive types, and that in any stage of the development of literature, writers may arise who rely for their power upon

modes of thought and feeling which the race
has apparently outgrown.

Limitations of
personality.   In studying the artistic productiveness of any man, it is necessary
to take into account the limitations of his
personality.   Browning's line, " and thus we
half-men struggle," may as pertinently be
applied to the novelist as to any other member of the human family.   Those limitations
of thought, experience, and emotion which
have just been discussed, as well as the de-
ficiencies in moral insight which we have still
to notice, must always be set down on the
debit side of an author's real accomplishment.   Even if he have the very highest endowment in the range of activities already
indicated, he may lack that final creative impulse, that surplusage of vitality, which drives
him to the making of a genuine book.

Limitations
of the age.   No less sharply defined limitations are to be traced in the influence of the author's generation upon his
own productiveness.   The history of literature furnishes abundant illustration of authors
born out of due time.   Matthew Arnold's
well known criticism of the poet Gray turns
not only upon the fact that Gray " never

spoke out," but upon the causes that un-
derlay this fact; namely, the influence of
a prosaic age upon the sensitive mind of
the academic poet. There have been many
belated romanticists like Cervantes, belated
Elizabethans like Charles Lamb, and few of
them have been able to say as Lamb did so
cheerily : " Hang the age ! I 'll write for
antiquity." It is only a rarely endowed intelligence that is thus able to make its own
choice of company. Ordinarily, a man is
forced to speak the speech and think the
thoughts of his own generation ; and a
novel-writer, let us say in France, in the
full tide of the scientific impulse of the
seventies, finds it quite impossible to compose such books as he might have written
had he been born in the romantic generation
of the thirties.

And every writer, furthermore, The novelist's
has a special public, — provided he special public.
be lucky enough to have any public at all,
— and this public soon develops a peculiar
capacity for requiring from the novelist a
certain product, and no other. It is in vain
for men like Defoe and Stockton to write
books differing essentially from those by

which their first and great reputation was
won.   Some writers grow cynical under this
enforced duty to produce a single kind of
composition, and it has not infrequently
happened that while the author's popular
reputation has been sustained by works
which he himself views in the light of " pot-
boilers " pure and simple, he has found his
deepest artistic satisfaction in producing a
limited amount of work appealing to the
most fastidious taste.   There died not long
ago a German artist who supported his family by painting comic little cherubic nudi-
ties, and satisfied his real artistic cravings,
meantime, by painting crucifixions which
the public never cared to buy.   This is only
an extreme instance of a distinction which
affects more or less directly the output of
every novelist who works for the public.
After he has become widely known, there
is a definite commercial demand that he
should turn out work in a particular vein,
and he departs from it at his peril.   Thackeray is not the only famous British novelist
who has complained of the limitations enforced by the British Public upon the free
presentation of the facts of life.   Yet it is

doubtless better that the British Public should warn a novelist that he must not trespass upon a certain territory, than that it should order him to confine himself to questionable topics if he would satisfy the popular taste. After all, those writers are not the least fortunate who, like Jane Austen and Oliver Goldsmith, have written masterpieces and quietly put them away in the drawer, leaving it to others, after an interval of years, to discover that these productions were masterpieces. No doubt it seemed at the moment as if " The Vicar of Wakefield " and "Pride and Prejudice" represented wasted time and effort. But work done in this tranquil fashion is often surer of immortality than the novel which is " syndicated " from one end of the country to the other.

The work of the novelist is very directly affected by his philosophy of life. Yet it is by no means necessary that he should be conscious of the view of the world which he in reality maintains. Here and there, indeed, there have been memorable examples of a novelist writing to illustrate, or to reduce to absurdity, some philosophical theory of the universe. Voltaire's " Can-

The novelist's philosophy.

dide " was written to ridicule the " whatever is, is right " theory, made famous by Leibnitz, Bolingbroke, and Pope. In Turgenieff's novels there is a tolerably complete exposition of political and philosophical nihilism. The philosophical theory of pessimism has never been more brilliantly exemplified than in the novels of Flaubert, and the middle and later stories of George Eliot drew much of their inspiration from the tendencies of positivism and agnosticism. These writers are all what Professor Masson would classify as " thought men " rather than " fact men." If they may not all have been able to pass an academic examination in the history of philosophy, each of them had a more or less distinct theory of the scheme of human life and its relations, or lack of relations, to the unseen world of spirit.

His practical doctrine. It frequently happens that novelists who have troubled themselves very little with philosophical theories and generalizations about human life have nevertheless with a fine unconsciousness delivered themselves clearly as to the meaning of life. Scott teaches us to be brave, Kingsley to be manly, Dickens to be kind. Mr. Henry

James instructs us that life is an art, and that to play the game properly requires infinite finesse. Such writers may not realize precisely the impression which they have conveyed. They do betray, however, consciously or unconsciously, the view of life which they have formed. They " give themselves away," not necessarily in any one book, nor in the productions of any one phase of their creative activity, but rather in the totality of their work. It is as impossible to mistake the every-day temper, the moral attitude of a writer who has expressed himself in a dozen books, as it would be to misunderstand entirely his action and his motives if we were to watch him through a dozen years of his life.

In discussing the ethical aim of "Art and morals." the fiction-writer, we trench upon the ground of the old debate concerning art and morality. Has art — the sphere of æsthetic enjoyment — anything at all to do with morals — the sphere of conduct? If these two fields do touch each other, what is the nature of their relations? These questions have been asked and answered

more insistently and more bitterly concerning
fiction than any other of the arts.

The artist is a human being. Let us begin by endeavoring to
trace the connection between the
general moral attitude of the novelist and
his excellence in his profession. We have
already quoted the definition of art : " A
bit of nature seen through a temperament."
It is true that this definition emphasizes but
a single function of the artist's complex task,
yet that function is an essential one. The
artist's own personality is as it were the
crucible through which the " bit of nature "
— the material for art — must pass in order
to be changed into the work of art. Whatever affects personality, therefore, instantly
and inevitably affects the work upon which
the artist is engaged. Now sin is the negation of personality. It turns a man into a
brute. It minimizes the life of the spirit,
until the spiritual faculties disappear. Nobody denies this. The artist is a man like
the rest of us. He is a moral being, and
running the same moral risks as you and I,
and presumably greater risks, owing to his
finer organization. To say that his personality is not affected by the morality or im-

morality of his life is to place the artist outside the pale of humanity. It is to deny
him the very attributes that make him a man.
To declare that an artist's art is in exact ratio
with the morality of his private life would be
an exaggeration, yet it would probably be
nearer the truth than to say that his life and
his art are wholly unrelated quantities.

We should note that the honest Labor itself a moral factor.
labor of the artist is in itself a
moral factor. We who are inclined to look
merely at the finished art product, and not
into the workshop where the product is
wrought, are constantly tempted to under-
rate the moral qualities which the excellent
workman must possess. One of the most
suggestive passages in Ruskin's lecture on
" Art and Morals " is this : —

"The day's work of a man like Mantegna or Paul
Veronese consists of an unfaltering, uninterrupted succession of movements of the hand more precise than those
of the finest fencer: the pencil leaving one point and
arriving at another, not only with unerring precision at
the extremity of the line, but with an unerring and yet
varied course — sometimes over spaces a foot or more
in extent — yet a course so determined everywhere
that either of these men could, and Veronese often
does, draw a finished profile, or any other portion of

the contour of a face, with one line, not afterwards changed. Try, first, to realize to yourselves the muscular precision of that action, and the intellectual strain of it; for the movement of a fencer is perfect in practiced monotony; but the movement of the hand of a great painter is at every instant governed by direct and new intention. Then imagine that muscular firmness and subtlety; and that instantaneously selective and ordinant energy of the brain, sustained all day long, not only without fatigue, but with a visible joy in the exertion, like that which an eagle seems to take in the wave of his wings; and this all life long, and through long life, not only without failure of power, but with visible increase of it, until the actually organic changes of old age. And then consider, so far as you know anything of physiology, what sort of an ethical state of body and mind that means! — ethic through ages past! what fineness of race there must be to get it, what exquisite balance and symmetry of the vital powers! And then, finally, determine for yourselves whether a manhood like that is consistent with any viciousness of soul, with any mean anxiety, any gnawing lust, any wretchedness of spite or remorse, any consciousness of rebellion against law of God or man, or any actual, though unconscious, violation of even the least law to which obedience is essential for the glory of life, and the pleasing of its Giver."

What Ruskin, with characteristic eloquence, has here said of the painter is scarcely less true of the novelist. A task honestly undertaken, patiently carried through, is in itself a bit of morality. There is something very fine in Emile Zola's steady devotion, for twenty long years, to a single artistic plan : the completion of the Rougon-Macquart series of novels. Fifteen hundred words a morning, every morning in the week, every week for twenty years ; no wonder M. Zola bears the worn, tired, patient face of the worker. Even though the Rougon-Macquart series proves, as time goes by, to have been a huge blunder, this does not lessen one's respect for such an example of fidelity to an imagined duty.

Fidelity to such a duty is of **"Laborare est** course a very different thing from **orare."** the religious consecration which made Fra Angelico breathe a prayer whenever he lifted his brush. " He who has not art," says Goethe, in a tone of Olympian condescension, " let him have religion." But Fra Angelico's painting was no worse for his preliminary prayer. The religious nature has often enough found a supreme expression through the arts. In a very true sense a man's art may be his religion, and where the religious element seems left out of an artist's nature, the great world's verdict commonly is that there is a defect in that man's art.

Witness the plays and poems of the Olympian Goethe himself.

A complete man.

In all this I am simply claiming that the novelist, like the poet or the painter, should be as far as possible a complete man. A defective moral organization, a deficient spirituality, will in the long run count as surely against him as a dull wit or a clumsy hand.

Immorality and technique.

But precisely how does an artist's immorality affect his work? George Eliot's dictum that " A filthy mind makes filthy art " is doubtless sound, but it does not explain the process in question. We must look for the results of immoral conduct at the point where the specific immorality affects the artist's handling of the medium in which he works. One may declare with absolute confidence that Paderewski is neither a drunkard nor an opium-eater; if he were, it would be physically impossible for him to retain his marvelously perfect control over the muscles of his fingers. He might perhaps be a miser or a thief without affecting his technique as a pianist; but no miser or thief ever had the freedom and serenity of mind which are essential for the composition of

great music. Benvenuto Cellini was a noto-
rious liar, sensualist, and murderer; yet as a
silversmith and designer he was one of the
most admirable workmen of the Renaissance.
Here one may perhaps say that the effect of
Benvenuto's immoralities was negative; if he
had not been so bad a man, he might have
cared to attempt some of the more noble
tasks to which contemporary artists devoted
themselves. In Browning's poem, theft and
treachery clip the wings of Andrea del Sarto's
imagination, although he remains, as he was
before his sin, the "faultless" painter. Such
discussions turn largely upon the importance
assigned to the element of technique in assess-
ing the value of an artist's work. The more
stress laid on technique the less important
does the question of morality become, unless
immorality results in actual unsteadiness of
eye or hand.

Or, to put the matter a little dif- The general
ferently, we may say that the moral law.
element enters into every art in proportion
as that art touches human life and character. All the arts, indeed, group themselves
about human life, but they do not all stand
towards life upon terms of equal intimacy. A

mediæval sculptor, chiseling grotesque gar-
goyles for the eaves of a cathedral, is working in a realm of art pretty thoroughly removed from human life and character. So
is an impressionist landscape painter who is
striving merely to reproduce, as cleverly as
may be, certain color tones; or a composer of
old-fashioned Italian opera, basing artificial
melodies upon the echoes of artificial feeling.
Such artistic activities as these may be compared with Cellini's exquisite cutting of
cameos; if the workman's hand and eye
retain their normal power, his goodness or
badness of heart is a matter of secondary
concern. But in the composition of great
music, or great poetry, or great fiction, mere
manual dexterity occupies a subordinate
place. The interpretation of life and character becomes now the artist's all-important
task, and a characterless, conscienceless man
has no apparatus wherewith to decipher character and conscience. He cannot interpret
what he cannot comprehend. The old argument of Quintilian that the good orator must
be a good man — an argument that has
never been successfully controverted — holds
with equal force in the realm of fiction. A

bad man cannot become a great novelist.
He might write excellent short stories; he
might even compose an excellent romance
of incident and adventure; but he could not
write " The Newcomes," or " David Copperfield," or " The Antiquary." The novel
would be beyond him.

In all this we must bear in mind, Allowances
however, that we are dealing with to be made.
relative rather than with absolute values.
The possession of rare literary gifts is no
warrant that the possessor is superior to
the weaknesses and vices of his own time,
or of his own individual nature. There is a
great deal of nonsense written about " the artistic temperament " and the allowances that
must be made for it. Yet the fact remains
that the professional artist has usually been
a somewhat specialized product of society.
In the case of the double hydrangea, as of
many other cultivated plants, beauty has been
developed at the expense of fertility; this
hydrangea does not bear fruit like the other
members of the family of plants to which
it belongs; it fulfills its purpose by performing the new function of producing beautiful flowers alone. By a similar analogy, we

are inclined to make certain allowances for
"genius," that is, for extraordinary endow-
ments of special capacity. As with a soldier
drafted for service, society tacitly excuses
the man of genius from some of the civic
duties and civic virtues. If he takes advantage of this freedom, however, we may be
sure that he and his work pay due penalty.
We may not be able to appreciate either the
force of his temptations or the degree of his
repentance; we do not know, as Burns has
pathetically reminded us, "what's resisted."
It is enough to remember that in a world of
erring men and women the "artist" has his
share of human weakness and struggle, and
that in the presence of such mysteries as
"sin" and "personality" and "creative
power" — all of which are involved in this
discussion — it is safer to avoid dogmatic
generalizations.

The moral in-
fluence of the
work itself:
it should be
judged as a
whole
When we pass from the moral
attitude of the artist to the moral
influence of the concrete work of
art, we are upon somewhat surer
ground. It is easier here to ascertain the
facts, and to base one's judgment upon a

wide comparison of experiences. We should note, for instance, that the influence of a book should be estimated by its effect as a whole, rather than by this or that detail. To select a familiar instance, it has frequently been pointed out that the sexual morality of Goethe's " Wilhelm Meister " is superficial, pagan, or bad, but yet that the influence of the book as a whole has been helpful to countless readers. There are some indecencies in Shakespeare's plays, and there is occasional grossness in Fielding's novels; but to emphasize such blemishes, and dwell upon them as if indecency and grossness were the characteristic qualities of Shakespeare and Fielding, is wholly to miss the splendid radiance, the robust humanity of these authors.

Furthermore, a work of art, whether painting, or statue, or novel, should be judged by artistically trained minds. *And by artistically trained minds.* Only such minds can determine the character of the work; can interpret the conventional language which the artist is forced to use. Artistic discipline alone, as sculptors find it necessary to remind us, can teach us to distinguish the nude from the naked, the undraped from the undressed. The vast majority of cultivated persons, in all civilized countries, feel that the undraped statue of the Venus of Melos, by its own inherent qualities, prohibits indecent suggestion. If here and there some excellent person is to be found declaring that this statue is improper, the prudishness is not so much a sign of finer moral feeling as of defective æsthetic discipline. There are plenty of novels that frankly appeal to prurient and depraved taste, but before condemning, on moral grounds, a novel which has given delight to generations of mature readers, it is wiser to ascertain whether we have perceived the author's point of view and properly interpreted his intention. There is rude common sense in Professor Raleigh's [1] blunt declaration " Books are written to be read by those who can understand them; their possible effect on those who cannot is a matter of medical rather than of literary interest."

"One man's meat." This will serve to remind us of the homely and useful proverb that " One man's meat is another man's poison."

[1] *The English Novel*, p. 171.

In feeding the mind as well as in feeding the
body, it must be remembered that the same
stimulus produces in different people very different reactions. There is such a thing as
dissolute music, but a musical ear and some
degree of musical training is necessary in
order to perceive it. Of two persons equally
responsive to the appeal of music, and listening to the overture to "Tannhäuser,"
the "Venusberg motif" will run riot in the
mind of one, and the "Pilgrims' Chorus motif" solemnize and uplift the other. Both
hearers are listening to the same orchestra,
but they are hearing and dreaming different
things. There are pages of fiction which
to some readers seem written in letters of
fire, so glowing is their passion, so intense
the subtle suggestions of the text; to other
readers — or to these same readers ten years
afterwards — those magic pages seem gray
and cold. In all imaginative art the spectator, the listener, the reader, plays an active
as well as a passive rôle; he too must become
for the moment a creator, a "maker;" he
lives, in a very true sense, in that imaginary
world; and the forms and potencies thus
created by the reciprocal activity of the

writer and the reader are as various and as
little capable of rigid classification as are
the infinite varieties of individual human
character.

**Sexual mo-
rality not the
sole morality
to be con-
sidered.**   Most discussions of the morals
of fiction drift back to the single
question of sexual morality. No
one who believes that "morality is
the core of life," and recognizes the profound
influence of sexual instinct in the actual
ordering of human institutions, will quarrel
with this tendency to scrutinize closely all
that a novel may portray of the relations of
the sexes. Yet such a scrutiny is apt to
overlook the fact that it deals with but a
single phase of morals. There are many
other things that count, both in the business
of this world and in the preparation for the
Kingdom of Heaven. There are thousands
of good people who are shocked — as perhaps they ought to be — by a story that
describes in plain terms the yielding of a
young man to sexual temptation, but who
are not shocked in the least by a story that
glorifies brute force, sings the praise of war,
and teaches that for the individual or the
nation it is might that makes right. Yet

which of these stories is really the more immoral? Which is more dangerous to the life of the Republic?

Another aspect of fiction, very frequently discussed, but never, in the nature of the case, capable of absolute, dogmatic statement, is suggested by the question of specific moral purpose. When a novelist sits down to write a story, should he have a specific moral intention? Mrs. Stowe is supposed to have had such a purpose in writing " Uncle Tom's Cabin," — to further the cause of abolition; Dickens in writing " Nicholas Nickleby," — to drive such schools as Dotheboys Hall out of existence; Mrs. Humphry Ward in writing " Robert Elsmere," — to preach Elsmerianism; and Miss Sewell in writing " Black Beauty," — to make people kind to their horses. Granting that these causes were praiseworthy, are the novels any better or greater because they were inspired by a definite moral purpose? Before I attempt to answer this question, two admissions should be made, one regarding the nature of fine art, and the other concerning the facts of literary history.

We must admit that fine art, as

Fine art has no practical end. such, has no practical end whatever. The pleasures which it affords are disinterested pleasures; it creates for us an object for delighted contemplation, nothing more. Its divorce from the world of action is absolute. And prose fiction belongs generically — in its highest reaches, at least — to the fine arts. The instant, therefore, that a work of fiction proposes as its end a definite action which is to be brought about through its influence — such as the acceptance of some creed, the reform of an abuse, the marshaling of certain social forces against other social forces — at that instant it ceases to be legitimate artistic fiction. It may be eloquent oratory, or clever pamphleteering, or effective sermonizing, but it is not the fine art of fiction any longer.

The other admission, which ap-

But fiction is not "un-moral." parently contradicts the first, is that as a matter of fact the " moral purpose " men have frequently written better novels than the " art for art's sake " men. In the words of Bernard Bosanquet, " History shows that hazardous to art as the didactic spirit is, the mood of great masters in great art epochs is nearer to the didactic spirit than to the conscious quest for abstract beauty."[1] The explanation is, I suppose, that the "moral purpose" men have on the whole been greater men, more adequately endowed in sympathy and imagination; and since prose fiction is more intimately concerned with human life and character than most of the other fine arts, this fuller endowment of moral sympathy has added a richness and vitality to the work of the "moral purpose" men. Art, as such, is indeed "unmoral;" an Indian basket, a Greek vase, a Morris wall-paper design, a Persian rug, are neither moral nor immoral. But to expect that a novelist can tell us the story of Arthur Dimmesdale or Arthur Pendennis or Arthur Donnithorne, and preserve the unmoral aloofness of the designer of a rug, is to fly in the face of the history of literature. The novelist is a man, and the men and women he describes are not alien to him. "Sunt lachrymæ rerum et mentem mortalia tangunt."

Let us now return to our question about the novel with a specific moral purpose. Is it likely to be

The novel with a purpose.

[1] Bosanquet, *History of Æsthetic*, p. 227.

on that account the better novel? The
chances are that it is not. If it has subordinated artistic considerations to the exigen-
cies of some ethical doctrine, it commonly
pays the penalty. Tolstoi's "Resurrection"
is a sermon; its point will disappear with
the changes in Russian society; his "Anna
Karénina" remains an enduring work of
art. The "novel with a purpose" has often
had the instantaneous influence, the wide
currency of a pamphlet, but in a few years
it shares the pamphlet's fate. The "novel
of the season" is not the novel of the generations. The cleverness of its adjustment
to the popular feeling or fad of the hour
makes it all the more hopelessly outlawed
when that hour is past. A "Pride and Prejudice," written for sheer love of the writing,
is surer of finding readers after another hundred years than any "novel with a purpose"
in our literature.

But is moral earnestness, then,
to be forbidden to the novelist?
Have indignation against injustice,
sympathy with the down-trodden, high ardor
for human progress, and passion for the
truth at whatever cost no place in the novel?

Moral passion has a place in the novel.

Have Fielding, Scott, Thackeray, Dickens, George Sand, Turgenieff, Daudet, no righteous indignation, no strenuous moral passion? To ask such a question is to answer it. But these great artists in fiction used their indignation and sympathy and zeal for human welfare as they used any other materials of their art. The artist in them — save in rare exceptions — controlled and directed the reformer. They wrote stories of human life, not merely tracts for the times. There is not in modern English poetry a profounder moral insight, a nobler spiritual aspiration, than in Tennyson's "Palace of Art." It affects the religious emotions more than a dozen sermons; yet it is not a sermon. It is a poem. The poet and not the preacher has held captive the ear and the soul; we are moved to the very depths of our nature, but we are not exhorted to go forth and accomplish a specific task. "The Palace of Art" is not a purposeless poem, but neither is it a "poem with a purpose;" and the creative power which used the elements of intellectual and moral passion in building "The Palace of Art" is the same power that wrought "The Scarlet Letter" and "The Bride of Lammermoor" and "Henry Esmond." In prose fiction, at least, if not always in the other arts, the laws of beauty sink deep into the structure of human life, and a novel that utilizes the deepest and strongest instincts of the heart is not the less likely, on that account, to possess consummate and enduring beauty.

The profession of moral purpose.

If, as I have tried to indicate, the presence of a specific purpose is usually a detriment to the artistic quality of a novel, it follows that the author's profession of a definite moral purpose is quite gratuitous. The eighteenth century men, with scarcely an exception, made the "moral purpose" plea in their prefaces. It became as conventional as the earlier dedication to a patron. Defoe did it, but we know that that imperturbable liar wrote to sell. Richardson claimed that his object in writing fiction was "to promote the cause of religion and virtue." Fielding gravely advertised himself as a "faithful historian of human nature." But readers of "Clarissa Harlowe" and "Tom Jones" heed very little what the prefaces say about the author's motive for composition. In practical life we distrust a man who talks much about the good influence which he is trying to exert; and the great public cares absolutely nothing about what the author believes to have been his purpose in writing. It cares only for what he has expressed in his book, and the novelists who write magazine articles and give lectures in order to explain their intentions would do well to profit by Goethe's advice to "create and not talk," — "Bilde, Künstler, rede nicht."

The total impression made by any work of fiction cannot be rightly understood without a sympathetic perception of the artistic aim of the writer. Consciously or unconsciously, he has accepted certain facts, and rejected or suppressed other facts, in order to give unity to the particular aspect of human life which he is depicting. No novelist possesses the impartiality, the indifference, the infinite tolerance, of nature. Nature displays to us, with an inveterate unconcern, the beautiful and the ugly, the precious and the trivial, the chaste and the obscene. If you lift up your eyes on a spring morning, you will see the bluebird flashing in the sun; but beneath your feet there may be miry ways and the foul winter's refuse

The novelist's artistic aim.

which nature, careless housekeeper, has not
yet troubled herself to put decently out of
sight.   And a writer must choose whether
he will look up or down; he must select the
particular aspects of nature and human nature
which are demanded by his work in hand.
A perfectly faithful " transcript of life " he
cannot make, not even if he is a Shakespeare; he is forced to select, to combine,
to create.   Stevenson wrote, in a characteristic passage : —

"Our art is occupied, and bound to be occupied, not
so much in making stories true as in making them
typical; not so much in capturing the lineaments of
each fact, as in marshalling all of them towards a common end.   For the welter of impressions, all forcible
but all discreet, which life presents, it substitutes a
certain artificial series of impressions, all indeed most
feebly represented, but all aiming at the same effect,
all eloquent of the same idea, all chiming together like
consonant notes in music, or like the graduated tints in
a good picture.   From all its chapters, from all its
sentences, the well-written novel echoes and reëchoes
its own creative and controlling thought ; to this must
every incident and character contribute ; the style must
have been pitched in unison with this ; and if there is
anywhere a word that looks another way, the book
would be stronger, clearer, and (I had almost said)
fuller without it."   *The Art of Fiction.*

Stevenson loved a paradox, and undoubtedly emphasized the principle of conscious artistic selection more than most men of his craft. It is enough, perhaps, for us to recognize that a selection of some sort must be made. Alike in the fairy stories of Hans Christian Andersen, the story for " the young person " by Frank Stockton, and the grossly naturalistic books of those novelists who " see the hog in nature and henceforth take nature for the hog," there is a deliberate suppression of whole departments of thought and feeling, there is the building up of a new world, which may be, according to the artist's choice, better or worse than the actual world, but which is in any case different.

This selection of subject, of material, is accompanied by a kindred instinct for the choice of form. Romantic and naturalistic epochs furnish constant illustration of the preference of content to form, of the desire to secure, at any price, the emotions of surprise and of recognition. But no epoch in the history of fiction is without illustration of the opposite tendency; namely, to subordinate the element of content to that of form, to secure " effect" through symbols

The instinct for beauty.

rather than by representation of objects. One sort of " effectivism " is as vicious as the other. The fiction that has yielded pleasure to generations of readers is that which reveals a deep synthesis of form and content, a fusion of those two elements that enter into the work of art. Such a synthesis must be traced back to the writer's spontaneous instinct. It is a process antedating the conscious choice of words, the conscious selection of this or that literary formula. After all, a man is born εὐφυής — with a beautiful, fair-proportioned mind — or he is not. Scott and Jane Austen and Hawthorne were εὐφυής, and their books reveal it. The desire to make beautiful things was an integral part of their personalities; and in such things, in spite of every difference in training and method and outward circumstance, was the true life of their spirits.

CHAPTER IX

REALISM

"Realism: the representation of what is real in fact . . . according to actual truth or appearance, or to intrinsic probability, without selection or preference over the ugly of what is beautiful or admirable; opposed to idealism and romanticism. . . .

"The observation of things as they are, . . . and the consequent faculty of reproducing them with approximate fidelity."

Century Dictionary.

"Courbet was the first or among the first to feel the interest and importance of the actual world as it is and for what it is, rather than for what it suggests."

W. C. BROWNELL, *French Art.*

WE are to discuss in this chapter a somewhat difficult theme, — one that has long occupied the attention of the reading public, and about which all the critics, and indeed most of the novelists, have at one time or another had their say. No term dealing with literary methods has been more current than "realism," and there is none that needs a more exact analysis. In connection with all the fine arts the word "realism" is used, but we do not

The need of defining "realism."

always use it in the same sense. In criticising works of art the term is employed with at least four distinct shades of meaning.

First, we speak of realism as op-
As opposed to conventionalism.
posed to conventionalism. In decorative work, for instance, there is usually no attempt to represent any particular flower or tree, but simply to repeat a conventional pattern. But if in the carvings around a cathedral door we find among the conventional trefoils and dragons an effort to represent an actual plant or animal of that neighborhood, we speak of the " realism " of the mediæval sculptor. In like manner, when the early Greek sculptors abandoned the stiff, purely conventional drapery that fell in wooden folds from the shoulders of men and women alike, and endeavored to give the effect of the actual garments then worn by the two sexes, it was, to that extent, a realistic movement, though of course very far removed from the painstaking labor of the modern sculptor to represent real lace and real buttonholes.

Secondly, we speak of realism in
As opposed to idealism.
distinction from idealism, meaning

by idealism the "effort to realize the highest type of any natural object by eliminating all its imperfect elements, — representing nature as she might be." Rosa Bonheur buys a horse, stables it next her studio, and paints it to the life. On the other hand, Regnault's "Automedon taming the Horses of Ulysses" is said to have called forth this comment from two visitors: "You never saw horses like those!" "No," said the other, "but I have been looking for them for forty years!" Rosa Bonheur's horse is more realistically painted; there is less idealism than in the horses of Regnault. Or, to take perhaps a better example, the Sistine Madonna is thought by many critics to be an idealization of a certain portrait by Raphael in the Pitti Palace at Florence. The slyness, the sensuality, has been taken out of the face, the features have been made more regular, the expression wonderfully purified, ennobled; the same woman is back of both pictures, but we speak of the "realism" of the Florence portrait, while the Sistine Madonna is so little of a portrait, is so idealized, that it becomes for most people a type of the Divine Motherhood.

In the third place, we talk of the realistic as opposed to the imaginative. Michelangelo took an extraordinary interest in anatomy, and was never weary of displaying his knowledge of the human figure. He has exhibited this knowledge, with equal mastery, let us say in his " Soldiers Bathing," and in the "Adam" of the Sistine Chapel, who stretches forth his hand to receive a living soul from the Creator. Both are admirable studies from the undraped figure, but the Sistine picture is infinitely more than that; it is a superb conception, a triumph of the imagination; and we mark this difference when we speak of the strong, healthy, admirable realism of the bathing soldiers. A cognate, although somewhat different, illustration may be drawn from the sphere of poetry. The " History of Dr. Faustus," which gave Marlowe the basis for his play, contains this description of the apparition of Helen of Troy : —

As opposed to the imaginative.

" This lady appeared before them in a most rich gown of purple velvet, costly embroidered; her hair hanging down loose, as fair as the beaten gold, and of such length that it reached down to her hams, having most amorous coal-black eyes, a sweet and

pleasant round face, with lips as red as any cherry ;
her cheeks of a rose-colour, her mouth small, her neck
white like a swan ; tall and slender of personage ; in
sum, there was no imperfect place in her ; she looked
round about her with a roling hawke's eye, a smiling
and wanton countenance."

We are told the texture·and color of her
robe, the length of her hair, the shape of her
face, the peculiarities of her features ; it is an
effort at realistic description ; but note how
the poet, with one beat of his pinions, rises
into the realm of the imagination, and describes by refraining from description : —

> " Was this the face that launched a thousand ships,
>   And burnt the topless towers of Ilium ? "

Lastly, it is customary, in speaking of the fine arts, to use the
term "realism" in contradistinction
to sentimentalism. We have this contrast
in mind when we put French painters in the
days of Louis XV., men like Watteau, Fra-
gonard, Van Loo, with their charming artificiality, their delicate and impossible combinations of Cupids and fountains and lawn-
parties, over against the Dutchmen who were
painting, as honestly as they knew how,
what Ruskin superciliously calls " fat cattle
and ditchwater."   We are conscious of the

As opposed to
sentimental-
ism.

same contrast in poetry when we turn from
" Childe Harold " to " Don Juan," from
Keats's " Endymion " to Crabbe's " Tales of
the Hall," from Rossetti's " Sister Helen "
to Browning's " Fra Lippo Lippi," or from
Tennyson's " Gardener's Daughter " to his
" Rizpah."

**Popular con-
ceptions of
realism in
fiction.** It will thus be seen that when
we attribute realism to a work of
art, we by no means always use the
word with the same signification.   It would be
hazardous to assert that the four uses I have
illustrated — namely, as in opposition to conventionalism, to idealism, to the imaginative,
and to sentimentalism — exhaust the possible
meanings of the term.   Realism in fiction
may mean realism in any of the senses applicable to the fine arts.   And furthermore, as
the result of the discussions of the art of
fiction which have been waged so continu-
ously and on every hand for the past twenty
years, there have been developed in the public mind three distinct conceptions of what
constitutes realism in fiction.   Let us note
them carefully.

**Copying
actual facts.** Perhaps the most wide-spread of
these popular conceptions is this :

that realism in fiction consists in copying
actual facts.   In the figure of speech most
often employed, the realist is a photographer.
He sets up his camera in front of you, without saying " By your leave," or " Now, a
pleasant expression, please," and he takes
you.   His grocer has a peculiar way of tying
up a package, his mother-in-law a trick of
lifting her left eyebrow; the indefatigable
realist secures a negative of each.   He can
do likewise with a railroad train, a line of
bricklayers, the side elevation of a tenement
house, or a landscape.   Once let him master
the mechanical process, and the world becomes an infinity of potential plates.   Those
to whom this metaphor of photography seems
too mechanical have another word to represent the copying of actual facts, the word
" transcribe."   Realism means a " transcript
of life " as it passes before you.   " You cannot take too many notes," says Henry James;
" the human documents " are the all-important thing, cry the French writers.

The second popular conception
of the realistic method is that it **Deliberate choice of the commonplace.**
does not photograph or transcribe
all the facts, but that it makes a deliberate

choice of the commonplace. The "Boston Herald" remarked, during one of the high tides of American realism : "In the bright lexicon of the new school of fiction the uninteresting means interesting, and persons having any particular strength of character are useful only as foils for the flaccid and colorless." As a less pungent but perfectly fair statement of the point at issue, I will quote from a personal letter of a professional musician, a pupil of Liszt, and himself a thorough romanticist.

"It seems to me that all art should idealize, and should select for embodiment characters and incidents which are raised by some unusual, inherent quality above the level of common every-day life, which we all experience *ad nauseam*. They need not be less realistic. The diamond is as real a natural product as a lump of coal; it is simply less common, more beautiful and valuable. I am aware that it is considered to-day the highest praise with a certain class of readers and critics, to pronounce a book strictly "true to life," by which is meant the every-day life of all. It seems to me it is better to take these experiences first-hand, in the original, as they come to us all in plenty, and to seek in literature for those equally real but rarer experiences, only found in the exceptional moments and in meeting exceptional characters ; experiences with the higher, intenser phases of life, not so readily obtainable elsewhere. I am well aware that these views are only those of the school to which I, as artist, naturally belong, and realize that you have the fullest right to adhere to the other."

I shall refer again to this extract from the musician's letter, and will ask the reader now simply to note the phrase "the every-day life of all," to the representation of which, he says, the " falsely called realistic school " devote themselves. In "the every-day life of all " there are a hundred chances to one that the horse does not run away, that the house does not burn down, that the long-lost will does not tumble out of the secret drawer. Therefore, as Mr. Howells has triumphantly argued, fiction should not concern itself with the hundredth chance, but with the ninety-nine: it should make deliberate choice of the commonplace.

The third of the current concep- The "un-
tions is not originally based upon pleasant."
the fiction of the Anglo-Saxon race, but has been imported from the continent, together with the books that have given rise to it. According to this conception, realism in fiction is synonymous with the "unpleasant." It deals with objects and relations which by

the common consent of well bred people are
tabooed in conversation. Its material may
be that which is physically repellent, or that
which offends the moral sense, or very likely
a combination of them both; and the prevailing British — and to some extent the
American — opinion about this phase of
realistic fiction is vigorously and exhaus-
tively, though not very poetically, expressed
in the line of Tennyson's second " Locksley
Hall " about " maiden fancies wallowing in
the troughs of Zolaism." It is to be noted
that this conception of realism, like the preceding one, is based upon the writer's choice
of material rather than upon his method.
We shall see later that it is quite possible for
a novelist like Stevenson to select romantic
material, but to depict it with realistic technique.

I should by no means wish to
assert that these three wide-spread
conceptions of the realistic novel
are necessarily misconceptions. Notable fiction has been produced by the method of
copying actual facts. The human spectacle
is one of extraordinary interest and variety,

These are not
misconcep-
tions.

and the hand can be taught a high degree of
skill in copying, or transcribing, those facts
that are apparent to the senses. It can never
be taught an absolute skill; a man is not a
machine — a camera raised to the nth power
— though he may try to make himself think
that he is. However faithfully he may attempt to copy the facts before him, some of
them will escape him. All unconsciously he
selects, modifies, adjusts; the camera has a
greater fidelity, a more perfect impartiality,
than the man ; and yet somehow the man's
work is better than the camera's. In other
words, the subjective element, which enters
necessarily into every product of man's artistic effort, however persistently the artist
tries to exclude it, is precisely the element
that gives the highest value to art, that gives
it enduring significance as the record of the
human spirit. And nevertheless, as to excel
in some forms of athletics a man must turn
himself into an animal for the time being
and renounce his higher faculties, so nothing is more common than to see the artist in fiction pride himself mainly upon his
lower gift, his manual dexterity. In pur-
suance of this theory of his own powers, or

a theory as to the limited province of his art, he may nevertheless do remarkable and valuable work on the level to which he restricts himself. The Dutch painters may have renounced the things of the spirit, — which are no doubt difficult to paint, — but they rendered their "fat cattle and ditchwater" with an accuracy and a sympathy that are worthy of high praise ; and it is in similar fashion that notable fiction has been produced by the method of copying actual facts, or by the allied method of selecting for representation certain facts which are uncompromisingly commonplace. Both these methods are properly enough called realistic; and it is also impossible to refuse that term to novels dealing with what we have called "unpleasant" phases of life. There are sensitive, highly cultivated people who cannot read books like "Anna Karénina" or "Madame Bovary," but it is idle to deny that these great books are realistic in method and that they are masterpieces of art.

The three conceptions of realism, then, are not misconceptions ; but they are partial conceptions if they are exclusive of one another. Is it possible

Is an inclusive definition possible ?

to find a definition which shall include them all? By taking a hint from Hawthorne's well known distinction between the romance and the novel, I think we may get this negative definition of realism in fiction : *It is that fiction which lacks the romantic atmosphere.* But it may be objected that " romantic atmosphere " is a somewhat vague term, and that it implies a preliminary discussion of romanticism. Here, then, is a more positive, working definition : *Realistic fiction is that which does not shrink from the commonplace* (although art dreads the commonplace) *or from the unpleasant* (although the aim of art is to give pleasure) *in its effort to depict things as they are, life as it is.*

Let me illustrate. I want, let us say, a live eagle for a pet. Now a live eagle is not an altogether pleasant thing to have in the house. I know beforehand that an eagle does not dine on bonbons ; there will be dried blood upon its beak, and filth upon its feathers, and the odor of carrion about its claws. A stuffed eagle would be for many reasons far nicer : an eagle carefully skinned, deodorized, and mounted, with insect powder in his plumage and varnish on

The live eagle.

his legs, and a pair of glass eyes. A stuffed eagle would be more artistic, would be more of an ornament to the library, would give more pleasure to one's friends, would be much safer for the children. Nevertheless, I am perverse enough to say, " I don't want a stuffed eagle ; I want a live one." And I have a right to choose the kind of eagle I prefer.

Choosing the fiction one wants. Is it not just like that in the matter of fiction ? I claim for myself, or for any one else, the privilege of saying to a novel-writer : " I am eager to know more about life. Literature, you say, is the interpretation of life. Therefore, by means of your art, interpret life to me. Only I am tired to-day — perhaps I may have been for many days — of reading about life as it used to be in the sixteenth century, or life as it is going to be in the twenty-first, or life as some one thinks it ought to be to-day ; tell me, you who have the eye and the tongue, about life as it is, about things as they are ! "

The field of fiction illimitable. One may demand this from a novel-writer without implying for a moment that realistic fiction is any better or greater than romantic fiction, or

historical fiction, or Utopian fiction. The
field of fiction is illimitable. It is a great pity
that some American champions of realism saw
fit to begin by sneering at their betters, or by
running round and round Sir Walter Scott,
barking at him. Hawthorne had as good a
right to construct a romance, laying the scene
in Rome, as had Mr. James to set a realistic
novel — or at least a chapter of a realistic
novel — in Albany, or to derive his heroine
from Schenectady ; and if Mr. James, who
knows the theory of fiction so much better
than Hawthorne, fails to make " The Portrait
of a Lady " as great a book as " The Marble
Faun," it simply proves, not that romance is
superior to realism, or that life in Albany is
any less suited to the novelist's art than life
in Rome, but simply that Nathaniel Hawthorne is a better story-writer than Henry
James.

In spite of the wide-spread interest in romantic fiction just at present, there is every reason for the
champion of realism to keep his temper, and
to read the books he likes best. No national
fiction gives more triumphant evidence than
the English of the success of the method that

*English
realism:
Defoe.*

does not shrink from the commonplace, the unpleasant, in its effort to render life as it is, things as they are. I turn at random the pages of the earliest master of English fiction, and come upon a passage like this : —

"When I came to open the chests, I found several things of great use to me ; for example, I found in one a fine case of bottles, of an extraordinary kind, and filled with cordial waters, fine and very good ; the bottles held about three pints each, and were tipped with silver. . . . I found some very good shirts, which were very welcome to me ; and about a dozen and a half of white linen handkerchiefs and colored neckcloths ; the former were also very welcome, being exceeding refreshing to wipe my face in a hot day. Besides this, when I came to the till in the chest, I found there three great bags of pieces-of-eight, which held about 1100 pieces in all ; and in one of them, wrapped up in a paper, six doubloons of gold and some small bars or wedges of gold ; I suppose they might all weigh near a pound."

The studied commonplaceness, the minute enumeration, the curious particularity, are of the very essence of realism ; they make up what we call the verisimilitude of " Robinson Crusoe," its life-likeness. These qualities will, perhaps, be even more apparent on reading Defoe's less known books, such as " Roxana." Here the tone is grave, frank ; the details circumstantial ; there is no fancy, no humor, no imagination, save the imagination that is directed upon things as they are, physically and morally ; never was there a book with less of a romantic atmosphere ; it is an absolutely realistic exposition of the sober, terribly earnest, Protestant theme that the wages of sin is death.

The attitude is the same, though the technique differs, in Richard- **Richardson.** son. At the age of fifty-one he wrote his first novel, " Pamela," whose heroine was a servant girl. He thought, he tells us, that if he wrote a story in an easy and natural manner — instead of a little book of familiar letters on the useful concerns of common life which his friends, the booksellers, had wished — he might possibly turn young people into a course of reading "different from the pomp and parade of romance writing, and dismissing the improbable and the marvelous, with which novels generally abound, might tend to promote the cause of religion and virtue."

" To promote the cause of religion and virtue " was somewhat os- **Fielding.** tentatiously announced by all the great eighteenth century novelists to be the object of

their labors.   Their theory was that it could
be accomplished by exhibiting men as they
are, showing vice and virtue in their true light.
" It is our business," says Fielding, " to dis-
charge the part of a faithful historian, and
to describe human nature as it is, not as we
would wish it to be."   " Alas," replies a critic
like Sidney Lanier, " if you confront a man
day by day with nothing but a picture of his
own unworthiness, the final effect is not to
stimulate, but to paralyze his moral energy.
. . . If I had my way with those classic books,
I would blot them from the face of the earth.
. . . I can read none of them without feeling
as if my soul had been in the rain, draggled,
muddy, miserable."   This is rather tropical
language for a professed critic.   Without
claiming for a moment that eighteenth century fiction shows perfect art or a perfect
morality, we may still assert that it is just as
legitimate for a novelist to base his work upon
human nature as it is, as upon human nature
as he would wish it to be.   If, following the
first of these methods, his books paralyze our
energy, then so much the worse for the novelist's conception of human nature.   As for
Fielding, who has to bear the brunt of the

attack, he is quite capable of fighting his
own battles. His readers will gladly sac-
rifice "the sublimities" if they may be allowed to observe Partridge in the theatre, or
"the postilion (a lad who hath been since
transported for robbing a hen-roost)" playing
the part of the Good Samaritan, or Sergeant
Atkinson when he supposes himself to be
dying and asks leave to kiss the hand of Mrs.
Booth, or Amelia in that chapter "In which
Amelia appears in a Light more Amiable
than Gay."

Such writing endures. It forms
the public taste, it is sure to be im- *The great
succession of
itated. Even when the influence of* realists.
Rousseau and the French Revolution brought
new types into English fiction, — embodying
the social aspirations of the Revolution, the
feeling for nature in her mildest and grandest
forms, the gloomy, Byronic individual, the romance of the picturesque and terrible, to say
nothing of the splendid series of historical
novels in which the genius of Sir Walter
Scott fascinated England and the continent,
— England was rarely without some writer
who did not shrink from the commonplace in
the effort to represent life as it is. The great

Sir Walter, whose own Scotch novels exhibit such admirable realism, noted in his diary, March 14, 1826 : —

> " Read again, and for the third time at least, Miss Austen's very finely written novel of *Pride and Prejudice*. That young lady had a talent for describing the involvements and feelings and characters of ordinary life, which is to me the most wonderful I ever met with. The Big Bow-Wow strain I can do myself like any now going ; but the exquisite touch, which renders ordinary commonplace things and characters interesting, from the truth of the description and the sentiment, is denied to me. What a pity such a gifted creature died so early ! "

Jane Austen wrote while the English romantic movement was at its height; then in the succession of the great novelists came Thackeray, who burlesqued the romantic movement and satirized it; Dickens, with his vivid social sense, his glorification of lowly life ; George Eliot, who completed her theory of fiction before she wrote a line, and who was realist to the core. Students of the realistic method as it existed in England in the latter half of the nineteenth century will never find more perfect harmony between critical theory and creative art than is found in " Adam Bede " and " The Mill on the Floss."

The key word of George Eliot's
art is sympathy; the key word of the French realists is detachment. *French realism: Madame Bovary.*
What is called realism or " naturalism " in
French fiction appeared shortly after 1850.
Some look upon Balzac as its founder, and
indeed as Balzac was by turns a little —
nay, a great deal — of everything, he was
now and again a capital realist.   But French
realism was beyond anything else a reaction
against the French romanticism of the thirties, and the book that voiced this reaction,
the book that has been called the " Don
Quixote " of romanticism — doing for it what
Cervantes did for chivalry — is Flaubert's
" Madame Bovary." The theme of this novel
which has exerted such a profound influence
upon French fiction is told in six lines at the
end of the fifth chapter: —

" Before her marriage, she believed herself in love,
but as the happiness which should have resulted from
that love did not come, she imagined that she must have
been mistaken.   And Emma endeavored to discover
exactly what people understood in life by those words
felicity, passion, intoxication, which had seemed to her
so beautiful in books."

A romantic temperament put into real dis-
tasteful surroundings, the fine false senti-

ment of books tested by life as it is: it is
no wonder that with such a theme "Madame
Bovary" is a masterpiece. Victor Hugo, De
Vigny, and the other romanticists had prided
themselves on their "local color," but the
localities were far away — in time or place:
Flaubert took the Normandy of his own
day, and studied its provincialism as Darwin
studied a pigeon; he was a passionate wor-
shiper of style; when he composed his book,
he agonized over every sentence. "Madame
Bovary" is incomparably written; it is absolutely realistic; its tone is cool, detached,
brutal; like "The Scarlet Letter," it is a piece
of work that some one ought to do, done once
for all.

Followers of Flaubert.   Flaubert's method has been followed—of course with some modi-
fications — by numberless pupils in the past
thirty years: by Zola, a man of undoubted
talent, of extraordinary imagination, who
would have distinguished himself in any
school of fiction, but who has offered himself
as the champion of realism in his critical essays, and in his writings has done more than
any dozen other men to bring realism into
disrepute; by Daudet, who had that gift of

sympathy which has always marked English
realism, and with it a delicacy of perception,
a mastery of language, a knowledge of technique, which placed him at the head of his
profession ; by Maupassant, who might apparently have done anything — that is, anything a pessimist can do in fiction — had
not his brain given way : and by a host of
lesser men, who have now broken up into
smaller groups or followed their individual
caprice or conviction, for plain realism has
long since gone out of fashion in Paris.

We must pass over the great
names and great books that realism **Realism in American fiction.**
may claim for itself in Spain and
Italy and Russia ; and likewise the names and
books of the American writers who have been
in fullest sympathy with the realistic movement.   Ours has been a day of international
influences in literature.   American authors
have been quick to learn from foreign masters, and better still, have been fertile enough
to write their own books in their own way.
Realism has shown its fairer side in the
American fiction of the last twenty - five
years.   It has betrayed its limitations, to be
sure, and nowhere so markedly as in the

novels of the men who have stood before the
public as the typical realists; but leaving that
aside for the moment, how observant, honest,
clever, sympathetic, delicate, in a word how
artistic, has been and is to-day the realistic
fiction of our own countrymen and country-
women!

The remaining questions. We have examined the theory
of realism and have glanced, how-
ever briefly, at its historical development. It
remains for us to inquire: What, after all,
has realism accomplished? What are its
limitations, its dangers? Finally, is the ultimate question in the art of fiction one of
method?

Realism has opened new fields. What, then, has realism accomplished? In the first place, it has
opened new fields to the artist.
Every great literary movement has indeed
done that. Romanticism cried "Back to
nature — to feeling," but what was meant
by "nature" was romantic nature, by "feeling," romantic emotions. There is but one
aspect of nature, one element of passion that
is romantic, to twenty that are not; and
realism has insisted that all of these are at

the disposal of the novelist. It has called
nothing common, and, alas, very few things
unclean. It has demolished the park wall
that used to divide themes unforbidden from
those forbidden to the artist ; it has advised
him to take his brush and palette and to stray
through the inclosure at will. It has given
him absolute liberty to portray things as he
finds them, and the range and freshness and
vividness of the artist's work have shown what
an immense stimulus there is in freedom.

And realism has created a new
technique. Tell a man he may
paint anything, provided he gives
Created a new technique.
you the sense of actuality, renders the subject as it is, and if he have the true artist's
passion for technical perfection, he will learn
to paint anything. In exact correspondence
with that marvelous technical power exhibited in modern French pictures of the realistic school, there has been developed in
realistic fiction a fidelity, a life-likeness, a
vividness, a touch, which are extraordinary
and new. Tolstoi describes a man standing
upon the steps of his club, drawing on his
gloves ; it is nothing, and yet the picture is
unforgettable. Hardy describes the gloves

of a working-woman gathering turnips on an English upland, and the image haunts you. Here are a few lines exemplifying this new method in English fiction. Tess of the D'Urbervilles, desolate and forsaken, is ringing the doorbell of the empty parsonage where the father and mother of her husband had lived.

"Nobody answered to her ringing. The effort had to be risen to, and made again. She rang a second time, and the agitation of the act, coupled with her weariness after the fourteen miles' walk, led her to support herself while she waited by resting her hand on her hip, and her elbow against the wall of the porch. The wind was so drying that the ivy-leaves had become wizened and gray, each tapping incessantly upon its neighbors with a disquieting stir of her nerves. A piece of blood-stained paper, caught up from some meat buyer's dust-heap, beat up and down the road without the gate ; too flimsy to rest, too heavy to fly away ; and a few straws kept it company."

We may look through the whole range of fiction, and we shall not find until our own day, and among the realists, a piece of blood-stained paper, beating impotently in the wind, used artistically, as a bit of the setting, to intensify the desolation, the horror, that are falling upon the spirit of the forsaken wife.

But realism has had relations to many other forces. It has been closely allied to that scientific temper which was discussed in the fourth chapter. Poetry and science, as we have seen, meet in the novel, and in many of the notable achievements of realism there is more science than poetry. The novels of so indubitable an artist as George Eliot would lose much of their quality if they lost the exact observation, the analytic power, the faculty for generalization, which she possessed in common with Pasteur. No one can doubt that certain positive benefits have accrued to realistic fiction in thus linking itself with the far-reaching scientific spirit of our time. It has gained in precision, solidity, breadth. But we must in a moment inquire whether it has gained, in relation to qualities even higher than these, through its association with science.

Realism and the scientific temper.

Realism, too, has had clearly marked lines of relationship with the democratic spirit. We must touch upon these in the chapter devoted to the tendencies of American fiction. Furthermore, I think it may fairly be claimed that the theory on which realism is based is in

Relations to democracy and Christianity.

close accord with the spirit of Christianity.
For the theory of realism teaches that the
" every-day life of all " is worth something
— if only worth describing ; it teaches the
reality of our present experiences, the significance of common things. In childhood,
perhaps, the real is too near, too obvious, to
be attractive. We have seen big boys ; tell
us the story of the Giants ! We have played
with the rocking-horse; please read to us about
Bucephalus and the Centaurs! The far-
away attracts us with a romantic charm ;
anywhere rather than here is where we child-
ishly long to be. These illusions fade as we
grow older ; it is perhaps after a long period
of disillusion that we turn suddenly to the
real. Here is our world,

> . . . " Here we find
> Our destined happiness, or not at all."

The actual grows spiritually significant.
The world becomes intelligible, interesting.
It is a live world — God's world. The forces
about us are real forces ; the men and women
we know are real personalities. Therefore
we say to the novelist : " Show us as much
of this most real of all worlds as you can.
Let us see how deep is your vision ; does it

penetrate as the Eternal Vision penetrates, is it as comprehensive as that, as loving as that?"

Said the Russian novelist Gogol: "I have studied life as it really is, not in dreams of the imagination; and thus I have come to a conception of Him who is the source of all life."

It is the sentimentalist, the romanticist, who exclaims: "I have enough of ordinary life; I experience it *ad nauseam;* give me the diamond, the unusual, the far-away, the exceptional." That was exactly the cry of Emma Bovary, poor Emma Bovary who, in Brunetière's words, is just like all of us, only a trifle too sensual and endowed with too little intelligence to accept the daily duty, to learn its charm and its latent poetry. The value of "the every-day life" to the more thoughtful type of mind has been well expressed by Richard Holt Hutton in his essay on Shelley:—

Realism and "the every-day life."

"Poets, and artists, and thinkers, and theologians, who hunger after reality, hold, we suppose, that the actual combination of qualities and substances and personal influences as God has made them, contains something much better worth knowing and imagining accurately, than any recast they could effect of their

own. They believe in the infinite significance of actual
ties. And those who feel this, as all realists do usually feel it, must cherish a certain spirit of faithful
tenacity at the bottom of their minds, a respect for the
mere fact of existence, a wish to see good reason before
they separate things joined together by nature, and
perhaps, they will think, by divine law; a disposition
to cling to the details of experience, as having at least
a presumptive sacredness; nay, they feel even a higher
love for such beauty as is presented to them in the
real universe, than for any which is got by the dissolv-
ing and recomposing power of their own eclectic idealism." *Literary Essays*, p. 174.

Now the great realists in fic-
**The signifi-
cance of the
present.** tion take the every-day life of all;
from the material furnished by the
average man in the ordinary situation they
form their work of art. They reveal — at
their best moments — the reality of things;
that is, the spiritual and enduring side of
things, the divine in the human, God's world
existing in and through our world. It is
in this sense that Christianity is on the side
of realism, because Christianity deepens our
sense of the actual, and of the eternal significance of the Here and Now, of the infinite potentialities of character. When we
have learned to look at men and women as
they are, the world as it is, to see in it some-

thing of perennial freshness and suggestiveness, to feel it beating with the Infinite Heart, then the writer of fiction who can interpret human life to us most closely, most sympathetically, bring it to us most intimately, is the realist. But if the actual world is *ennuyeux* to us, then we should logically take refuge in another sort of fiction, — in the stories of other times and other places, of other orders of beings, acting under conditions different from our own. If the sunlight, the clear, frank sunlight, is too strong for us, or too colorless, let us by all means spread a purple awning, and diffuse a romantic atmosphere of our own.

In what has just been written, I have made the very highest claim Limitations of realism. for the possibilities of realistic art. Yet it is easy to see the limitations of realism. The realist says : " I paint things as they are, the world as it is ; " but by this he means necessarily things as they are to him, the world as it is to him. However objective he strives to be, he looks out upon the world through the lens of his own personality. His art is conditioned upon his vision, his physical

vision, his psychical vision. In the very
nature of the case, that vision is more or less
contracted, blurred. What he takes for
reality may not be reality. There is but one
real world, and that is God's world. The
novelist's world, depend upon it, will be but
an imperfect copy ; what he calls the real
world will be his own world, not God's world,
but a Turgenieff world, a Thomas Hardy
world, a Miss Wilkins world. Alas ! what
distortion ! what pitiful limitation ! A realist with well-nigh perfect physical vision
may have what the brain specialists call psy-
chic blindness, — inability to perceive the
meaning of the visual impression. He may
be a pure materialist, seeing only the animal
side of life, devoting great talents to the
analysis of wrath and love as functions of the
bodily organism. He may steadfastly ignore
those hopes and aspirations that reach out
beyond the confines of mortality, that lay
hold upon the world to come.

And realism has its dangers as
Its dangers : well as its limitations. The realist
lack of sym-
pathy.   must represent actualities ; he must
study them objectively ; he must be an observer ; and nothing is easier than for him

to learn to observe without sympathy. This is, as the reader may remember, what Hawthorne dreaded ; it is the theme of his "Ethan Brand." It is the "detachment" which has been one of the catchwords of French realism, and which explains why so much of the fiction of the last generation in France, with all its wonderful qualities, has nevertheless been so pitiless.

Another danger for realism lies in that very technical excellence which the French writers have brought to such perfection. To the vivid rendering of the appearances of things, other qualities equally important to artistic work of a high rank have been sacrificed. Technique and nothing back of it is a besetting foe to the realist. It is so much easier to start with painting the surface, to be content with outdoing one's rivals in cleverness, in tricks of the brush, in "impressionism." But the cleverest record of fact, the most sensitive rendering of atmosphere, fails, by itself, to make fiction vital. The lack of imagination in some of those books whose technical workmanship seems beyond praise is startling. By imagination I do not mean a journey into

Technique and nothing more.

cloudland, but the power of seeing real things imaginatively. One of the Goncourt brothers puts forth this request in a preface to a novel : —

"I want to write a novel which shall be the study of a young girl, — a novel founded on human documents. I find that books about women, written by men, lack feminine collaboration. The impressions of a little girl, confidences as to her feelings at the time of confirmation, her sensations when she first goes into society, the unveiling of the most delicate emotions, — in a word, all the unknown femininity at the depths of a woman, these are what I need. And I ask my feminine readers, in those unoccupied hours, when the past, in its gloom or happiness, rises before them, to write these thoughts or memories down for me, to send them to me anonymously at the address of my publisher."

Comment upon the delicacy of this proposition is quite needless, but did ever a professed artist make a more pitiful confession of his own imaginative sterility? To put yourself in another person's place is the first law of the novelist's creative imagination; this disciple of Flaubert stretches forth his hands impotently for the other person's documents.

Facts not enough. It is just here that the alliance of realism with the scientific spirit,

which, as we have seen, has given fiction
precision, solidity, breadth, has nevertheless
with some schools of fiction wrought irrepa-
rable mischief. The scientific temper, un-
transmuted by artistic feeling, has never been
of value in any of the fine arts ; the application of scientific methods to fiction has time
and again crowded the creative imagination
off the field to make room for the documents.
There is of course an endless variety in nature and in human nature, but an endless
succession of realists, working merely by scientifically accurate observation and record,
can never produce a great novel any more
than an endless succession of photographers
can produce a great picture. They can give
us a marvelous array of facts, but fact is not
fiction. Science cares for facts, art, in the
high sense, for facts only as they reveal truths ;
and unless the writer of fiction uses facts to
explain truths, his work is like the dead iron
before it is carbonized into steel, like prose
uncrystallized into poetry.

The last danger that the realist
runs is perhaps the most obvious, if **Animalism.**
it be not the worst.   It is the danger, already
alluded to in a previous chapter, of represent-

ing the body rather than the mind, the physi-
ological to the exclusion of the psychological.
A reviewer in the " New York Evening Post "
has put this sharply, but not unjustly.

" It is only fair to say that what we have called animalism others pronounce wonderful realism.   We use
the word animalism for the sake of clearness, to denote
a species of realism which deals with man considered
as an animal, capable of hunger, thirst, lust, cruelty,
vanity, fear, sloth, predacity, greed, and other passions
and appetites that make him kin to the brutes, but
which neglects, so far as possible, any higher qualities
which distinguish him from his four-footed relatives,
such as humor, thought, reason, aspiration, affection,
morality, and religion.   Real life is full of the contrasts
between these conflicting tendencies, but the object of
the animalistic school seems always to make a study of
the *genus homo* which shall recall the menagerie at
feeding-time rather than human society."

There is plenty of animalism in human society, as everybody knows ; but this does not
justify a man of talent in writing as if there
were nothing but animalism.   The novelists
who have followed their morbid-minded lead-
ers over the park wall, in search of material
which has hitherto been considered too sacred
or too horrible to be used by fiction, have
been so severely taken to task for it by the
best critics, that we may content ourselves

with a single remark. Crossing the park wall leaves a man no better painter than he was before. He may sit outside, with brushes and colors and palette, and sigh for the forbidden subjects. He may then cry,

" Down with Reticence, down with Reverence — forward " —

and follow his indefatigable leader across the broken wall; he may select his forbidden fruit and begin to paint it. Very well; he is just the same painter as ever : no more true of eye, no more skillful of hand; indeed, since the man must often cross the barrier between decency and indecency with the artist, the hand may not be so steady, nor the eye so clear. What then is gained? The picture, the book, sells to a debased public, which it helps still further to debase ; but to a sensitive writer of fiction there can scarcely be a worse Inferno than the thought that a book has sold at the expense of the artistic capacity of the writer himself.

No more powerful protest against this naturalism has yet appeared than the one uttered by the Spanish novelist Valdés in the preface to his " Sister St. Sulpice : " —

The testimony of Valdés.

" I believe firmly with the naturalist writers that man represents on this planet the ultimate phase of animal evolution, and that on this supposition the study of his animal instincts and passions is interesting, and explains a great number of his actions. But this study has for me only a historic value, because if man proceeds directly from animality, every day he goes farther and farther away from it, and this and nothing else is the basis of our own progress. We come surely from the instinctive, the unconscious, the necessary, but we are going forward toward the rational, the conscious, and the free. Therefore the study of all that refers to the rational, free, and conscious mind as the explanation of a great proportion of human acts, the only noble and worthy ones, is far superior to the first. It is more interesting to study man as man than as an animal, although the naturalist school thinks otherwise. . . . In order that there should be beauty in man, it is necessary that he show himself as man, and not as brute."

The bankruptcy of realism in France. It is to such causes that we must assign the bankruptcy of realism in France. It has ventured as far into forbidden territory as any fiction is ever likely to go, and it has brought back pictures that defile the imagination and sicken the heart. It has made disreputable an artistic method which in other countries, and in the hands of many a French writer, has served great ends. The limits have long since been reached, and before the close of the nine-

teenth century the Paris critics began coolly
to balance the assets and liabilities of realism,
as with the ledgers of a wrecked concern.

Yet in England and America, **The future of**
and indeed everywhere outside this **realism.**
eddy in a single European city, the currents of
realism have by no means spent their force.
Realism has wrought itself too thoroughly
into the picture of the modern world, it is too
significant a movement, to allow any doubt
as to the permanence of its influence. It is
true that in the opening years of the twentieth century we Americans are witnessing a
sort of "Romantic Revival," whose devotees
are complaisant toward any books that excite
and entertain them. In the face of this unappeasable and perfectly legitimate thirst for
romance, has the realistic method vitality
enough to hold its own?

In art, no method, of itself, has
vitality; it is men that have vitality. **A question**
of men, not
The only promise of permanent **of method.**
life for a novel is in the creative imagination
of the writer. Everything else has been
proved transient. No "ism" can save a
book beyond an hour. The ultimate question in the art of fiction, therefore, is not

what is the method of to-day, of the future ; it
is, what are the men who are to be back of the
method ?   In place, therefore, of speculating
as to the future of realism, let us turn to the
future realist, and assert what manner of man
he must be if realism is to be credited with
any coming triumphs.   The assertion may
be made very positively, it seems to me, and
in very simple terms.

Seeing, feel-
ing, and
thinking.
"Guy de Maupassant sees," said
a recent magazine writer, "Pierre
Loti feels, Paul Bourget thinks."
Each of these admirable but highly specialized
artists represents a quality that is essential to
the greatest writers of fiction.   How clearly
Maupassant sees, how sensitively Pierre Loti
feels, how delicate and grave is the thinking
of Bourget !   The organization, let us say, is
perfect.   But what does this one see, and that
one feel, and the other one think ?   Does
Maupassant bring to us nothing more than
the pitilessness of life, Loti the pathos of life,
Bourget a sense of the confusion of life ?   We
have a right to demand of the future novelist
that he shall see *and* feel *and* think.   But he
shall see things as they are, the world as it
is ; God's world.   He shall feel in the men

and women around him the pulsation of the
Infinite Heart. He shall think nobly, because truly.   And his shall be such mastery of
his material that no technical resource shall
be unknown to him, no feat of creative imagination too hard for him ; and by virtue of
that mastery he shall make us see and feel
and think, so that when we read his book it
may be with the joy of deeper insight and
quicker sympathy and a new hold on truth.
Truth shall be the key word of his art, and
the truth that he reveals shall be seen of us
as beauty.

When that man comes, I should call him a
realist : but he is welcome to call himself an
idealist, a romanticist, or any other name he
likes.   And while we are waiting, we can
turn once more the pages of " Amelia " and
" Henry Esmond " and " Adam Bede."

CHAPTER X

ROMANTICISM

" I cannot get on with Books about the Daily Life which I find rather insufferable in practice about me. I never could read Miss Austen, nor (later) the famous George Eliot. Give me People, Places, and Things which I don't and can't see ; Antiquaries, Jeanie Deans, Dalgettys, etc. . . . As to Thackeray's, they are terrible ; I really look at them on the shelf and am half afraid to touch them. He, you know, could go deeper into the Springs of Common Action than these Ladies ; wonderful he is, but not Delightful, which one thirsts for as one gets old and dry."

Edward FitzGerald to S. Laurence, December 30, 1875.

" The discussion is quite vain, into which so many fishermen have gone, on the question whether the artificial fly is to be used on the imitation theory. Trout take some flies because they resemble the real fly on which they feed. They take other flies for no such reason. And in this they are like men."

W. C. PRIME, *I Go A-Fishing.*

Its various meanings. IN the discussion of romanticism, as of realism, one is first of all confronted by the fact that the word is capable of many varieties of meaning. Its significance shifts as the critic passes from one country, one generation, one group of men, to another. Fortunately for the student of literature, however, there have been many brilliant and scholarly treatises upon the character and history of romanticism. Some of the most important books and articles upon the subject are mentioned in the bibliography for the present chapter in the Appendix. It will be sufficient for our present purpose to explain the more general meanings which have been attached to the word, and to indicate briefly the rôle which romanticism has played in various national literatures. We can then pass to the discussion of romanticism in fiction, and endeavor to see what qualities it implies in the writer, the book, and the public.

One of the most famous discussions of romanticism is to be found **Hegel.** in Hegel's " Æsthetics." He points out that in the evolution of art there are three phases which characterize different stages of its development. The first of these phases is the symbolic, in which, according to Hegel, the material element overmasters the spiritual element. Most architecture may be said to remain permanently in this symbolic stage. Next comes the classic phase, where the material and spiritual elements are in equilibrium. This phase is best represented by

sculpture.   Finally comes the romantic phase,
where the spiritual element predominates over
the material, and which is best exemplified
by the arts of music, painting, and poetry.
Hegel points out, furthermore, that these
three phases may be illustrated in the history
of any one art.   In sculpture, for instance,
although as a whole it is predominantly
classic, there may be traced distinctively symbolic, classic, and romantic periods.   While
later critics have shown that this analysis of
Hegel's must be subjected to many modifications, it remains an extremely suggestive
one, and affords a convenient starting point
for our own discussion.

"Classic" Every educated person is more
and "ro- or less distinctly aware of certain
mantic"
qualities. qualities which, when evidenced in
a work of art, are by common consent called
" classic."   These classic qualities may be
indicated by terms like " purity of feeling,"
" reserve," " perfection of form."   It is true
that these qualities are often accompanied by
such defects as coldness and formalism.
There are likewise certain " romantic " qualities suggested by the very word itself ; for instance, freedom, warmth, expressiveness.   In

attaining these qualities the artist frequently runs the risk of falling into lawlessness, into the caprices of a disordered imagination. What seems significant to him may be vague or even meaningless to us; for the romantic artist, generally speaking, deals more with the emotional element than with the purely intellectual factors that enter into the work of art.

But, however one may choose to define classic and romantic charac- Illustrations. teristics, it is apparent that in all the arts it is possible to point out specific objects which are characterized by one or the other group of qualities already mentioned. Thus the Parthenon is classic; Cologne Cathedral romantic; the Apollo Belvedere classic; Rodin's " Apollo " romantic; the " Antigone " of Sophocles classic; " A Midsummer Night's Dream " of Shakespeare romantic; Beethoven's music — in its general features at least — classic; Chopin's romantic. However widely critics may be inclined to differ in their assessment of the value of such representative works of art as those just named, they would agree in the general classification here given. We find, then, that it is possible to apply to literature, as well as to the other arts of expression, the term romantic. Let us try to see still more precisely what the word connotes.

Romantic movements in literature: England. The last century is rich in examples of romantic movements in literature. In England, Germany, and France there have been sharply defined romantic periods, illuminated by great names and producing memorable works. These periods have had their special characteristics, their peculiar modes of development and channels of expression. Yet underneath all these differences it is easy to see that common factors have been at work. In England, for instance, we can trace far back in the eighteenth century the beginnings of the romantic temper. Professor Beers [1] and Professor Phelps [2] have devoted interesting chapters to the first impulses, feeble and imitative as these were, to break away from the frigid conventions into which the great Augustan tradi-

[1] *A History of English Romanticism in the Eighteenth Century.* By H. A. Beers. New York : Henry Holt, 1899. See also *A History of English Romanticism in the Nineteenth Century.* By the same author. New York : Holt, 1901.

[2] *The Beginnings of the English Romantic Movement.* By W. L. Phelps. Boston : Ginn, 1893.

tions had degenerated. The English romantic
movement came to its perfect flowering in
such men as Coleridge and Keats, Scott,
Byron, and Shelley. Curious as were the
differences that divided the leading English
romanticists, making many of them bitter
personal enemies, these men all held to certain
tenets of a common creed. Like true children
of Rousseau, they cried, "Back to nature,"
emphasizing particularly the picturesque and
terrible aspects of natural scenery. But they
cried also, "Back to simple, elemental feeling." From this point of view, two such
apparently diverse poems as Wordsworth's
"We are Seven" and Byron's "The Cor-
sair" are in fundamental accord. And the
English romanticists insisted, and with increasing fervor as the romantic movement
drew toward its close, "Let us go back to
history, to the manners and institutions of
our forefathers." Yet curiously enough,
though all the English romanticists were
strongly interested in politics, the romantic
movement in Great Britain left politics and
religion practically untouched.

The German romantic movement,
however, was, as many critics have **In Germany.**

pointed out, a Catholic renaissance. It was a revolt against the classic paganism of Goethe, Lessing, Winckelmann, and Schiller. It idolized Roman countries, such as Italy; the authors of southern Europe, such as Calderon. In such representative German romanticists as Tieck, the Schlegel brothers, and Novalis, there is everywhere to be found a love of warmth and color, the worship of enthusiasm, the desire to become like little children in sensitiveness to impressions, in naïveté of emotion. Professor Francke[1] has pointed out the three phases through which the German romantic movement swiftly ran its course: first, that of individual caprice; second, fantastic sensualism; and third, a flight into the land of the supernatural and miraculous. In politics, as it is scarcely necessary to say, the German romantic movement was reactionary. It strengthened the hands of absolutism in government as in religion.

In France. In France, on the other hand, the romantic movement was pagan and republican. Instead of worshiping the

---

[1] *Publications of the Modern Language Association.* New series, Vol. III, No. 1.

authors of southern Europe, it was most
strongly influenced by such men as Scott,
Byron, and Shakespeare. That is to say, it
was a German, a gothic romanticism, grafted
upon the French stock. The French writers
who came in the generation of the thirties,
such as Victor Hugo, DeVigny, Musset,
George Sand, and Balzac, rescued the French
language from the classic formalism into
which it was in danger of declining. They
produced a wonderful literature, glowing with
colors like those of the great romantic painters Delacroix and Delaroche, and echoing
with fantastic music like that of Berlioz and
Chopin. They performed a great patriotic
service likewise, and in their common worship
of art they sustained the French tradition of
intelligent, capable workmanship. Such romantic literature as this is sure to have in its
own day and generation an immense vogue.
Whether it meets the literary canons of succeeding generations, whether it contains in
itself those elements which may one day be
recognized as classic, is quite another matter.
How slender, how colorless a literary product
seems Goldsmith's " The Vicar of Wakefield "
when compared with Victor Hugo's " Les

Misérables " !   And yet, as the years go by,
it does not seem hazardous to assert that
" The Vicar of Wakefield " possesses certain
qualities which are likely to insure for it a
more enduring life than was imparted to
" Les Misérables " by the splendid exuber-
ance, the affluent fancy, the poignant tragic
power of the great Frenchman.

Critical terms are relative. It is only through wide acquaintance with the books written during
one or all of these representatively
romantic periods that one becomes gradually
aware of the elasticity of meaning, as well as
the persistent drift of meaning, that abides
in the term " romanticism."   One perceives
the justice of some of the famous definitions
which make it synonymous with "aspiration,"
" mystery," "the spirit of Christianity," "the
emancipation of the ego," " liberalism in
literature," " the renaissance of wonder,"
and " strangeness in beauty, rather than
order in beauty."   Yet many of these definitions reveal their inadequacy the moment
they are applied to other phases of romanticism than the particular one which has
evoked the definition.   Romantic material
may be treated with the spirit of classicism ;

and conversely the romantic method may be
applied to subjects that are severely classical.
And there is a true and a false romanticism,
just as there is a true and a false classicism.
Professor Beers, in the preface to his "English
Romanticism in the Nineteenth Century," re-
affirms his right to use romanticism as synonymous with "mediævalism," making it, in other
words, the reproduction in modern art or literature of the life or thought of the middle ages.
The working value of this definition is indisputable, although it needs, perhaps, the further explanation of mediævalism which is
given in these words of Walter Pater : —

"The essential elements, then, of the romantic spirit
are curiosity and the love of beauty ; and it is only as
an illustration of these qualities that it seeks the Middle Age, because, in the overcharged atmosphere of
the Middle Age, there are unworked sources of romantic effect, of a strange beauty, to be won, by strong
imagination, out of things unlikely or remote." [1]

There is another passage in this essay of
Pater's which becomes particularly suggestive
as one approaches the study of romanticism
in fiction : —

"There are the born classicists who start with *form*,
to whose minds the comeliness of the old, immemorial,

[1] *Appreciations*, p. 261.

well-recognized types in art and literature have revealed themselves impressively ; who will entertain
no matter which will not go easily and flexibly into
them ; whose work aspires only to be a variation upon,
or study from the older masters.   ' 'T is art's decline,
my son ! ' they are always saying to the progressive
element in their own generation ; to those who care for
that which in fifty years' time every one will be caring
for.   On the other hand there are the born romanticists, who start with an original, untried *matter*, still in
fusion ; who conceive this vividly, and hold by it as
the essence of their work ; who, by the very vividness
and heat of their conception, purge away, sooner or
later, all that is not organically appropriate to it, till
the whole effect adjusts itself in clear, orderly, proportionate form ; which form, after a very little time, becomes classical in its turn.   The romantic or classical
character of a picture, a poem, a literary work, depends then on the balance of certain qualities in it ;
and in this sense, a very real distinction may be drawn
between good classical and good romantic work.   But
all critical terms are relative ; and there is at least a
valuable suggestion in that theory of Stendhal's, that
all good art was romantic in its day." [1]

Romanticism in fiction. Bearing in mind, therefore, that
" all critical terms are relative," let
us turn more definitely to the field of fiction.
What is meant by romantic fiction, as compared with realistic and other types ?   The
definition of " romance " given in the Century Dictionary will be helpful : —

[1] *Appreciations*, p. 271.

"A tale in verse in one of the Romance dialects, as early French or Provençal. A popular epic. A fictitious story of heroic, marvelous, or supernatural incidents derived from history or legend. A tale or novel dealing *not so much* [*sic*] with real and familiar life as with extraordinary and often extravagant adventures ('Don Quixote'); with rapid and violent changes in scene and fortunes ('Count of Monte Cristo'); with mysterious and supernatural events ('Dr. Jekyll and Mr. Hyde'); or with morbid idiosyncrasies of temperament ('Caleb Williams'); or picturing imaginary conditions of society influenced by imaginary characters (Fouqué's 'Undine')."

The reader will note that I have taken the liberty of italicising the words "not so much." We are concerned with a question of relative emphasis. According to the relative amount of stress which it lays upon the extraordinary, the mysterious, the imaginary, does the romance differ from the novel. What is the reason for this difference in emphasis?

For answer we must look to the writer of romance, and endeavor to see why he turns away from the **The mood of the romantic writer.** common facts of experience. It is a question of mood. The romantic writer, as such, is dissatisfied with the artistic material furnished by every-day life. This is not saying that, **as a man,** he is dissatisfied with life; that he

is a pessimist or a cynic. Poe was this, and
Hawthorne was not, although both were
romanticists.   It is simply saying that when
he wishes to construct a story, the romanticist desires to weave it out of different material from that which his every-day experience offers.   In the words of Don Quixote's
niece, he wants " better bread than wheaten."
He seeks not the violet that grows in common fields, but some mysterious " blue
flower," which forever eludes him.   He portrays, not some woman whom he has met that
morning on the street, but a woman of his
dreams.   The images, the sounds that haunt
his imagination, are not those of wearisome,
reiterated reality.   And it should be needless
to say that all this is perfectly legitimate,
that it is wholly in keeping with one mode
of the artistic temperament.

The romantic   It is to this characteristic of the
atmosphere.   romantic writer that is due what we
call the " atmosphere " of romantic works of
fiction.   No better description of it can be
given than that which was penned by one of
the most perfect masters of it — Nathaniel
Hawthorne — in the well known preface to
" The House of the Seven Gables."

" When a writer calls his work a Romance, it need hardly be observed that he wishes to claim a certain latitude, both as to its fashion and material, which he would not have felt himself entitled to assume had he professed to be writing a Novel. The latter form of composition is presumed to aim at a very minute fidelity, not merely to the possible, but to the probable and ordinary course of man's experience. The former — while as a work of art, it must rigidly subject itself to laws, and while it sins unpardonably so far as it may swerve aside from the truth of the human heart — has fairly a right to present that truth under circumstances, to a great extent, of the writer's own choosing or creation. If he think fit, also, he may so manage his atmospherical medium as to bring out or mellow the lights and deepen and enrich the shadows of the picture. He will be wise, no doubt, to make a very moderate use of the privileges here stated, and, especially, to mingle the Marvellous rather as a slight, delicate, and evanescent flavor than as any portion of the actual substance of the dish offered to the public. He can hardly be said, however, to commit a literary crime even if he disregard this caution.

" In the present work, the author has proposed to himself — but with what success, fortunately, it is not for him to judge — to keep undeviatingly within his immunities. The point of view in which this tale comes under the Romantic definition lies in the attempt to connect a bygone time with the very present that is flitting away from us. It is a legend prolonging itself, from an epoch now gray in the distance, down into our own broad daylight, and bringing along with it some of its legendary mist, which the reader, according to his pleasure, may either disregard, or allow it to float almost imperceptibly about the characters and events for the sake of a picturesque effect."

It is needless to say that, in books like " The House of the Seven Gables," " The Scarlet Letter," or " The Marble Faun," the reader sees the personages and events of the story through the warm or sombre romantic medium, — the special atmosphere which the author has created for him.   In the most successful stories of Mr. Howells, on the other hand, the atmosphere is precisely that of Boston or New York during the year or decade described in the story.   The realist has succeeded with singular skill in making a vertical sunlight strike upon his pages.   To turn from such novels as these to the romances of Hawthorne is to pass from the clear, frank sunlight of high noon into the mist of dawn, the glow of the sunset, the wavering outlines of moonlight.   Which atmosphere is more attractive depends upon the temperament, the momentary mood, the literary training of the individual reader.   It is foolish to endeavor to prove that one type of book — as a type — is better than the other.   All that we are now concerned to see is that there is a difference ; that the presence or absence of the romantic atmosphere largely determines the nature of a work of fiction.

How is this atmosphere to be se- Remoteness of time. cured ? The writer frequently com- passes it by the simple expedient of placing his story in a remote period, where the very distance enhances the atmospheric effect. Mr. Crawford's "Zoroaster" will serve to illus- trate this type of romantic novel. The mere remoteness in time from our own day and generation is sufficient to give such a romance an appeal to the historic imagination. In- deed, almost all historical fiction is in this sense of the word romantic fiction. Now and again surprising efforts have been made, as in the Egyptian novels of George Ebers, to paint the personages and the scenes of re- mote antiquity with all the detailed accuracy of a chronicle of the present day. Such experiments in applying the realistic method to the depiction of historical personages and events have commonly failed, however, to im- part either any sense of reality or any roman- tic charm. It is surely wiser to follow the course of the great writers of historical ro- mance in avoiding a too curious consideration

of exact details. " Quentin Durward " and
" The Talisman " are all wrong archæologi-
cally, yet they are triumphs of fiction-writing
none the less.

Strangeness of scene.   There is, too, a romanticism which
owes its atmosphere to strangeness
of place rather than remoteness of time.   We
know how the imaginations of Southey and
Coleridge were affected by the sound of the
syllables in the word Susquehanna, upon the
banks of which unvisited, romantic stream
they were desirous of founding a Utopian
colony.   That element of our human nature
which constantly tempts us to belittle what
is actually present, and to idealize and glo-
rify what is beyond the field of our own vision, is constantly playing into the hands of
the romance-writer.   Mr. Crawford's " Mr.
Isaacs," for instance, seems, to one reading
the story in England or America, to move in
a sort of fairyland.   But the traveler familiar
with the East is likely to have met the actual
Mr. Isaacs in his jewelry shop in Delhi, and
to smile at the mere romance of place which
has so moved the imagination of the untrav-
eled reader.

But remoteness of time and place do not contribute more perfectly to the creation of romantic atmosphere *The atmosphere of passion.* than do quite modern and present circumstances, provided these are viewed through an atmosphere of intense emotion. Let passion enter, let fury or pathos or tragedy brood over the personages of a story, and it matters little how sordid and prosaic the world in which the characters move. We have used Mr. Crawford's "Zoroaster" and "Mr. Isaacs" to exemplify certain types of romantic atmosphere. There is a chapter of his "Casa Braccio" where he describes the interior of an Italian restaurant in a fashion that would do credit to any realistic writer, but the vulgar interior is flooded with the intense light of passion and crime. The familiar outlines, the scents and odors and sights of the place are filled, as it were, by the mist of anguish and terror. To be able to accomplish such a feat as this is to prove one's self a master of the methods of romance.

We have been looking at the writer of romances and at those qualities in his books which make *Romantic sentiment in the public.*

it possible for them to convey an atmosphere
of romantic sentiment.   This sentiment would
be ineffectual, however, if it were not for the
corresponding, the reciprocal, sentiment on
the part of the public itself.   The public is
never more like a healthy child than in its
thirst for the exceptional and the exotic.   I
have chosen as one of the mottoes for this
chapter the verdict of a veteran fisherman,
who declares that " trout take some flies because they resemble the real fly on which they
feed.   They take other flies for no such reason.   And in this they are like men."   In
truth, we all like, at certain seasons, the
strange, bright-colored creations of a novelist's fancy, and the more vividly they differ
from the sober colors of reality the greater
the pleasure they afford.

In youth and   To youth, colored as it is with
age.   romantic hues of its own devising,
no fiction seems so improbable as to forbid
acceptance.   Old age, disillusionized by many
adventures, by many voyages into far-off
seas, loves to cheat itself once more with the
swiftly spun web of romantic delusion.   The
first motto for the present chapter is a passage from one of the letters of Edward Fitz-

Gerald regarding the novels of Thackeray.
It was written in December, 1875, when Fitz-
Gerald felt himself " old and dry," and in no
mood for the fiction that deals with human
life in its profounder aspects. Yet only three
years before he was writing about Disraeli's
romantic novel " Lothair : " —

" Altogether the Book is like a pleasant Magic Lan-
tern : when it is over I shall forget it : and shall want
to return to what I do not forget ; some of Thackeray's
monumental Figures of ' pauvre et triste Humanité,'
as Old Napoleon called it : Humanity in its depths,
not in its superficial Appearances."

There could scarcely be a better illustration of the shifting moods of a sympathetic,
sensitive reader than that given by these
two passages from FitzGerald's letters.

All of us, in certain hours of A literature
weariness, of relaxation from the of evasion.
daily toil, of twilight dreaming, desire to
forget the disappointments of actual experience. Romantic fiction furnishes a literature
of evasion. It allows us to escape from
the complications, the fret, the strain of living. In such hours one is willing to leave
the reading of realistic fiction to the strong,
the courageous persons who have no fear of

the facts of life; who prefer to face them,
with all their terrible implications. It is
enough for the rest of us, for the time being,
at least, to wander away into some enchanted
land "far from this our war."

It is easy to understand, there-
The "neo-romantic movement." fore, how the modern "neo-romantic" movement has arisen as a re-
action against realism. It is impossible to
analyze exactly these changes in the reading
public's temper. They are as unaccountable,
apparently as whimsical, as the variations in
any other human appetite. But there are
few sympathetic readers of modern English
fiction who do not feel grateful for the books
written by the younger men who, with Stevenson as their gallant leader, came into prominence during the last twenty years of the
nineteenth century. Few or none of these
men have revealed themselves as great personalities seriously engaged in interpreting
the more vital aspects of human experience.
Sometimes one is even inclined to doubt
whether most of them have very much to
say. But they have at least performed the
useful service of giving delight to their con-
temporaries. Many of them have been mas-

ters of the story-telling art; they have learned
brevity of description, brilliancy of narrative,
ready invention of situations and events.
Their task, after all, is far less difficult than
that of the author of great realistic fiction.
The Spanish novelist Valdés has remarked,
in the previously quoted preface to his novel
" Sister St. Sulpice," —

> " The talent of dazzling with strange events, of in-
> teresting by means of complicated intrigues and im-
> possible characters, is possessed to-day in Europe by
> several hundreds of writers, while there are not much
> more than a dozen of those who can awaken interest
> with the common acts of existence, and with the paint-
> ing of characters genuinely human."

But these " hundreds of writers " have
learned at least to avoid certain pitfalls into
which the authors of realistic fiction have
been apt to stumble. They have learned not
to preach, not to go too far in depicting unpleasant phases of life, and not to let a love
of accuracy of detail persuade them into the
composition of pages that are only weariness
to the reader. In the long history of the
English novel there has been no period when
so many readable books have been written as
in the last twenty-five years. Whether many

of these books are destined to last beyond the
moment may naturally be doubted.   The very
variety and originality which captures the
public attention for the season are often an
obstacle to permanent literary fame.   To
quote once more from the preface to " Sister
St. Sulpice : " —

" Extremely original works produce a lively impression upon the public for the moment, but are speedily
forgotten.   And this is because their originality frequently lies in a deviation from the truth, and truth is
not slow in reasserting its sway, because it alone is eternal and beautiful.   The public does not admire the poet
or novelist who holds the reins of his imagination and
makes it serve his purpose, who understands how to give
fit preparation to his work and writes with naturalness
and good sense.   And yet as a general rule these are
the ones that become immortal."

**Romanticism
and idealism.**   No discussion of romantic fiction is adequate which leaves out
of view the relation of romanticism to idealism.   Idealism is necessary, is inevitable, in
every true work of art.   It means building
up a whole in accordance with the artist's
idea ; it means freeing his material from accidental elements so that he may express its
real significance.   There is as profound and
far-reaching idealism in a realistic novel like

" Middlemarch " as there is in a romance like
Sienkiewicz's " Fire and Sword." But many
discussions of realism have devoted themselves to pointing out a supposed antagonism
between realism and idealism, as if no realistic novel could possibly express an ideal. By
far the more vital contrast is, as we have seen,
between realism and romanticism. That is to
say, along what lines is the artist to work out
his ideal? Is he to stand solidly upon the
earth, to base his work upon the actualities
of mortal experience, or is he to leave the
earth behind him and go voyaging off into
the blue? Tolstoi's " Resurrection," with
its frank inclusion of many repellent and
painful aspects of human experience, is a
thoroughly realistic piece of fiction. Yet its
main theme is to show what sort of recon-
struction of human society would be necessary if the teachings of the New Testament
were really to be accepted as an actual rule
of life. There could be no theme more idealistic than this. On the other hand, Miss
Johnston's " To Have and to Hold " is a
frankly romantic story, one in which the men
are brave and the women beautiful; where
there are pirates and shipwrecks, sword and

saddle, battle, murder, and sudden death. It
portrays such a state of society as never existed in Colonial Virginia or anywhere else
upon the face of the earth. It likewise is a
piece of pure idealism ; it " leaves the ground
to lose itself in the sky." But it is as truly
romantic in its entire texture as Tolstoi's
study of contemporary Russia is realistic.

What does the novelist think of life ? In the last analysis, therefore,
the question becomes simply this :
What does the artist in fiction think
of life ? If he believes it to be a good thing,
the best thing God has given us, he may
wish, and probably will wish, to keep his art
close to it. Provided he have ideas, there is
no danger that his work will lack idealism.
But if, on the other hand, he desires " better bread than wheaten," if life does not seem
to him very good, then he must surely dream
out something different. He must create an
imaginary world, whether in Colonial Virginia or elsewhere, and keep his art close to
that. He too, provided he have ideas, will
not lack idealism. But whatever he thinks
about life itself, about the conditions in which
plain men and women move and form the
shifting figures in the pattern of the eternal

human comedy, it is his task to make something beautiful.   He must give pleasure, no matter from what materials the texture of his craft is woven, no matter what method he chooses to adopt.   Which material or which method gives the higher pleasure, the more permanent delight, to generations of readers, will depend entirely upon the readers themselves.   It can never be settled by any theoretical discussion of the advantages and disadvantages of realistic or romantic art.

CHAPTER XI

THE QUESTION OF FORM

"The form, it seems to me, is to be appreciated after the fact: then the author's choice has been made, his standard has been indicated; then we can follow lines and directions, and compare tones and resemblances. Then, in a word, we can enjoy one of the most charming of pleasures, we can estimate quality, we can apply the test of execution."

HENRY JAMES, *Partial Portraits.*

To be well written.

In one of the most genial passages of his "Partial Portraits," Mr. Henry James has described those Sunday afternoon gatherings of a famous group of novelists in Flaubert's little salon, where the talk concerned itself mainly with the methods of the art of fiction. These men had long since passed beyond the point where they interested themselves with questions of morals or conscious purpose; to them "the only duty of a novel was to be well written; that merit included every other of which it was capable."

Matter, man, and manner.

What does "well written" mean? It is a question of form, of adapt-

ing means to ends. In the earlier chapters
of this book we have been considering the
material used by the novelist in its relations to the material used by cognate arts,
as well as with a view to its adaptability
for the structural purposes of the fictionist.
We have seen how the elements of character,
plot, and setting lend themselves to the mould-
ing imagination of the fiction-writer. We
then studied the fiction-writer himself, endeavoring to estimate the influence of his
personality upon his conscious or unconscious
selection of material. In the chapters devoted
to realism and romanticism we saw that these
tendencies — these general fashions of envis-
aging one's material — are to be traced back
to the writer's attitude towards life, as well
as to the influence of the literary fashions
prevailing in different periods of a national
literature. We have now to observe the final
step in the production of a work of fiction,
that is to say, the writer's choice of form,
his mastery of language, — in short, his skill
in execution. The matter, the man, and the
manner ; that, for better or worse, has been
the order we have followed.

The province of rhetoric.   In analyzing a writer's manner, that is, his personal adaptation of the literary means at his disposal to the end he has in view, we enter upon the territory of rhetoric. It is the students of rhetoric, of style, who have made the clearest exposition of those various kinds of composition which are to be observed in prose fiction. They have furnished special treatises upon "The Literature of Feeling," [1] upon narration [2] and description,[3] and they have illustrated every variety of technical method from the practice of the modern fiction-writer. They have balanced the stylistic advantages and difficulties of such varying fictional forms as the romance and the novel, the allegory and the short story. It is not the purpose of the present chapter to take up such questions in detail. All that I shall endeavor to do is to point out to the serious reader of fiction some of the paths which he may follow, if he will, and then, in the succeeding chapter, to select one typical form of

[1] J. H. Gardiner, *The Forms of Prose Literature.* New York : Scribners.

[2] W. T. Brewster, *Prose Narration.* New York : Holt.

[3] C. S. Baldwin, *Prose Description.* New York : Holt.

fiction, the short story, for more detailed treatment.

For it is only the reader who takes his fiction rather seriously who is likely to interest himself in questions of form. The great public concerns itself chiefly with the " stuff " of a novel; it simply asks : Does this new book impart any thrills of emotion ? Is it interesting ? Does it have a good " story " ? Does it give a glimpse of people and places worth knowing : Lincoln, Napoleon, Richard the Lion Heart; California, India, London, Paris ? Whether the book is " well written," in the technical sense, is a question concerning which the general public is quite indifferent. And it is a wholesome thing for the student of style in fiction to place himself, now and again, frankly on the territory occupied by the great public ; to remember that the " stuff " in itself has æsthetic values that are never to be neglected or underrated, that there are sound human reasons for that preference of the untrained public for the " picture that tells a story " over the picture that is simply well painted. I have known novelists to hesitate and agonize over the

The student and the public.

question of writing a certain story in the first person or the third person ; drafting it now under one form, now under another ; rejoicing over the technical opportunities of the autobiographical method, and mourning over its necessary limitations ; liking the objective, impartial " third person " point of view, yet finding it perhaps too cold and colorless for that particular story. This is a good example of those questions of pure form in which students of fiction and some writers of fiction take a natural interest, but towards which the public remains blandly indifferent. If " Esmond " is a " good story," thinks the public, what earthly difference does it make whether it is written in the first person or the third person, or now in one and now in the other ? The present chapter, however, is written for the comparatively few people who believe that the choice of form is significant, as bearing upon the total impression made by the story.

But it should be remembered, in the first place, that the forms of prose fiction are extremely flexible. It is impossible, as we have seen, to apply to them the comparatively rigid rules that are

The infinite variety of forms.

exemplified in the epic, the lyric, the drama. And even after a general choice of fictional form has been made — let us say, for instance, in favor of the short story rather than the novel as the better artistic medium for the conveyance of a certain idea, a certain impression of life — there are infinite possible modifications of form, due to the varying personal power of expression possessed by different writers. Turgenieff and Mr. Kipling, let us say, will both exercise an unerring instinct in determining that a given theme can be better presented in a dozen pages than in a hundred. But there the similarity of choice ends. The two men have different eyes, minds, hands. The brush-work is not the same ; no trained reader can possibly mistake a page of Turgenieff for a page of Kipling. The selection of words, the ordering of sentences, the arrangement of events, reveal the style of the individual workman. The contrast between two works in different *genres* — for instance Trollope's "Barchester Towers" and one of Hardy's "Wessex Tales" — involves not only all those differences in material and in personality which we have already discussed, but countless subtleties of

style, of manner. Such a comparative study
implies, on the one hand, a knowledge of
the technique of prose fiction considered as
an abstract medium of expression, and on
the other, the closest scrutiny of the command of language, the individual power over
words, possessed by these two writers.

The analysis of style: Minto. How is the student of fiction to
train himself in such analysis?   I
know of no better method than
that followed in such excellent handbooks as
Minto's " Manual of English Prose Literature " [1] or Clark's " English Prose Writers." [2]
In Professor Minto's book, for example, there
are careful studies of representative British
authors, who are minutely examined under
such headings as Life, Character, and Opinions, in order to insure, first of all, an intelligent knowledge of the man behind the book.
Then the Elements of Style are considered :
the Vocabulary, its constituents and characteristics, the Sentences and Paragraphs ; then
the Qualities of Style, such as Simplicity,

[1] William Minto, *A Manual of English Prose Literature.*
New York and Boston : Ginn.

[2] J. Scott Clark, *A Study of English Prose Writers : A
Laboratory Method.*   New York : Scribners.

Clearness, Strength, Pathos, the Ludicrous, Melody, Harmony, Taste. His Figures of Speech are then analyzed and classified, and finally, taking a broader outlook, there is an estimate of the author's accomplishment in the varying kinds of composition, such as Description, Narration, Exposition, and Persuasion.

Professor Clark's method of analytic study is similar in aim, although it differs in details. In *Clark's laboratory method.* his own words, " the method consists in determining the particular and distinctive features of a writer's style (using the term "style" in its wide sense), in sustaining that analysis by a very wide consensus of critical opinion, in illustrating the particular characteristics of each writer by voluminous and carefully selected extracts from his works, and in then requiring the pupil to find in the works of the writer parallel illustrations." In the section devoted to Dickens, for example, there is first a brief Biographical Outline, followed by a Bibliography on Dickens's style. Then follows a list of Particular Characteristics as pointed out by competent critics, each characteristic being also illustrated by extracts from the novels. They are grouped under eleven heads : 1. Fondness for Caricature — Exaggeration — Grotesqueness. 2. Genial Humor. 3. Incarnation of Characteristics — Single Strokes. 4. Descriptive Power — Minuteness of Observation — Vividness. 5. Tender, sometimes Mawkish, Pathos. 6. Gayety — Animal Spirits — Good-Fellowship. 7. Sincerity — Manliness — Earnestness. 8. Broad Sympathy — Plain, Practical Humanity. 9. Dramatic Power. 10. Vulgarity — Artificiality. 11. Diffuseness.

The value of such discipline. Does all this sound rather schoolmasterish? It is schoolmasterish if done pedantically, with over-literalness, and considered as an end in itself. But it is only by some such exact discipline in the appreciation of a literary product that "we can enjoy one of the most charming of pleasures, we can estimate quality, we can apply the test of execution." Let the reader take a single book of any of the masters of fiction, and devote a few days or weeks to writing out, with the most scrupulous care, such critical notes upon it as Minto and Clark have suggested. He will not only never regret the labor, but unless he is a born pedant, he will read fiction thereafter with new eyes and a new delight. If he be a born pedant, unwilling to look beyond his own critical categories, unable to see the wood for the trees, then his soul has gone blind already, and a little more rhetorical analysis will not do it any harm.

The standpoint of the present chapter, it will be observed, has hitherto been that of the reader of fiction. It is based upon the belief that the pleasure to be derived from novel reading is enhanced in proportion to one's intelligent perception of the nature of the writer's problems and of the skill with which he has overcome them. Let us now shift our point of view, and endeavor to place ourselves in the position of the writer of fiction. Does his understanding of the theory and technique of his art contribute to his practical mastery of it? Understanding is not mastery, of course; yet for all except the geniuses — who may be trusted to find their road across country — it is the straightest path to mastery. It was to some purpose that George Eliot had perfected her theory of fiction at thirty-five, before she had written a line of fiction herself. If the

"young writer" has objectively studied the
laws of fiction, as they have been commented
upon by such skilled workmen as Mr. Henry
James, Stevenson, Bourget, and many more,
it is his own fault if he has not gained a clearer
knowledge of what he is doing, as well as
some measure of inspiration for his task.

How far is technical excellence in
What training is necessary? the composition of fiction a matter
of training?   It is surely a miscon-
ception that no training at all is required, that
if "you have it in you," all that is necessary
is to take pen and paper and begin.   One is
about as likely to turn out a great work of fiction by following that programme as he would
be to paint a great picture the first time he
handled the brush.   Yet it is certainly easier
to write a tolerable novel the "first time trying" than to paint a tolerable picture.   The
reason is, obviously, that the artistic medium
of fiction, namely, language, is a tool with
which all of us are somewhat familiar.   And
if, besides possessing resources of language,
one has already trained himself, consciously
or unconsciously, in the observation of varied types of character, in vivid narration and
description, in the dramatic, the imaginative

way of confronting human life, he may without suspecting it be already a matured novelist in everything except the actual writing of the story. How many letter-writers still possess these gifts in perfection! From this point of view, such famous " first books " as Scott's " Waverley," written at forty-three, Richardson's " Pamela," written at fifty-one, and George Eliot's " Scenes from Clerical Life," written at thirty-five, are not such pertinent examples of " the first time trying " as of the long general preparation for an unforeseen, specific task.

It should be noted, furthermore, that technical excellence in composition is often gained more quickly **Maturing of hand and mind.** than the intellectual processes which are also involved in the production of notable fiction. The early work of Thackeray, Hawthorne, Stevenson, and Mr. Kipling is an illustration of the hand maturing before the mind. Hawthorne and Stevenson, in particular, wrote admirable English before they really had anything to say. The ultimate question concerning a novelist is, of course, a two-fold one : What does he have to say ? and how does he say it ? In the case of many novelists who have achieved great things, the second part of the question can be answered favorably long before one can reply with any confidence to the first. There is a charming story of the youthful Tennyson brothers, Charles and Alfred, to the effect that they stayed at home from church one Sunday, and Charles, the elder, assigned to Alfred the roses in the rectory garden as a subject for a poem. Alfred, who was not many years out of the cradle, obediently filled his slate with verses. Whereupon his elder brother remarked with grave finality, " Alfred, you can write ! " That verdict can be rendered upon many men up and down the world to-day, who seem, nevertheless, to find nothing worth writing about. But in the mean time it is something, at least, to be a master of the instrument.

Can the art of fiction be taught? This may throw some light upon the question first brought before the public by Sir Walter Besant's lecture upon " The Art of Fiction," namely, whether that art can be taught. If by this question one means the technical handling of narration and description as media of expression, it should be answered in the affirmative.

In that sense fiction-writing can be taught, precisely as versification or essay and oration writing are taught. Thousands of young people are practicing it every day in this country, under the eye of competent instructors in rhetoric. How far the pupil may go will naturally depend more upon the pupil himself than upon the mere method of instruction. In the class in " description " there will be now and then a young Daudet, or a Sentimental Tommy with a preternatural instinct for the *mot juste;* and in the class in " narration " some Charles Reade or Clark Russell will exhibit an astounding facility in spinning a yarn. But as a rule this deliberate effort to apprentice one's self to the novel-writing trade gives the "young writer" very much what the " young reader" may also gain from it, that is, merely a quickened perception of the nature of the novelist's craft.

I venture to add without comment Sir Walter Besant's " Rules for Novel-Writers," as an interesting contribution from a writer who has won honorable recognition for his work : 1. Practice writing something original every day. 2.

Besant's "Rules for Novel-Writers."

Cultivate the habit of observation. 3. Work regularly at certain hours. 4. Read no rubbish. 5. Aim at the formation of style. 6. Endeavor to be dramatic. 7. A great element of dramatic skill is selection. 8. Avoid the sin of writing about a character. 9. Never attempt to describe any kind of life except that with which you are familiar. 10. Learn as much as you can about men and women. 11. For the sake of forming a good natural style, and acquiring command of language, write poetry.

Fewer books, and better. But it may honestly be doubted if these rules, or any rules or course of discipline, will turn a naturally poor workman into a good one. If some one could devise a set of rules that would discourage mediocrity from rushing into print, and reduce the ranks of fiction-writers instead of swelling them, he would deserve well of his generation. What we need, surely, is not more novels, but higher tests of excellence. The training suggested in this chapter is primarily that which helps the reader to discern the good from the bad, the genuine product of thought and passion from the shoddy sentimentality, the empty sound and fury of the fiction that perishes in a day. That instinct for form which gives the final perfection to a novel cannot be imparted by the study of form; it is born and not made; it comes from some glimpse of enduring beauty as revealed to the true artist soul.

CHAPTER XII

THE SHORT STORY

"For here, at least [in the short story], we have the conditions of perfect art; there is no subdivision of interest; the author can strike directly in, without preface, can move with determined step toward a conclusion, and can — O highest privilege! — stop when he is done."

THOMAS WENTWORTH HIGGINSON.

A hint from Thackeray. THE initial difficulty in discussing the short story is that old danger of taking one's subject either too seriously or else not seriously enough. If one could but hit upon the proper key at the outset, one might possibly hope to edify the strenuous reader, and at the same time to propitiate the frivolous. Let us make certain of our key, therefore, by promptly borrowing one! And we will take our hint as to the real nature of the short story from that indisputable master of the long story, Thackeray. In his "Roundabout Paper" "On a Lazy Idle Boy" there is a picture, all in six lines, of "a score of white-bearded, white-robed warriors, or grave seniors of the city, seated at the gate of Jaffa or Beyrout, and listening to the story-teller reciting his marvels out of The Arabian Nights." That picture, symbol as it was to Thackeray of the story-teller's rôle, may well hover in the background of one's memory as he discourses of the short story as a form of literary art.

Is it a distinct form, with laws Is it a dis-
and potencies that differentiate it tinct form?
sharply from other types of literature? This question is a sort of turnstile, through which one must wriggle, or over which one must boldly leap, in order to reach our field of investigation. Some of my readers are familiar with a magazine article, written many years ago by Mr. Brander Matthews, entitled "The Philosophy of the Short-Story," and recently revised and issued as a little volume.[1] It will be observed that Professor Matthews spells "short-story" with a hyphen, and claims that the short-story, hyphenated, is something very different from a story that merely happens to be short. It is, he believes, a distinct

[1] *The Philosophy of the Short-Story.* By Brander Matthews, D. C. L. New York : Longmans, Green and Company, 1901.

species ; an art form by itself ; a new literary *genre*, in short, characterized by compression, originality, ingenuity, a touch of
fantasy, and by the fact that no love interest
is needed to hold its parts together. Mr.
Matthews gives pertinent illustrations of
these characteristics, and comments in an interesting fashion upon recent British and
American examples of the short-story.   But
one is tempted to ask if the white-bearded,
white-robed warriors at the gate of Jaffa were
not listening, centuries and centuries ago, to
tales marked by compression, originality, ingenuity, a touch of fantasy, and all the other
" notes " of this new type of literature.

A new form ?   The critical trail blazed so plainly
by the professor of dramatic litera-
ture at Columbia has been followed by several authors of recent volumes devoted to
the modern art of short story writing.[1]   But
story-telling, surely, is as old as the day when
men first gathered round a camp-fire or women huddled in a cave ! The study of comparative folk-lore is teaching us every day
how universal is the instinct for it.   Even
were we to leave out of view the literature of

[1] See the Bibliography for the present chapter.

oral tradition, and take the earlier written literature of any European people, — for instance, the tales told by Chaucer and some of his Italian models, — we should find these modern characteristics of originality, ingenuity, and the rest in almost unrivaled perfection, and perhaps come to the conclusion of Chaucer himself, as he exclaims in whimsical despair, "There is no new thing that is not old!" And yet if the question be put point-blank, "Do not such short story writers as Stevenson, Mr. Kipling, Miss Jewett, Bret Harte, Daudet — not to mention Poe and Hawthorne — stand for a new movement, a distinct type of literature?" one is bound to answer "Yes." Here is work that contrasts very strongly, not only with the Italian *novella,* and other mediæval types, but even with the English and American tales of two generations ago. Where lies the difference? For Professor Matthews is surely right in holding that there is a difference. It is safer to trace it, however, not in the external characteristics of this modern work, every feature of which can easily be paralleled in prehistoric myths, but rather in the attitude of the contemporary short story writer toward his material, and in his conscious effort to achieve under certain conditions a certain effect. And no one has defined this conscious attitude and aim so clearly as Edgar Allan Poe.

Poe's view. In that perpetually quoted essay upon Hawthorne's "Tales," written in 1842 — one of the earliest and to this day one of the best criticisms of Hawthorne — Poe remarks : —

" Were I bidden to say how the highest genius could be most advantageously employed for the best display of its own powers, I should answer, without hesitation — in the composition of a rhymed poem, not to exceed in length what might be perused in an hour. Within this limit alone can the highest order of true poetry exist. I need only here say, upon this topic, that in almost all classes of composition, the unity of effect or impression is a point of the greatest importance. It is clear, moreover, that this unity cannot be thoroughly preserved in productions whose perusal cannot be completed at one sitting. We may continue the reading of a prose composition, from the very nature of prose itself, much longer than we can persevere, to any good purpose, in the perusal of a poem. This latter, if truly fulfilling the demands of the poetic sentiment, induces an exaltation of the soul which cannot be long sustained. All high excitements are necessarily transient. Thus a long poem is a paradox. And without unity of impression the deepest effects cannot be brought about. . . .

" Were I called upon, however, to designate that class of composition which, next to such a poem as I have suggested, should best fulfill the demands of high genius — should offer it the most advantageous field of exertion — I should unhesitatingly speak of the prose tale, as Mr. Hawthorne has here exemplified it. I allude to the short prose narrative, requiring from a half hour to one or two hours in its perusal. The ordinary novel is objectionable, from its length, for reasons already stated in substance. As it cannot be read at one sitting, it deprives itself, of course, of the immense force derivable from totality. Worldly interests intervening during the pauses of perusal, modify, annul, or counteract, in a greater or less degree, the impressions of the book. But simple cessation in reading would, of itself, be sufficient to destroy the true unity. In the brief tale, however, the author is enabled to carry out the fullness of his intention, be it what it may. During the hour of perusal the soul of the reader is at the writer's control. There are no external or extrinsic influences — resulting from weariness or interruption.

" A skillful literary artist has constructed a tale. If wise, he has not fashioned his thoughts to accommodate his incidents ; but having conceived, with deliberate care, a certain unique or single effect to be wrought out, he then invents such incidents, — he then combines such events as may best aid him in establishing this preconceived effect. If his very initial sentence tend not to the outbringing of this effect, then he has failed in his first step. In the whole composition there should be no word written, of which the tendency, direct or indirect, is not to the one preëstablished design. And

by such means, with such care and skill, a picture is at
length painted which leaves in the mind of him who
contemplates it with a kindred art, a sense of the fullest satisfaction.   The idea of the tale has been presented unblemished, because undisturbed ; and this is
an end unattainable by the novel."

The starting point.   If we assent to Poe's reasoning,
we are at once upon firm ground.
The short story in prose literature corre-
sponds, then, to the lyric in poetry ; like the
lyric, its unity of effect turns largely upon its
brevity ; and as there are well known laws of
lyric structure which the lyric poet violates
at his peril or obeys to his triumph, so the
short story must observe certain conditions
and may enjoy certain freedoms that are peculiar to itself.   Doubtless our professional
story-tellers seated before the gate of Jaffa
or Beyrout had ages ago a naïve, instinctive
apprehension of these principles of their art ;
but it is equally true that the story-writers
of our own day, profiting by the accumulated
experience of the race, responding quickly to
international literary influences, prompt to
learn from and to imitate one another, are
consciously, and no doubt self-consciously,
studying their art as it has never been studied

before.   Every magazine brings new experiments in method, or new variations of the
old themes ; and it would speak ill for the intelligence of these workmen if there could be
no registration of results.   Some such registration may, at any rate, be attempted without
being unduly dogmatic, and without making
one's pleasure in a short story too solemn and
heart-searching an affair.

Every work of fiction, long or
short, depends for its charm and
power — as we have already seen
— upon one or all of three elements : the
characters, the plot, and the setting.   Here
are certain persons, doing certain things, in
certain circumstances ; and the fiction-writer
tells us about one or another or all three of
these phases of his theme.   Sometimes he
creates vivid characters, but does not know
what to do with them ; sometimes he invents
very intricate and thrilling plots, but the men
and women remain nonentities ; sometimes
he lavishes his skill on the background, the
milieu, the manners and morals of the age,
the all-enveloping natural forces or historic
movements, while his heroes and heroines are

Characters, plot, and setting.

hurriedly pushed here and there into place,
like dolls at a dolls' tea-party. But the masters of fiction, one need hardly say, know
how to beget men and women, and to make
them march toward events, with the earth
beneath their feet and overhead the sky.

Character-drawing. Suppose we turn to the first of
these three potential elements of
interest and ask what are the requirements
of the short story as regards the delineation
of character. Looking at the characters
alone, and not, for the moment, at the plot
or the setting, is there any difference between
the short story and the novel? There is this
very obvious difference : if it is a character-
story at all, the characters must be unique,
original enough to catch the eye at once.
Everybody knows that in a novel a commonplace person may be made interesting by a
deliberate, patient exposition of his various
traits, precisely as we can learn to like very
uninteresting persons in real life if circumstances place them day after day at our elbows. Who of us would not grow impatient
with the early chapters of " The Newcomes,"
for instance, or " The Antiquary," if it were
not for our faith that Thackeray and Scott

know their business, and that every one of those commonplace people will contribute something in the end to the total effect? And even where the gradual development of character, rather than the mere portrayal of character, is the theme of a novelist, as so frequently with George Eliot, how colorless may be the personality at the outset, how narrow the range of thought and experience portrayed! Yet, in George Eliot's own words, " these commonplace people have a conscience, and have felt the sublime prompting to do the painful right." They take on dignity from their moral struggle, whether the struggle ends in victory or defeat. By an infinite number of subtle touches they are made to grow and change before our eyes, like living, fascinating things.

But all this takes time, — far more time than is at the disposal of the short story writer. If his special theme be the delineation of character, he dare not choose colorless characters; if his theme is character-development, then that development must be hastened by striking experiences, — like a plant forced in a hothouse instead of left to the natural conditions of sun and

Swift development.

cloud and shower. For instance, if it be a
love story, the hero and heroine must begin
their decisive battle at once, without the advantage of a dozen chapters of preliminary
skirmishing. If the hero is to be made into
a villain or a saint, the chemistry must be of
the swiftest; that is to say, unusual forces are
brought to bear upon somewhat unusual personalities. It is an interesting consequence
of this necessity for choosing the exceptional
rather than the normal that, so far as the
character-element is concerned, the influence
of the modern short story is thrown upon the
side of romanticism rather than of realism.

Plot alone will serve. And yet it is by no means necessary that the short story should
depend upon character-drawing for its effect.
If its plot be sufficiently entertaining, comi-
cal, novel, thrilling, the characters may be
the merest lay figures and yet the story remain an admirable work of art. Poe's tales
of ratiocination, as he loved to call them, like
"The Gold-Bug," "The Purloined Letter,"
or his tales of pseudo-science, like "A Descent into the Maelstrom," are dependent for
none of their power upon any interest attach-
ing to character. The exercise of the pure

logical faculty, or the wonder and the terror of the natural world, gives scope enough for that consummate craftsman.   We have lately lost one of the most ingenious and delightful of American story-writers, whose tales of whimsical predicament illustrate this point very perfectly.   Given the conception of "Negative Gravity," what comic possibilities unfold themselves, quite without reference to the personality of the experimenter! I should be slow to assert that the individual idiosyncrasies of the passengers aboard that remarkable vessel, The Thomas Hyke, do not heighten the effect produced by their singular adventure, but they are not the essence of it.   "The Lady or the Tiger?" remains a perpetual riddle, does it not, precisely because it asks: "What would *a woman* do in that predicament?"   Not what this particular barbarian princess would do, for the author cunningly neglected to give her any individualized traits.   We know nothing about her; so that there are as many answers to the riddle as there are women in the world.   We know tolerably well what choice would be made in those circumstances by a specific woman like Becky Sharp or Dorothea

Casaubon or Little Em'ly ; but to affirm what
a woman would decide ? Ah, no ; Mr.
Stockton was quite too clever to attempt
that.

**Obliteration
of personal
traits.** Precisely the same obliteration
of personal traits is to be noted in
some tales involving situations that
are meant to be taken very seriously indeed.
The reader will recall Poe's story of the
Spanish Inquisition, entitled " The Pit and
the Pendulum." The unfortunate victim of
the inquisitors lies upon his back, strapped
to the stone floor of his dungeon. Directly
above him is suspended a huge pendulum, a
crescent of glittering steel, razor-edged, which
at every sweep to and fro lowers itself inch
by inch towards the helpless captive. As he
lies there, gazing frantically upon the terrific
oscillations of that hissing steel, struggling,
shrieking, or calculating with the calmness
of despair, Poe paints with extraordinary
vividness his sensations and his thoughts.
But who is he ? He is nobody — anybody,
— he is John Doe or Richard Roe, — he is
man under mortal agony — not a particular
man ; he has absolutely no individuality,
save possibly in the ingenuity by means of

which he finally escapes. I should not wish to imply that this is a defect in the story. By no means. Poe has wrought out, no doubt, precisely the effect he intended: the situation itself is enough without any specific characterization; and yet suppose we had Daniel Deronda strapped to that floor, or Mr. Micawber, or Terence Mulvaney? At any rate, the sensations and passions and wily stratagems of these distinct personalities would be more interesting than the emotions of Poe's lay figure. The novelist who should place them there would be bound to tell us what they — and no one else — would feel and do in that extremity of anguish. Not to tell us would be to fail to make the most of the artistic possibilities of the situation. Poe's task, surely, was much less complex. "The Pit and the Pendulum" is perfect in its way; but if the incident had been introduced into a novel, a different perfection would have been demanded.

Nor is it otherwise if we turn to that third element of effect in fic- *The background.* tion; namely, the circumstances or events enveloping the characters and action of the tale. The nature of the short story is such

that both characters and action may be almost without significance, provided the atmosphere — the place and time — the background — is artistically portrayed.   Here is
the source of the perennial pleasure to be
found in Mr. P. Deming's simple " Adiron-
dack Stories."   If the author can discover
to us a new corner of the world, or sketch
the familiar scene to our heart's desire, or il-
lumine one of the great human occupations,
as war, or commerce, or industry, he has it
in his power, through this means alone, to
give us the fullest satisfaction.   The modern
feeling for landscape, the modern curiosity
about social conditions, the modern æsthetic
sense for the characteristic rather than for
the beautiful as such, all play into the short
story writer's hands.   Many a reader, no
doubt, takes up Miss Wilkins's stories, not
because he cares much about the people in
them or what the people do, but just to breathe
for twenty minutes the New England air —
if in truth that be the New England air!
You may even have homesickness for a place
you have never seen, — some Delectable
Duchy in Cornwall, a window in Thrums, a
Californian mining camp deserted before you

were born, — and Mr. Quiller Couch, or Mr. Barrie, or Bret Harte will take you there, and that is all you ask of them.   The popularity which Stephen Crane's war stories enjoyed for a season was certainly not due to his characters, for his personages had no character — not even names — nor to the plot, for there was none.   But the sights and sounds and odors and colors of War — as Crane imagined War — were plastered upon his vacant-minded heroes as you would stick a poster to a wall, and the trick was done.   In other words, the setting was sufficient to produce the intended effect.

It is true, of course, that many stories, and these perhaps of the highest rank, avail themselves of all three of these modes of impression.   Bret Harte's "The Luck of Roaring Camp," Mr. Cable's "Posson Jone," Mr. Aldrich's "Marjorie Daw," Mr. Kipling's "The Man who would be King," Miss Jewett's "The Queen's Twin," Miss Wilkins's "A New England Nun," Dr. Hale's "The Man without a Country," present people and events and circumstances, blended into an artistic whole, that defies analysis.   But because we sometimes receive full measure, pressed down and running over, we should not forget that the cup of delight may be filled in a simpler and less wonderful way.

Opportunities afforded to the writer. This thought suggests the consideration of another aspect of our theme; namely, the opportunity which the short story, as a distinct type of literature, gives to the writer. We have seen indirectly that it enables him to use all his material, to spread before us any hints in the fields of character or action or setting which his notebook may contain. Mr. Henry James's stories very often impress one as chips from the workshop where his novels were built, — or, to use a less mechanical metaphor, as an exploration of a tempting side path, of whose vistas he had caught a passing glimpse while pursuing some of his retreating and elusive major problems. It is obvious, likewise, that the short story gives a young writer most valuable experience at the least loss of time. He can tear up and try again. Alas, if he only would do so a little oftener ! He can test his fortune with the public through the magazines, without waiting to write his immortal book. For older men in whom the creative impulse is comparatively feeble, or manifested at long intervals only, the form of the short story makes possible the production of a small quantity of highly finished work. But these incidental advantages to the author himself are not so much to our present purpose as are certain artistic opportunities which his strict limits of space allow him.

In the brief tale, then, he may be didactic without wearying his *Didacticism.* audience. Not to entangle one's self in the interminable question about the proper limits of didacticism in the art of fiction, one may assert that it is at least as fair to say to the author, " You may preach if you wish, but at your own risk," as it is to say to him, " You shall not preach at all, because I do not like to listen." Most of the greater English fiction-writers, at any rate, have the homiletic habit. Dangerous as this habit is, uncomfortable as it makes us feel to get a sermon instead of a story, there is sometimes no great harm in a sermonette. " This is not a tale exactly. It is a tract," are the opening words of one of Mr. Kipling's stories, and the tale is no worse — and likewise, it is true, no better — for its profession of a moral purpose. Many a tract, in this generation so suspicious of its preachers, has disguised itself as a short story, and made good reading, too. For that matter, not to grow quite unmindful of our white-robed, white-bearded company sitting all this time by the gate of Jaffa, there is a very pretty moral even in the artless tale of Aladdin's Lamp.

Posing problems. The story-writer, furthermore, has this advantage over the novelist, that he can pose problems without answering them. When George Sand and Charles Dickens wrote novels to exhibit certain defects in the organization of human society, they not only stated their case, but they had their triumphant solution of the difficulty. So it has been with the drama, until very recently. The younger Dumas had his own answer for every one of his problem-plays. But with Ibsen came the fashion of staging the question at issue, in unmistakable terms, and not even suggesting that one solution is better than another. "Here are the facts for you," says Ibsen; "here are the modern emotions for you; my work is done." In precisely similar fashion does a short story writer like Maupassant fling the facts in our face, brutally, pitilessly. We may make what we can of them; it is nothing to him. He poses his grim problem with surpassing skill, and that is all. A novel written in this way grows intolerable, and one may suspect that the contemporary problem-novel is apt to be such an unspeakable affair, not merely for its dubious themes and more than dubious style, but because it reveals so little power to " lay " the ghosts it raises.

Again, the short story writer is always asking us to take a great _{Arbitrary premises.} deal for granted. He begs to be allowed to state his own premises. He portrays, for instance, some marital comedy or tragedy, ingeniously enough. We retort, " Yes; but how could he have ever fallen in love with her in the first place ? " " Oh," replies the author off-hand, " that is another story." But if he were a novelist, he would not get off so easily. He might have to write twenty chapters, and go back three generations, to show why his hero fell in love with her in the first place. All that any fiction can do — very naturally — is to give us, as we com-

monly say, a mere cross-section of life.   There
are endless antecedents and consequents with
which it has no concern ; but the cross-section of the story-writer is so much thinner
that he escapes a thousand inconveniences,
and even then considers it beneath him to
explain his miracles.

What is more, the laws of brevity
Omission of unlovely details. and unity of effect compel him to
omit, in his portrayal of life and
character, many details that are unlovely.
Unless, like some very gifted fiction-writers
of our time, he makes a conscientious search
for the repulsive, it is easy for him to paint a
pleasant picture.   Bret Harte's earliest stories
show this happy instinct for the æsthetic, for
touching the sunny places in the lives of extremely disreputable men.   His gamblers are
exhibited in their charming mood; his outcasts are revealed to us at the one moment
of self-denying tenderness which insures our
sympathy.   Such a selective method is perfectly legitimate and necessary ; " The Luck
of Roaring Camp " and " The Outcasts of
Poker Flat " each contains but slightly more
than four thousand words.   All art is selective, for that matter ; but were a novelist to

take the personages of those stories and exhibit them as full-length figures, he would be
bound to tell more of the truth about them,
unpleasant as some of the details would be.
Otherwise he would paint life in a wholly
wrong perspective. Bret Harte's master,
Charles Dickens, did not always escape this
temptation to juggle with the general truth of
things ; the pupil escaped it, in these early
stories at least, simply because he was working on a different scale.

The space limits of the short story
allow its author likewise to make **The horrible.**
artistic use of the horrible, the morbid, the
dreadful — subjects too poignant to give any
pleasure if they were forced upon the attention throughout a novel. " The Black Cat,"
" The Murders in the Rue Morgue," " A
Descent into the Maelstrom," are admirable
examples of Poe's art ; but he was too skillful a workman not to know that that sort
of thing if it be done at all must be done
quickly. Four hundred pages of " The
Black Cat " would be impossible.

And last in our list of the dis- **Impression-**
tinct advantages of the art form **ism.**
we are considering is the fact that it allows

a man to make use of the vaguest suggestions, a delicate symbolism, a poetic impressionism, fancies too tenuous to hold in the
stout texture of the novel. Wide is the
scope of the art of fiction ; it includes even
this borderland of dreams. Poe's marvelous
" Shadow, a Parable," " Silence, a Fable ; "
Hawthorne's "The Hollow of the Three
Hills," or " The Snow - Image ; " many a
prose poem that might be cited from French
and Russian writers, — these illustrate the
strange beauty and mystery of those twilight
places where the vagrant imagination hovers
for a moment and flutters on.

The under-lying principle. It will be seen that all of the
opportunities that have been enu-
merated—the opportunity, namely,
for innocent didacticism, for posing problems
without answering them, for stating arbitrary
premises, for omitting unlovely details and,
conversely, for making beauty out of the horrible, and finally for poetic symbolism — are
connected with the fact that in the short story
the powers of the reader are not kept long
upon the stretch. The reader shares in the
large liberty which the short story affords to
the author. This type of prose literature,

like the lyric in poetry, is such an old, and simple, and free mode of expressing the artist's personality ! As long as men are interesting to one another, as long as the infinite complexities of modern emotion play about situations that are as old as the race, so long will there be an opportunity for the free development of the short story as a literary form.

Is there anything to be said upon the other side ? Are the distinct advantages of this art form accompanied by any strict conditions, upon conformity to which success depends ? For the brief tale demands, of one who would reach the foremost skill in it, two or three qualities that are really very rare.

What it demands: imagination.

It calls for visual imagination of a high order : the power to see the object ; to penetrate to its essential nature ; to select the one characteristic trait by which it may be represented. A novelist informs you that his heroine, let us say, is seated in a chair by the window. He tells you what she looks like : her attitude, figure, hair and eyes, and so forth. He can do this, and very often seems to do it, without really seeing that individual woman or making us see her. His trained pencil merely sketches some one of the same general description, of about the equivalent hair and eyes, and so forth, seated by that general kind of window. If he does not succeed in making her real to us in that pose, he has a hundred other opportunities before the novel ends. Recall how George Eliot pictures Dorothea in "Middlemarch," now in this position, now in that. If one scene does not present her vividly to us, the chances are that another will, and in the end, it is true, we have an absolutely distinct image of her. The short story writer, on the other hand, has but the one chance. His task, compared with that of the novelist, is like bringing down a flying bird with one bullet, instead of banging away with a whole handful of birdshot and having another barrel in reserve. Study the descriptive epithets in Stevenson's short stories. How they bring down the object! What an eye! And what a hand! No adjective that does not paint a picture or record a judgment! And if it were not for a boyish habit of showing off his skill and doing trick shots for us out of mere superfluity of cleverness, what judge of marksmanship would refuse Master Robert Louis Stevenson the prize?

An imagination that penetrates to the very heart of the matter; a *Style.* verbal magic that recreates for us what the imagination has seen, — these are the tests of the tale-teller's genius. A novel may be high up in the second rank — like Trollope's and Bulwer-Lytton's — and lack somehow the literary touch. But the only short stories that survive the year or the decade are those that have this verbal finish, — " fame's great antiseptic, style." To say that a short story at its best should have imagination and style is simple enough. To hunt through the magazines of any given month and find such a story is a very different matter. Out of the hundreds of stories printed every week in every civilized country, why do so few meet the supreme tests? To put it bluntly, does this form of literature present peculiar attractions to mediocrity?

For answer, let us look at some of the qualities which the short *What it fails to demand: sustained power.* story fails to demand from those who use it. It will account in part for the number of short stories written.

Very obviously, to write a short story requires no sustained power of imagination. So accomplished a critic as Mr. Henry James believes that this is a purely artificial distinction; he thinks that if you can imagine at all, you can keep it up. Ruskin went even farther. Every feat of the imagination, he declared, is easy for the man who performs it : the great feat is possible only to the great artist; yet if he can do it at all, he can do it easily. But as a matter of fact, does not the power required to hold steadily before you your theme and personages and the whole little world where the story moves correspond somewhat to the strength it takes to hold out a dumb-bell? Any one can do it for a few seconds; but in a few more seconds the arm sags ; it is only the trained athlete who can endure even to the minute's end. For Hawthorne to hold the people of " The Scarlet Letter " steadily in focus from November to February, to say nothing of six years' preliminary brooding, is surely more of an artistic feat than to write a short story between Tuesday and Friday. The three years and nine months of unremitting labor devoted to " Middlemarch " does not in itself afford any criterion of the value of the book; but given George Eliot's brain power and artistic instinct to begin with, and then concentrate them for that period upon a single theme, and it is no wonder that the result is a masterpiece. "Jan van Eyck was never in a hurry," says Charles Reade of the great Flemish painter in "The Cloister and the Hearth," — "Jan van Eyck was never in a hurry, and therefore the world will not forget him in a hurry." This sustained power of imagination, and the patient workmanship that keeps pace with it, are not demanded by the brief tale. It is a short distance race, and any one can run it indifferently well.

Nor does the short story demand of its author essential sanity, **Sanity.** breadth, and tolerance of view. How morbid does the genius of a Hoffmann, a Poe, a Maupassant seem when placed alongside the sane and wholesome art of Scott and Fielding and Thackeray! Sanity, balance, naturalness; the novel stands or falls, in the long run, by these tests. But your short story writer may be fit for a madhouse and yet compose tales that shall be immortal. In other words, we

do not ask of him that he shall have a philosophy of life, in any broad, complete sense.
It may be that Professor Masson, like a true
Scotchman, insisted too much upon the intellectual element in the art of fiction when he
declared, " Every artist is a thinker whether
he knows it or not, and ultimately no artist
will be found greater as an artist than he was
as a thinker." But he points out here what
must be the last of the distinctions we have
drawn between the short story and the novel.
When we read " Old Mortality," or " Pendennis," or " Daniel Deronda," we find in
each book a certain philosophy, " a chart or
plan of human life." Consciously or unconsciously held or formulated, it is nevertheless
there. The novelist has his theory of this
general scheme of things which enfolds us
all, and he cannot write his novel without be-
traying his theory. " He is a thinker whether
he knows it or not."

Deals with fragments. But the short story writer, with all
respect to him, need be nothing of
the sort. He deals not with wholes, but with
fragments ; not with the trend of the great
march through the wide world, but with some
particular aspect of the procession as it passes.

His story may be, as we have seen, the merest
sketch of a face, a comic attitude, a tragic
incident; it may be a lovely dream, or a hor-
rid nightmare, or a page of words that haunt
us like music. Yet he need not be consistent; he need not think things through. One
might almost maintain that there is more of
an answer, implicit or explicit, to the great
problems of human destiny in one book like
" Vanity Fair " or " Adam Bede " than in
all of Mr. Kipling's one hundred and sixty
short stories taken together — and Mr. Kipling is perhaps the most gifted story-teller of
our time.

Does not all this throw some light
upon the present popularity of the
short story with authors and public alike?
Here is a form of literature easy to write and
easy to read. The author is often paid as
much for a story as he earns from the copy-
rights of a novel, and it costs him one tenth
the labor. The multiplication of magazines
and other periodicals creates a constant market, with steadily rising prices. The qualities of imagination and style that go to the
making of a first-rate short story are as rare
as they ever were, but one is sometimes

Easy litera-
ture.

tempted to think that the great newspaper
and magazine reading public bothers itself
very little about either style or imagination.
The public pays its money and takes its
choice.   And there are other than these mechanical and commercial reasons why the
short story now holds the field.   It is a kind
of writing perfectly adapted to our over-
driven generation, which rushes from one
task or engagement to another, and between
times, or on the way, snatches up a story.
Our habit of nervous concentration for a
brief period helps us indeed to crowd a great
deal of pleasure into the half-hour of perusal ; our incapacity for prolonged attention
forces the author to keep within that limit,
or exceed it at his peril.

Affecting other forms.   It has been frequently declared
that this popularity of the short
story is unfavorable to other forms of imaginative literature.   Many English critics have
pointed out that the reaction against the
three-volume novel, and particularly against
George Eliot, has been caused by the universal passion for the short story.   And the
short story is frequently made responsible for
the alleged distaste of Americans for the

essay. We are told that nobody reads magazine poetry, because the short stories are so
much more interesting.

In the presence of all such brisk   Does anybody
generalizations, it is prudent to ex-   know?
ercise a little wholesome skepticism.   No one
really knows.   Each critic can easily find the
sort of facts he is looking for.   American
short stories have probably trained the public
to a certain expectation of technical excellence in narrative which has forced American
novel-writers to do more careful work.   But
there are few of our novel-writers who exhibit
a breadth and power commensurate with their
opportunities, and it is precisely these qualities of breadth and power which an apprenticeship to the art of short story writing
seldom or never seems to impart.   The wider
truth, after all, is that literary criticism has
no apparatus delicate enough to measure the
currents, the depths and the tideways, the
reactions and interactions of literary forms.
Essays upon the evolution of literary types,
when written by men like M. Brunetière,
are fascinating reading, and for the moment
almost persuade you that there is such a
thing as a real evolution of types, that is,

a definite replacement of a lower form by a higher. But the popular caprice of an hour upsets all your theories. Mr. Howells had no sooner proved, a few years ago, that a certain form of realism was the finally evolved type in fiction, than the great reading public promptly turned around and bought " Treasure Island." That does not prove " Treasure Island" a better story than " Silas Lapham ; " it proves simply that a trout that will rise to a brown hackle to-day will look at nothing but a white miller to-morrow ; and that when the men of the ice age grew tired of realistic anecdotes somebody yawned and poked the fire and called on a romanticist. One age, one stage of culture, one mood, calls for stories as naïve, as grim and primitive in their stark savagery as an Icelandic saga ; another age, another mood, — nay, the whim that changes in each one of us between morning and evening, — chooses stories as deliberately, consciously artificial as "The Fall of the House of Usher." Both types are admirable, each in its own way, provided both stir the imagination. For the types will come and go and come again ; but the human hunger for fiction of some sort is never sated.

Study the historical phases of the art of fiction as closely as one may, there come moments — and perhaps the close of an essay is an appropriate time to confess it — when one is tempted to say with Wilkie Collins that the whole art of fiction can be summed up in three precepts: " Make 'em laugh ; make 'em cry ; make 'em wait."

The important thing, the really *The wonder-* suggestive and touching and won- *world.* derful thing, is that all these thousands of contemporary and ephemeral stories are laughed over and cried over and waited for by somebody. They are read, while the " large still books " are bound in full calf and buried. Do you remember Pomona in "Rudder Grange " reading aloud in the kitchen every night after she had washed the dishes, spelling out with blundering tongue and beating heart: " Yell — after — yell — resounded — as — he — wildly — sprang," — or "Ha — ha — Lord — Marmont — thundered — thou — too — shalt — suffer "? We are all more or less like Pomona. We are children at bottom, after all is said, children under the story-teller's charm. Nansen's stout-hearted comrades tell stories to one another while the Arctic ice drifts onward with the Fram; Stevenson is nicknamed The Tale-Teller by the brown-limbed Samoans; Chinese Gordon reads a story while waiting — hopelessly waiting — at Khartoum.   What matter who performs the miracle that opens for us the doors of the wonder-world?   It may be one of that white-bearded company at the gate of Jaffa; it may be an ardent French boy pouring out his heart along the bottom of a Paris newspaper; it may be some sober-suited New England woman in the decorous pages of " The Atlantic Monthly ; " it may be some wretched scribbler writing for his supper.   No matter, if only the miracle is wrought; if we look out with new eyes upon the many-featured, habitable world; if we are thrilled by the pity and the beauty of this life of ours, itself brief as a tale that is told ; if we learn to know men and women better, and to love them more.

CHAPTER XIII

PRESENT TENDENCIES OF AMERICAN FIC-TION.

" The literature of a people should be the record of its joys and sorrows, its aspirations and its shortcomings, its wisdom and its folly, the confidant of its soul. We cannot say that our own as yet suffices us, but I believe that he who stands, a hundred years hence, where I am standing now, conscious that he speaks to the most powerful and prosperous community ever devised or developed by man, will speak of our literature with the assurance of one who beholds what we hope for and aspire after, become a reality and a possession forever."

> JAMES RUSSELL LOWELL, *Our Literature.* (1889.)

" Democracy in literature, as exemplified by the two great modern democrats in letters, Whitman and Tolstoi, means a new and more deeply religious way of looking at mankind, as well as at all the facts and objects of the visible world. It means, furthermore, the finding of new artistic motives and values in the people, in science and the modern spirit, in liberty, fraternity, equality, in the materialism and industrialism of man's life as we know it in our day and land — the carrying into imaginative fields the quality of common humanity, that which it shares with real things and with all open-air nature, with hunters, farmers, sailors, and real workers in all fields."

> JOHN BURROUGHS, *Democracy and Literature.*

In concluding this study of the art of prose fiction, let me attempt a survey of the present tendencies

Difficulties of an adequate survey.

of the fiction of our own country. It goes without saying that such a survey presents difficulties of no ordinary kind. The field at which one must glance is so vast, the varieties of production are so numerous, the characteristics of the phenomena to be examined so changeable in their nature from year to year, that anything like an exact appreciation of our national fiction is out of the question. One must content himself with suggestions, rather than with any detailed exposition; with a statement of some of the conditions that enter into the question, rather than with any elaborate attempt at reaching a fixed formula.

A knowledge of the past. One danger should be avoided at the outset — a danger never so insistent in its pressure as at present — the danger, namely, of being too contemporaneous in one's point of view. Even in trying to take account of contemporary tendencies, a historic sense is the most valuable equipment for the task of criticism. A knowledge of what has been already accomplished in the world of fiction is essential if one is to have any sense of perspective, any power of valuing new claimants to the honors of the craft.

The heavens are full of literary comets in
these days, and their course can be measured
only by reference to the fixed stars. Those
trite sentences of advice to young readers,
" When a new book comes out, read an old
one," " Read no book until it is fifty years
old," were never more applicable than now,
and in the field of fiction. The multiplication of periodicals issued in the interest of
publishing houses, and for very practical
reasons devoted to the glorification of new
writers more or less at the expense of old
ones, the personal gossip about the literary
heroes of the hour, tend to confuse all one's
ideas of proportion. A people gifted, like
ourselves, with a sense of humor will sooner
or later discount the extravagant adjectives
used in the commercial exploitation of new
books. But meanwhile there is a mischief
in it all ; and the mischief is that the mind
of the reading public is systematically journalized. The little men, by dint of keeping
their names before us, pass in many quarters
for great men. The historic sense is bewil-
dered, benumbed ; and when we attempt an
appreciation of fiction-writers and of the art
of fiction itself our opinions are sadly contemporaneous.

Go back
fifty years.

Before our judgment of a current book or a current tendency can have any particular value, we must understand the work of American novelists for at least the last half century. And it is a somewhat curious fact that if we wish to point to American fiction-writers who have won a secure place in the world's literature, we must go back fifty years or more to find our men. When an intelligent foreign critic asks us what writers of fiction America has to show, of quality and force worthy to be compared with the masters of the art elsewhere, whom can we name? Fenimore Cooper for one : the author of "The Leather Stocking Tales," "The Spy," and "The Pilot ; " the creator of Natty Bumppo, and Chingachgook, and Long Tom Coffin. His rank is unquestioned. And so is the rank of Nathaniel Hawthorne, who has a reserved seat for immortality if any one has. And there is a third candidate for universal honors, a short story writer, Edgar Allan Poe. Hawthorne, Cooper, Poe ; these men are beyond the need and the reach of literary logrolling.

But when we have mentioned The other names.
these three Americans, we have
nearly or quite exhausted, not indeed our
riches in native fiction, but the roll-call of
those who by common consent have won
through the art of fiction a permanent fame.
Irving's reputation is rather that of an essay-
ist, pioneer in a certain field of fiction though
he was. One would hesitate to place beside
the names of Cooper, Hawthorne, and Poe
the name of the author of " Uncle Tom's
Cabin," although no American book has ever
had so wide a vogue in other countries, or
wakened such intense emotion in our own.
Bret Harte would have some suffrages, no
doubt ; and many a critic would linger in-
quiringly and affectionately over the names
of Mark Twain, Howells, Aldrich, Stockton,
James, Cable, Crawford, and many another
living writer of admirable workmanship and
honorable rank. But I suppose that there
are few critics who would deliberately select
among these later men a fourth to be placed
in equality of universal recognition with that
great trio who more than half a century ago
were in the fullness of their power.

Quantity and quality.   However, three such men are enough to give distinction to the first hundred years of American fiction-writing. If we institute a comparison in quality between American and English and Continental fiction, we have simply to point to Hawthorne alone. In bulk his contribution to the world's pleasure in the form of books is slender when set alongside the volumes of Scott or Dickens or Dumas, but in point of quality the quiet New Englander is easily the peer of the greatest story-writers of the world. Even when judged by the more unsatisfactory test of quantity of production, American fiction can nearly or quite hold its own with the fiction of England, France, or Germany. The figures of the book market, while interesting enough to the curious minded, are vitiated, for one who is trying to estimate the American output of fiction, by the fact of the immense circulation of some novels which are literature only by courtesy, but which affect statistics just as much as if they were literature. If we apply the test of mere quantity of production, we must take into account not only all these books that are " borderland dwellers" between literature and non-literature, but an immense supply of fiction that does not even pretend to be literature any more than a clever space-reporter for a Sunday newspaper pretends that his work is literature. But putting all such books aside, it is still possible to select twenty or twenty-five American story-writers of the past forty years who have published enough good books to place American fiction well alongside of American poetry, and certainly far in advance of American music, painting, sculpture, or architecture.

From this body of work is it possible to draw any conclusions as to the character of our fiction? Can we indicate the tendencies which have been prevalent in the past, which are now operative, and which consequently are likely to characterize to a greater or less extent the American novel of the future? There are at least three tendencies to which attention should be drawn. I cannot do better than follow here the suggestions of Professor Richardson,[1] who thinks that the first is the production of novels of the soil, that is, the

Prevalent tendencies: novel of the soil.

[1] Charles F. Richardson, *American Literature.* 2 vols. New York: Putnam, 1889.

presentation of American types and scenes.
The service of Fenimore Cooper in this direction was a most important one. Before his
time, Brockden Brown, for instance, had
treated American themes, yet in so romantic a
fashion as to disguise the reality. But Fenimore Cooper's backwoodsmen and sailors and
frontier landscapes have the verity of nature
herself. Hawthorne, too, did for New England, by very different methods, but with an
equal honesty of rendering, what Cooper did
for northern New York. Before the war,
notes Professor Richardson, there were few
attempts to delineate American home life in
the various sections of the country; but the
improvement in American minor fiction since
1861 is largely owing to the attempt to describe American life as it is. This tendency
is growing more and more marked with every
year; it is very little, if at all, affected by the
present revival of romanticism; it has been
helped, rather than hindered, by the sudden
crop of historical novels. If every American
county has not its novelist, its painter of
manners, — as Scotland is said to have had,
— at least every state can show fiction-writers who aim to delineate local conditions as

faithfully as they may, and there is every reason for thinking that this movement will be permanent.

A second characteristic which has hitherto marked American fic- **Excellence in a limited field.** tion, and one that follows closely upon the first, is its excellence in a limited field, rather than any largeness of creative activity. The qualities which a foreign critic would be inclined to postulate theoretically about our fiction, reasoning from our immense territory, our still youthful zest, our boundless faith in ourselves, our resources, — in short, the general "bigness" of things American, — are precisely the qualities which our fiction has hitherto lacked. Instead of fertility of resource, consciousness of power, great canvases, broad strokes, brilliant coloring, we find a predominance of small canvases, minute though admirable detail, neutral tints, an almost academic restraint, a consciousness of painting under the critic's eye. American fiction lacks breadth and power. What Walt Whitman tried, with very imperfect success one must admit, to do in the field of "All-American" poetry, if I may use the phrase, no one has even attempted to do in

fiction. Some magazine critics have expressed
the opinion that the cause of this is to be
found in the fact that the conventional standards, the critical atmosphere, of the effete Atlantic seaboard have hitherto been dominant
in our literature. They profess to believe
that when the "literary centre" of the country is established at Chicago, or Indianapolis,
or thereabouts, our fiction will assume a scale
proportionate to the bigness of our continent.
But this matter is not so simple as it looks,
and the question whether excellence in a
small way rather than largeness of creative
activity will continue to characterize American fiction is still to be solved. We may
find some light thrown upon it in considering
the relation of sectional to national fiction.

Fundamental morality. A third fact impressed upon the
student of the American novel is
its fundamental morality. It is optimistic.
Its outlook upon life is wholesome. The
stain] of doubtful morality or flaring immorality which has often tinged English and Continental fiction, and made both the English
and the American stage at times unspeakably
foul, has left scarcely any imprint as yet upon
the better known American story-writers.

Our greater magazines have remained for the most part unsoiled. Bad as our " yellow " newspapers are, brazen as our stage often is, people who want the sex-novel, and want it prepared with any literary skill, have to import it from across the water. The outlook for the morality of the distinctively American novel seems assured. If our professional novelists have, in the last five years, withstood the temptation to win notoriety and money by *risqué* books, we can confidently say of the American fiction of the future, that while it may not be national, and may not be great, it will have at least the negative virtue of being clean.

We are now in a position to esti- The "repre-
mate the conditions which must be sentative"
met by an American writer who book.
hopes that his books may be in some true sense representative of the national life. Why does not the " great American novel " which we talk about, and about which we prophesy, get itself written? One difficulty in the path of the representative American novel has already been pointed out indirectly. It lies in the immensity of the field

to be covered; the complexity of the phenomena which literature must interpret; the mixture of races, customs, traditions, beliefs, ideals, upon this continent. We are a united nation, and have never been more conscious of the national life and more proud of it than since the twentieth century began its course. But literature is an affair of race as well as of nationality. Study the variety of names upon the signboards of any city; watch the varying racial types in the faces of your fellow citizens as you travel east or west, north or south. Who can be an adequate spokesman for all this? Homer is Greece, but Greece was a hand's breadth in comparison with us; Dante is Florence, a single city; Molière, Paris, another city; even Shakespeare, the "myriad-minded," was the spokesman of but one little island, though that was the England of Elizabeth. But the truth is that not one of these men was probably conscious of speaking for his country and his time. It is only a Balzac, a sort of gigantic child, who dares to set himself deliberately to the task of representing all France, and thereby the entire Human Comedy. As civilization widens, as more and more subtle differentiations

make themselves manifest in society, the task
becomes increasingly greater. In a Walt
Whitman rhapsody a man might venture to
speak for " these States," but a writer of
prose, in possession of his senses, would per-
force decline any such prophetic function.

Then, too, the tendency to the Sectional
production of sectional fiction, to fiction.
which allusion has just been made, has pre-
vented our fiction from taking on even the
semblance of national quality. By dint of
keeping their eyes on the object, many of our
best writers have studied but the narrowest
of fields. They do not represent, or pretend
to represent, with adequacy the entirety even
of that limited province for which they stand
as representative authors. We speak, for instance, of Mr. Cable, Miss Murfree, Mr. Page,
Mr. Allen, Miss Johnston, Mr. Harris, Miss
King, and a half dozen more, as representatives of the South in contemporary fiction ;
but they exhibit as many Souths as there are
writers. Who can select any one book of
these skilled story-tellers and say, " Here is
the South represented through the art of
fiction " ? Or take New England, as interpreted by such excellent and such different

writers as Mrs. Stowe, Miss Jewett, Miss
Wilkins, Mrs. Elizabeth Stuart Phelps Ward.
Mrs. Stowe shows one New England, Miss
Wilkins another; each is marvelously true
to the local color selected; but you cannot
take " Old Town Folks " and " Deephaven "
and " Pembroke " and " A Singular Life "
and say " Here is New England." At best
you can say " Here is a part of New England."
Now if there is a difference in passing from the
Vermont or Massachusetts of Miss Wilkins to
the Maine of Miss Jewett, think of the difference in passing from these to the Virginia
of Mr. Page, the Northwest of Mr. Garland,
the California of Bret Harte, the Alaska of
Mr. Jack London ! If we can scarcely find
a thoroughly representative sectional novel,
how shall we expect a representative national
novel ?

International influences.   An additional element in the
denationalizing of our fiction lies
in the fact that ours is peculiarly a day of
international influences in literature. Communication between the book-producing countries of the world is now so easy, the work
of foreign authors so accessible, international
gossip so entertaining and necessary to us,

that it sometimes seems as if literature were adopting the socialists' programme of doing away with national lines altogether, of creating a vast brotherhood of letters in which the accident of residence in Belgium or Scotland or South Dakota counts for nothing. So far as Continental fiction makes its influence felt in this country, it touches not so much the mass of readers as those who themselves are producers of fiction. In some interesting statistics showing the hundred novels most often drawn from American public libraries, in the order of their popularity, gathered by Mr. Mabie for "The Forum" a few years ago, the absence of modern French and Russian masters from the list was most noticeable. The American public does not read Turgenieff and Tolstoi, Flaubert and Daudet, Björnson and D'Annunzio so very much ; indeed it reads them very little. But wherever writers of fiction gather, it is names like these that are discussed. And even for the general public, a book's foreign reputation is impressive, although the book may be little read here. A London reputation, particularly, may make the fortune of a novel on this side of the Atlantic. For all our

talk about outgrowing colonialism, we have
never been more colonial than at present,
though we call this spirit cosmopolitanism. A
very pretty essay might be written to prove
that the much-praised cosmopolitanism of
some of our successful young novelists is
only a sort of varnished provincialism, the
real fibre of it differing not so very much
from the innocent provincialism of the man
who comes back from his first ten weeks' trip
abroad and tells you buoyantly that he has
" been everywhere and seen everything."

Genuine pro-   Now a genuine provincialism, as
vincialism.   the history of literature abundantly
proves, is not a source of weakness.   It is a
strength.   Carlyle was provincial.   Scott was
provincial.   Burns and Wordsworth and Whit-
tier were provincial.   They were rooted in the
soil, and by virtue of that they became representative.   In our own political life, who have
been our most truly representative men?
Webster, the rugged son of New Hampshire
and Massachusetts, spoke as no other man
spoke, "for the country and the whole country."   It was the gaunt rustic President from
Kentucky and Illinois who has become, in
Lowell's noble phrase, " our first American."

Perhaps these figures outside the field of literature will help us to see the conditions for a representative *A representative man of letters.* national figure in literature. Those conditions can be met only by a powerful personality in harmony with its age. The personality must be great enough to take up into itself the great thoughts and feelings of its time, and transform them, personalize them, use them, and not be overwhelmed by them. Such a personality represents its age and country, not by the method of extension so much as by the method of intension, not by a wide superficial acquaintance with cities and with men, but by seeing deeply, and thinking deeply, and feeling deeply. It is by means of such power that Cooper and Hawthorne are American, as Fielding is English, Victor Hugo French, and Turgenieff Russian. If the future grants us sufficiently powerful individuals, thoroughly Americanized, we shall have representative American novelists.

A further question forces itself upon us, and one by no means easy *Democracy.* to answer. How is our fiction to be affected by the vast democratic movement which is

changing the face of society throughout the
civilized world? There is at the present
moment a reaction against liberalism in
England and upon the continent, and a corresponding reaction against republicanism here.
These reactions are more wide-spread than at
any time for sixty years past, but they have
been brought about by peculiar conditions,
and no one supposes that they will ultimately
block the wheels of advancing democracy.
"The people will conquer in the end," as
Byron prophesied as long ago as 1821. Now
how will this triumph of the people affect
literature? Are we to have an epoch of
distinctively democratic art, and if we are,
what sort of fiction can we imagine as flourishing in that epoch? Said J. A. Symonds, in
his essay on "Democratic Art," —

"In past epochs the arts had a certain unconscious
and spontaneous *rapport* with the nations which begat
them, and with the central life-force of those nations
at the moment of their flourishing. Whether that central energy was aristocratic, as in Hellas, or monarchic,
as in France, or religious, as in mediæval Europe, or
intellectual, as in Renaissance Italy, or national, as in
Elizabethan England, or widely diffused like a fine
gust of popular intelligence, as in Japan, signified
comparatively little. Art expressed what the people

had of noblest and sincerest, and was appreciated by the people."

Can there be anything like this in the new era toward which we are hastening? Mr. Symonds himself was compelled to give up the question as at present unanswerable. It is undeniable that the aristocratic tradition still holds firm in almost all the arts. "Kings, princesses, and the symbols of chivalry," says the English critic Mr. Gosse, "are as essential to poetry as we now conceive it, as roses, stars, or nightingales," and he does not see what will be left if this romantic phraseology is done away with. "We shall certainly have left," retorted John Burroughs, "what we had before these aristocratic types and symbols came into vogue, namely, nature, life, man, God." But can poets and novelists find new artistic material in the people, the plain people who are so soon to hold the field? Walt Whitman declared, in a fine passage of his "Democratic Vistas," —

"Literature, strictly considered, has never recognized the People, and whatever may be said, does not to-day. I know nothing more rare even in this country than a fit scientific estimate and reverent appreciation of the People — of their measureless wealth of latent power and capacity, their vast artistic contrasts of lights and shades, with, in America, their entire reliability in emergencies, and a certain breadth of historic grandeur, of peace or war, far surpassing all the vaunted samples of book-heroes . . . in all the records of the world."

"The divine average."

The question is simply this: "How will all the phenomena of a great democratic society be able to touch the poet or novelist imaginatively?" And I think no one has felt the significance of this question more adequately than Whitman. He has tried to answer it in his not very clearly expressed phrase about recognizing "the divine average." What he means by the divine average is simply the presence of the divine in average human beings. If we grant the presence of that element in the "average sensual man," — an element which appeals to the sense of beauty and sublimity, which fires the imagination of the artist, — then democratic art is possible. Without it there can never be any democratic art, and we had better stick to kings and princesses, to Prisoners of Zenda and Gentlemen of France. But if one has read Dickens or George Eliot or Kipling, or any of the Ameri-

can novelists who have been faithful to the
actual life of these United States, one knows
that an art of fiction is even now in existence
which does recognize the people, which reveals, however imperfectly, the diviner qualities in the life of the ordinary man.

How is the art of fiction destined Future
to be changed as this recognition is types.
more and more widely made? Will the realistic or romantic type of fiction be best fitted
to the needs of the coming democracy? Perhaps this question, too, cannot be answered,
and yet one or two assertions may fairly be
made. Democracy insists increasingly upon
conformity to ordinary types. It is a pitiless
leveler, whether up or down. It is fatal to
eccentricities, to extravagant personal characteristics, in a word, to a large part of the
field from which romantic fiction draws its
power. Romantic types of character, as far
as they have external marks of peculiarity,
are probably destined to extinction. And
our sense of wonder at outward things is
steadily diminishing. Marvels have grown
stale to us. We no longer gape over the
telegraph, the telephone, the " wireless ; " we
shall gape at the flying machine for a few

days at longest.   There will be one day no
more unexplored corners of the world, no
" road to Mandalay."   We shall be forced
to turn inward to discover the marvelous ;
" Cathay and all its wonders " must be found
in us or nowhere.   The effect of all this
upon fiction will be unmistakable.   If novels
of the outward life, of conformity to known
facts and types, are written, they will be realistic in method ; the old romantic fiction
machinery will become the veriest lumber.
There will come again an age of realism in
fiction, if a fiction is desired which keeps close
to life.   We may imagine that the readers
of that age will smile at Victor Hugo and
praise " Middlemarch."   But the history of
literature has taught us that men have always craved what I may call the fiction of
compensation, the fiction that yields them
what life cannot yield them.   And as the
inner world will then be the marvelous world,
I imagine the fiction of compensation will
take the form, not of adventures in South
Seas and Dark Continents, but of the psychological romance, pure and simple.   Readers
will then smile at " Treasure Island " and
praise " Dr. Jekyll and Mr. Hyde."

If all this appears, as perhaps it Future themes. well may, too fanciful a picture, let us turn to the kind of subjects with which American novelists of the immediate future seem likely to occupy themselves. That there will be very shortly — if indeed there is not already — a reaction against over-production of Colonial, Revolutionary, and other types of American historical fiction, cannot be doubted. But this is chiefly because the supply has temporarily outrun the demand. The story of our own ancestors and their struggles upon American soil will never lose its essential fascination when depicted, not by a horde of imitative weaklings, but by masters of the fictive art. The marvelous epic of the settlement of the western half of the continent still waits an adequate reciter. We have had already a legion of Civil War stories, and yet we have not begun to see the wealth of material which that epoch holds for the true imaginative artist. The romance of labor, of traffic, of politics, in our strangely composite civilization, has been perceived by a few writers ; but how much is still to be told !

For American social life is chan- A changing world. ging, taking account of itself before our eyes, readjusting itself, and a thousand subtle, delightful, forceful themes are thus laid open to the novelist. He will follow in the wake of all these social movements of the twentieth century as the sea-birds follow the steamer, sure of finding the fit morsel soon or late. But that simile is inapt; the novelist is not like a creature watching the course of a mechanism; he is a creature enraptured with something that is itself alive, changing from hour to hour, unfolding, perfecting itself from generation to generation. We talk of human nature being ever the same; but nothing is falser to the facts of life and the process of the world's growth. Brute nature does remain the same. The ape and tiger of this hour are, so far as we know, exactly the same ape and tiger that our ancestors fought in the stone age. But the ape and tiger in us dies, though slowly; the brute passions are not destined forever to sway the balance in our lives. The human spirit changes, widens, grows richer and more beautiful with the infinite years of man's history upon this planet. And over against this wonderful process of development stands the novelist, himself a part of it all, and yet one of its interpreters. If, watching that changing human spectacle, he finds no stories to tell, discovers no charm or beauty or solemnity, it is not because these things are not there, but because his eyes are holden.

We need have no fear that the future American novelist will fail in power of expression. The technical finish of his work is assured by the standard that has been already reached. Decade by decade one can mark the steady development of the American novelist in all that pertains to mere craftsmanship. But the value of his work will not turn primarily upon its technical excellence on the side of form. Cleverness of hand he will certainly possess ; but as I have said more than once already, cleverness of hand is not enough. If his work is to have any significant place in the literature of the world, he must learn to see and feel and think, and what he sees and feels and thinks will depend solely upon what he is himself. The " great American novel " will probably never be written by a man who suspects that he is doing anything of the sort. It is quite likely to come, as other greater things than novels come,

Technique and imagination.

"without observation." You and I — Gentle Reader with whom I am parting company — may never see it, but ultimately nothing is so certain as the triumph of the things of the spirit over the gross material forces of American civilization. Summer itself is not so sure in its coming as the imagination in its own time.

APPENDIX

APPENDIX

SUGGESTIONS FOR STUDY

THE first chapter of this book gives an outline of
the method of studying fiction which has been followed throughout the volume. Teachers and students
who may desire to do further work for themselves
along the lines here suggested, or in other fields of
investigation, are advised to give that first chapter a
second reading, in the light thrown upon it by the
book as a whole. It will help them to remember the
specific purpose of this volume, and to see the relation between its method and that of other works to
which the attention of the student should now be
called. Some of my readers will be solitary students,
free to follow any path they like into the pleasant fields
of the theory and practice of story-writing. Others will
be members of reading circles and clubs, where there
is a definite although perhaps not very strenuous line
of study mapped out in advance. Still others will, I
hope, belong to school and college classes, bent upon
serious endeavor to learn as much as possible about an
art which has established its significance and value as
an interpreter of modern life. In the bibliographies
and other aids and suggestions for study which I shall
now give, I have endeavored to keep in mind these

varying requirements of my readers. Some of the work outlined is extremely elementary. But I have also indicated some tasks which will need the full powers of the student. The arrangement of this supplementary work is such, however, that teachers will find no difficulty, I trust, in selecting from it such courses of reading and topical exercises as shall best suit the specific needs of their classes. I cannot urge too strongly the advisability of a detailed analytic study of some one representative novel, and, if possible, an acquaintance with the entire production of one of the greater novelists, before attempting more than a bird's-eye view of any national fiction as a whole. The average college student, in particular, needs training in the analysis of a single work, and in steady reflection upon the problems presented by it, far more than he needs a greater familiarity with the novelists of his own day. Most of us will remain readers of fiction all our lives long, but the chosen time for the serious study of fiction is in those golden years when we first perceive the treasures of thought and imagination, the breathing images of passionate human life, revealed to us by the novelists.

I

BIBLIOGRAPHY

a. Introductory : Æsthetics. Since the method followed in our study is primarily that of æsthetic criticism, the student of the art of fiction should, if possible, acquaint himself in some degree with the theory of the Fine Arts and their place in human life. For a general survey of the field of Æsthetics, see the articles " Æsthetics," by James Sully, and " Fine Arts," by Sidney Colvin, in the *Encyclopædia Britannica*. Baldwin Brown's *The Fine Arts* (University Extension Manuals, Scribners) is a useful handbook. Bosanquet's voluminous *History of Æsthetic* (Macmillan) is extremely valuable to the advanced student. Most of the standard treatises upon Æsthetics are indicated in the card catalogue of any good library; for an extended bibliography, consult Gayley and Scott, *Methods and Materials of Literary Criticism* (Ginn & Co., 1899), Knight's *Philosophy of the Beautiful* (University Extension Manuals), and the Appendix to Bosanquet.

b. Introductory: Poetics. After this preliminary survey of the field of Æsthetics, the student is recommended to acquaint himself with some of the many helpful discussions of poetic theory. How closely the field of Poetics is allied to that of Prose Fiction we have already seen in the second and third chapters. The most famous of all treatises on Poetics is that of Aristotle. There are many good translations; the admirable one by Professor S. H. Butcher (Macmillan, 2d ed., 1898) is enriched by interpretative essays dealing with the disputable passages. A general bibliography for Poetics, with brief comment upon the important treatises, will be found in Gayley and Scott. The article on " Poetry " by Theodore Watts in the *Encyclopædia Britannica* is noteworthy. Gummere's *Poetics* (Ginn & Co.) is an excellent brief handbook ; see also his *Beginnings of Poetry* (Macmillan, 1901) and W. J. Courthope's *Life in Poetry — Law in Taste* (Macmillan, 1901). Volumes like Stedman's *Nature and Elements of Poetry* (Houghton, Mifflin & Co.) and C. C. Everett's *Poetry, Comedy, and Duty* (Houghton, Mifflin & Co.) are stimulating. But teachers who are provided with Gayley and Scott can easily make such reference lists as will be adapted to the needs and capacity of their pupils.

That portion of the territory of Poetics which is occupied with the Theory of the Drama is especially important for the student of fiction. Useful books are Freytag's *Technique of the Drama* (Eng. trans., S. C. Griggs & Co.), Elizabeth Woodbridge's *The Drama; its Law and Technique* (Allyn & Bacon), Alfred Hennequin's *Art of Play Writing* (Houghton, Mifflin & Co.), Price's *Technique of the Drama* (Brentano), Moulton's *Ancient Classical Drama* and *Shakespeare as a Dramatic Artist* (Macmillan).

c. Prose Fiction : Historical. Two admirable sketches of the history of English prose fiction are Walter Raleigh's *The English Novel* (Scribners, 1894) and Wilbur L. Cross's *The Development of the English Novel* (Macmillan, 1899). Dunlop's *History of Prose Fiction* (2 vols., revised edition by Wilson, Bohn, 1896) is a standard work of reference. Professor David Masson's *British Novelists and their Styles* (Boston, 1859) is still a fresh and suggestive volume. W. E. Simonds's *Introduction to English Fiction* (D. C. Heath, 1894) is a useful handbook for a preliminary survey. Consult also Bayard Tuckerman's *History of English Prose Fiction* (Putnam, 1882), F. M. Warren's *History of the Novel Previous to the Seventeenth Century* (Holt, 1895), Jusserand's *English Novel in the Time of Shakespeare* (London, 1890), the Bibliographical Notes in

the Appendix to Cross, and the Bibliography prefaced
to the first volume of Wilson's edition of Dunlop.

d. Prose Fiction: Philosophical and Critical.
Suggestive discussions of general tendencies in modern
fiction are found in F. H. Stoddard's *The Evolution of the English Novel* (Macmillan, 1899), Sidney Lanier's *The English Novel* (Scribners, revised
edition, 1897), D. G. Thompson's *Philosophy of Fiction
in Literature* (Longmans, 1890), Zola's *Le Roman
Expérimental* (Eng. trans., Cassell, N. Y.), Brunetière's *Le Roman Naturaliste* (Paris), Spielhagen's
Beiträge zur Theorie und Technik des Romans (Ber-
lin), C. T. Winchester's *Principles of Literary Criticism* (Macmillan), Howells's *Criticism and Fiction*
(Harpers), F. Marion Crawford's *The Novel: What
It Is* (Macmillan), Sir Walter Besant's lecture on "The
Art of Fiction" (Cupples, Upham & Co., Boston, 1885),
Henry James's essay in rejoinder on "The Art of Fic-
tion" in *Partial Portraits* (Macmillan), R. L. Steven-
son's "A Humble Remonstrance" addressed to Mr.
James (reprinted in *Memories and Portraits*), Brander Matthews's *The Historical Novel and other Es-
says* and *Aspects of Fiction* (Scribners), Paul Bourget's
"Réflexions sur l'Art du Roman" in *Études et Por-
traits*. For younger students, Miss Charity Dye's
The Story-Teller's Art (Ginn, 1898) is a useful book;
and for such pupils May Estelle Cook's *Methods of
Teaching Novels* (Scott, Foresman & Co.) and Alfred
M. Hitchcock's *Journeys in Fiction* (Allyn & Bacon)
also afford profitable hints.

e. Prose Fiction: Special Topics. Articles upon the
various aspects of fiction have been frequent in periodical literature, especially since 1880. For these, consult

Poole's *Index to Periodical Literature.* W. M. Griswold's *Descriptive Lists of American and Foreign Novels* (Cambridge, Mass.) is useful, as are also the lists of selected fiction issued by the public libraries of Boston, Providence, and other cities. Some of the best comment upon novels and novelists is to be found in reviews and critical articles in periodicals ; if Poole's *Index* is not at hand, the index to the periodical itself will often put the student upon the track of helpful material. Biographies of the great novelists, and their Notebooks and Letters, are full of suggestive comment upon their art.

The footnotes to the various chapters of the present work give occasional references to books bearing particularly upon the subject of each chapter ; but as I have wished to keep the text as free as possible from notes, I will add here a few suggestions for special reading in connection with some of the main topics of the book.

In studying chapter iii. for instance, it will be well to take as supplementary reading some of the books already mentioned under *b*, and especially Gummere's *Poetics* and Watts's article. For chapter iii., note especially Freytag, Woodbridge, and Hennequin.

For chapter iv., note Edward Dowden's *Studies in Literature*, J. Wedgwood on "The Ethics of Literature" in *Contemporary Review*, January, 1897, and W. J. Stillman on "The Revival of Art" in the *Atlantic*, vol. lxx.

In connection with chapters v., vi., and vii., the most profitable work is a first-hand study of the practice of various novelists, as indicated below under II. *Topics for Study.*

For chapter viii., see Ruskin's "Art and Morals" in *Lectures on Art*, D. G. Thompson, chapter xiii., Lanier, chapter xii., Stoddard, chapter v., John La Farge's *Considerations on Painting*, Lecture II. (Macmillan), Charles F. Johnson's *Elements of Literary Criticism*, chapter iv. (Harpers).

In connection with the discussion of Realism in chapter ix., see Howells's *Criticism and Fiction*, the chapter on Realism in W. C. Brownell's *French Art* (Scribners), Valdés's Preface to *Sister St. Sulpice* (Crowell), and Cross, chapters v. and vi.

Romanticism (chapter x.) is discussed in many recent volumes, such as the books of Beers and Phelps referred to on page 262. See also Pater's essay in the Postscript of *Appreciations*, F. H. Hedge's article in the *Atlantic*, vol. lvii., T. S. Omond's *The Triumph of Romance* (Scribners), W. P. Ker's *Epic and Romance* (Macmillan), and consult the Bibliography furnished by Professor Beers.

For chapter xi., see the references in the text to Minto, Clark, Gardner, Brewster, and Baldwin, and the critical essays of James, Stevenson, Brunetière, Bourget, and other acute contemporary students of literary form.

For chapter xii., compare Poe's criticism of Hawthorne in *Graham's Magazine*, 1842 (in vol. vii. of the Stedman-Woodberry edition ; Stone & Kimball), Brander Matthews's *The Philosophy of the Short-Story* (Longmans, 1901), C. R. Barrett's *Short Story Writing* (Baker and Taylor), Sherwin Cody's *The World's Greatest Short Stories* (McClurg, 1902), G. S. Nettleton's *Specimens of the Short Story* (Holt), W. M. Hart's *Hawthorne and the Short*

Story (Berkeley, Cal., 1900), and H. S. Canby's " The Short Story " (*Yale Studies in English ;* Holt, 1902).

For chapter xiii., see Walt Whitman's " Democratic Vistas," Lowell's address on " Democracy," J. A. Symonds's " Democratic Literature " in *Essays Speculative and Suggestive*, W. H. Crawshaw's *Literary Interpretation of Life*, chapters v.–vii. (Macmillan), C. F. Richardson's *American Literature* vol. ii. (Putnam, 1889), W. C. Bronson's *Short History of American Literature* (Heath, 1901), Barrett Wendell's *History of Literature in America* (Scribners, 1901), and A. G. Newcomer's *American Literature* (Scott, Foresman & Co., 1901).

f. Representative English Novels. To students desiring to understand the historical development of English fiction in its main outlines, the following list of typical productions is suggested : Sir Philip Sidney's *Arcadia* (1590), Bunyan's *Pilgrim's Progress* (1678–84), Swift's *Tale of a Tub* (1704), Defoe's *Captain Singleton* (1720), Richardson's *Pamela* (1740), Fielding's *Amelia* (1751), Goldsmith's *Vicar of Wakefield* (1766), Ann Radcliffe's *Mysteries of Udolpho* (1794), Jane Austen's *Pride and Prejudice* (1812), Sir Walter Scott's *Ivanhoe* (1820), Charlotte Brontë's *Jane Eyre* (1847), Thackeray's *Vanity Fair* (1847–48), Dickens's *David Copperfield* (1849–50), Trollope's *Barchester Towers* (1857), George Eliot's *Middlemarch* (1871–72), Stevenson's *Treasure Island* (1883).

g. Representative American Novels. The following stories are fairly representative of the tendencies of American fiction : Brockden Brown's *Wieland* (1798), Irving's *Sketch Book* (1819), Cooper's *Last of the Mohicans* (1826), Poe's *Tales of the Grotesque and Arabesque* (1839), Hawthorne's *Scarlet Letter* (1850), Mrs. Stowe's *Uncle Tom's Cabin* (1852), Bret Harte's *Luck of Roaring Camp* (1870), Eggleston's *Hoosier Schoolmaster* (1871), Clemens's [Mark Twain] *Tom Sawyer* (1876), Henry James's *The American* (1877), Howells's *Rise of Silas Lapham* (1885), Cable's *Grandissimes* (1880), Miss Wilkins's *Humble Romance* (1887), Weir Mitchell's *Hugh Wynne* (1897), Owen Wister's *The Virginian* (1902).

II

TOPICS FOR STUDY

It cannot be emphasized too often that the aim of this *Study of Prose Fiction* is to help students to use their own eyes and minds. Topics for independent study may be assigned in connection with almost all the chapters in the book, but v., vi., and vii. are particularly well adapted for this kind of work. For instance, the student may be asked to write a brief paper, as the result of independent study in any author, of one or more of the following topics : —

1. *Character-Studies.*   (See chapter v.)

A character embodying but one quality or passion. A complex character with one trait in predominance. A complex character consisting of evenly balanced opposing forces.   A character involved in a conscious moral struggle, successful or otherwise ; in an unconscious moral struggle.   Deterioration, with or without a struggle.   A character developing under prosperity ;

adversity; old age; influence of other personalities; of religion, art, philosophy. A character illustrating professional, class, or national traits. A character fulfilling the requirements of its rôle as villain, lover, heroine, etc. A "plot-ridden" character. Character-contrasts: in the family; among friends; in wider relations. Character-grouping: as regards the unifying principle, subordination of parts, place in the book as a whole.

2. *Studies in Plot*.   (See chapter vi.)

An incident as revealing character. A situation as determining character. A climax in its relation to the theme. A catastrophe as poetic justice; as illustrative of the individual philosophy of the writer; as unsatisfactory to the reader. Plot complication and resolution as dictated by character. Accident as a complicating force; a resolving force. Fate as a resolving force. Mystification in plot. Anticlimax in plot. Plot as determined by the characters. Sustaining of plot-interest. A perfect plot. A sub-plot as reflecting, depending upon, or artificially joined to the main plot. A plot as influenced by the setting.

3. *Studies in Setting*.   (See chapter vii.)

A given novel as illustrating the time and place of its setting; for instance, the Egyptian, Oriental, Greek, Roman, or mediæval world. The setting of a novel whose scenes are laid in a part of America with which you are personally familiar; for instance, a Tennessee, Virginia, New York, New England, California story. A setting making artistic use of one of the great occupations of men: as politics, war, commerce, manufac-

turing, farming, mining, travel, student life, life of the
unemployed poor, the unemployed rich. A setting furnished by institutions or ideas prevalent in society : as
feudalism, democracy, socialism, patriotism, religion.
The sea, the mountains, the city, the village, the country, as setting for a given story. A landscape setting
which harmonizes with the characters ; contrasts with
the characters ; affects the incidents ; determines the
situations ; gives unity to the book.

III

ORIGINAL WORK IN CONSTRUCTION

This book is not designed, of course, to give training
to "young writers" in practical craftsmanship. But it
is often a stimulus to the intelligent and sympathetic
reading of fiction to attempt for one's self some of the
practical problems with which novelists are constantly
called upon to deal. For class-room work, in particular, some such exercises as the following will be found
interesting : —

1. Read the opening chapters of any novel until you
feel sure that the main characters are all introduced ;
then block out a plot which shall accord with your view
of the characters.

2. Read until the complication is well advanced ; then
block out the remainder of the plot.

3. Read until you are sure the catastrophe is immi-
nent ; then sketch in detail a catastrophe which shall
harmonize with the foregoing plot.

4. Construct a diagram of a plot involving but two
or three persons, indicating the lines of complication,
the climax or turning point, and the dénoûment.

5. Construct a similar diagram, indicating the situations or steps by which the action advances to the climax, and thence to the catastrophe.

6. Describe a room or a house so that each detail shall serve to indicate the character of the occupant.

7. Write a conversation which indirectly reveals a character; describe an action which directly reveals a character.

8. Describe an important situation, sketching briefly the antecedent and subsequent plot-movement.

9. Write a closing chapter, indicating the steps by which it is reached.

10. Describe a group of characters suitable for a sub-plot, with the briefest indication of their connection with the main plot.

IV

PRACTICE IN ANALYSIS

In studying representative novels, whether in the class-room or by one's self, it is well to read with pencil in hand, and to endeavor to sum up, as clearly as possible, the outline of the story, as regards plot, characters, and design. A simple method of analysis is here given, as applied to Thackeray's *Vanity Fair*.

Vanity Fair.

I. *Aim.* Where did Thackeray get his title? What light is thrown by the title, the author's preface, and the references to Vanity Fair throughout the novel, upon the aim and spirit of the book? In other words, what is Thackeray trying to do?

II. (a) *Characters*. Fiction exhibits characters in

action, by means of narration and description. Study
the opening chapters of *Vanity Fair* with the aim of
getting a clear conception of the characters there presented, before the complication of the story really
begins.

(b) *Plot.* After doing this we must study the characters as they are thrown together, influenced by one
another, and developed by means of the action. It
will therefore be necessary, before examining the characters in complication with one another, to trace the
action, or plot, of the novel. The plot of *Vanity
Fair* may, for convenience, be summarized under seven
divisions.

1. *Introduction.* (Chapters 1–11, inclusive.) The
opening six chapters are concerned with Amelia, Rebecca, the Osbornes, the Sedleys, and Dobbin; the next
five chapters describe the Crawleys.

2. *Development.* (12–26.) This division treats mainly
of Miss Crawley, Rebecca's conquests, the Sedley failure,
Dobbin's affection for Amelia, and George Osborne's
disinheritance.

3. *The Waterloo Campaign.* (27–32.) Here is the
first great crisis of the book. Its significance in the
plot, aside from George Osborne's death, lies in its
definite revelations of character, particularly of Joseph
Sedley, Dobbin, and Rebecca.

4. *Struggles and Trials.* (33–46.) This division cov-
ers many years of time. Rebecca is successfully fighting her way up in the world, and Amelia is struggling
vainly against poverty. Chapter 39 is important as
affecting Rebecca's position. Note that chapter 37
prepares the way for division 5, just as chapter 43 is
a preparation for division 6.

5. *Lord Steyne.* (47–55.) Here is the second and greatest crisis of the story. It contains the culmination of Rebecca's success, and the catastrophe. Chapter 50 is inserted here to show the lowest point of Amelia's fortunes.

6. *Our Friend the Major.* (56–61.) The re-introduction of two characters, and the deaths of two others, mark the turning point in Amelia's struggles, just as division 5 shows the turn in Rebecca's.

7. *Dénoûment.* Note Rebecca's degradation, her temporary influence over Amelia, Dobbin's departure, recall, and marriage, the end of Joseph Sedley, and Rebecca's final position in the world.

(c) *Setting.* Having mastered the plot, in its main and subordinate features, it will be well to review definitely the circumstances of time and place in which the action is laid ; as for instance, London life in the period 1814–30, Queen's Crawley under Sir Pitt, Brussels in 1815, the Rawdon Crawley establishment in Curzon Street, Gaunt House, or the town of Pumpernickel. Be able to reproduce this historical and local setting as far as possible.

(d) Review each character, first by itself, then in contrast with the other characters with which it is most closely grouped, and determine lastly what is the function of each character in the plot as a whole. Distinguish carefully between the characters that are unmodified by the action of the story, as Sir Pitt or Mrs. O'Dowd, and those whose development is affected by the action, as Rawdon Crawley or Rebecca.

III. *Style.* If we understand what Thackeray aimed to do in writing *Vanity Fair*, and what he has actually done, we are ready to criticise his manner of doing it, that is, his style. Judging from *Vanity Fair* alone, what inferences can you draw as to Thackeray's (a) creation of character, (b) invention of plot, and (c) power of narration and description; in other words, his gifts as a story-teller?

V

REVIEW QUESTIONS

The questions to be asked of the student, in reviewing the works of fiction selected for his study, will naturally vary widely. The queries made by one teacher will not suit another at every point. But I have thought it worth while to give here a few examples of review questions, based upon such different material as Scott's *Ivanhoe*, some selected short stories of Poe and Hawthorne, and George Eliot's *Middlemarch*. They may serve as hints for better questions, if nothing more.

a. Ivanhoe.[1]

I. The function of the opening chapter of a novel is ordinarily to give a picture of the time or place in which the story is to move, or to introduce some of the minor — occasionally the leading — characters, or to strike the keynote of the dramatic action. If it is prevailingly narrative, rather than descriptive, it usually deals with an event from which the subsequent events of the book distinctly take their origin, or an event or scene which must be explained before the reader can advance into the story, or one to the explanation of which the entire book is to be devoted. Which of

[1] Reprinted by permission from the annotated edition of *Ivanhoe*, edited by Bliss Perry. Longmans, Green & Co., 1897.

these various purposes does the first chapter of *Ivanhoe* seem to you to fulfill ? Compare it, for effectiveness, with the opening chapter of Scott's earliest novels, such as *Waverley* and *Guy Mannering ;* with some of his later novels, such as *Kenilworth* and *Quentin Durward*. Study this first conversation of the jester and the swineherd as an example of character-contrast.

II. What do you think of Scott's habit of describing in minute detail the personal appearance of his characters, before he has made them reveal their nature by speech or action ? Do you recall any other novels in which Scott has depicted a worldly minded ecclesiastic ? Compare the Templar with Marmion, in external traits and character, as far as this chapter reveals the Templar to us. Are the references to Cedric and Rowena, designed of course to prepare us for the following chapter, skillfully introduced ?

III. Compare Cedric with other fiery old people in Scott's novels, as Sir Geoffrey in *Peveril of the Peak*, Baron Bradwardine in *Waverley*, Lady Bellenden in *Old Mortality*, and Sir Henry Lee in *Woodstock*. Notice how his talk is designed to heighten the reader's interest in the coming chapter.

IV. Note the opportunity of which Scott here avails himself to describe again the personal appearance of two of his leading characters. Does the delay in Rowena's entrance add to its effectiveness ? Can you give a clear account, from memory, of her features and dress? What is gained by having the entrance of a stranger announced at the very end of the chapter ?

V. For prototypes of Isaac of York, read Shakespeare's *Merchant of Venice* and Marlowe's *Jew of*

Malta. Can you find other strongly drawn Jewish figures in the drama or in fiction? Note that the quarrel between the Templar and the Palmer furnishes a sort of "inciting moment;" that is, an action which involves and leads to the subsequent plot-movement. Does Rowena's loyalty to the reputation of Ivanhoe indicate anything as to the relation between these two characters? What interest is added to the story by the fact that the Palmer appears obviously in disguise? What other instances of disguise can you recall in Scott's poems and novels?

VI. Note how the close of this chapter, as that of the preceding one, is designed to stimulate the reader's interest in the coming tournament. Review the first six chapters, all of which centre in Rotherwood, and see if you have the characters and the plot (as thus far outlined) clearly in mind. Notice carefully whether the main characters develop as the story progresses, or are left stationary as regards mental and moral growth, as is usual with minor characters in fiction. In a romance of adventure, is there much gained by insisting upon this character-development?

VII. Can you draw a plan of the lists from memory of the description just given? Note the points of contrast between the figures of Rebecca and Rowena at their first presentation to the reader.

VIII. In connection with this chapter the description of the tournament in Chaucer's *Knight's Tale* may be read with advantage. Notice the very skillful fashion in which Scott leads up to the entrance of the Disinherited Knight, and the artistic effect of "the solitary trumpet." By what various means does he secure the reader's sympathy for the unknown champion?

IX. What is the value, in this chapter, of the fiction-writer's privilege of explaining what is passing in the minds of his characters? Can you criticise the dialogue in any respects?

X. Note the successive stages by which the manly character of Gurth is revealed to the reader; also the effective race-contrast between him and Isaac. Is anything gained by the reference to the Knight's " perplexed ruminations " which it is not now " possible to communicate to the reader " ? Can you point out any passages where Isaac's talk seems too rhetorical to be altogether natural?

XI. The forest scene delineated in chapter xi. furnishes a sort of comic interlude, midway in the eight chapters that centre around the tournament at Ashby. What are the devices by which Scott secures our respect for Gurth and also for the outlaws? What were the elements in Scott's nature, as far as you understand it, that would make the writing of a chapter like this a thoroughly congenial task to him?

XII. The foregoing chapter is one of the most famous in English fiction, and will repay the closest study. Note that the unlooked-for prowess of the Black Knight, and the discovery of the identity of the Disinherited Knight, furnish it with two distinct points of climax. In the first of these, what is gained by the unexpectedness of the incident? Can you recall similar feats of arms, as described by other novelists? If you find Scott superior as a describer of such things, in what points does his superiority seem to you to lie? Does the dropping of Ivanhoe's disguise suggest anything to you about the danger of over-using disguise as an element of interest in fiction? Does Scott altogether escape the danger in *The Talisman*, *The Abbot*, and elsewhere?

XIII. This is another very famous chapter. The effect of climax, in Locksley's successive shots, is in its way as finely artistic as Scott's management of the tournament in chapter xii. Study it closely. Similar feats of archery are described in Roger Ascham's *Toxophilus* (1545) and Maurice Thompson's *Witchery of Archery*. A mark like Locksley's, and an equal skill, is credited to various personages (Robin Hood, Clym of the Cleugh, William of Cloudesley) in old English ballads. For a discussion of these Robin Hood ballads, see Professor F. J. Child's *English and Scottish Ballads*, vol. v. Do you remember any other characters depicted by Scott who have, like Hubert, "one set speech for all occasions"? (See *Woodstock*, *Waverley*, etc.)

XIV. Note how this chapter furnishes concrete illustration of those differences between Saxon and Norman which it was Scott's purpose to emphasize wherever possible. Why does Cedric's toast to Richard increase the reader's sympathy for both of these characters?

XV. This is a good example of an intrigue chapter, as distinguished from one devoted to the exposition of character or to the depiction of a situation. Its purpose is to furnish a link between two stages of the narrative, and explain the events of the chapters immediately succeeding. What do you think of Waldemar's soliloquy, as compared with similar ones in *Richard III.*, *Othello*, etc., where the villain outlines his scheme? Is a soliloquy, as such, better suited to the drama than to the novel?

XVI. This is another comic interlude, in Scott's richest vein, and is the first of five forest chapters which separate the Rotherwood and Ashby groups of chapters from the eleven chapters that deal with the siege of Torquilstone. For the rôle played by Friar Tuck in the Robin Hood ballads, see the previous references to them. Scott's fondness for exhibiting the human — not to say worldly — side of his clerical figures is noticeable. Can you recall any instances of it?

XVII. It is only an artificial division, of course, which separates this chapter from the preceding one. From your knowledge of Scott's poetry, do you consider the songs in this chapter a fair representation of his skill in that field?

XVIII. Does the language put into Gurth's mouth seem to you invariably in keeping with the character? Notice the relatively slight interest, whether of plot or characterization, that this chapter affords, and then see how the interest is heightened, from point to point, during the next two chapters.

XIX. Note the ease and precision of the character-drawing here, and the rapidity of the forward movement of the story.

XX. The reader should observe how this chapter, like the two preceding ones, directs the attention forward, rather than concentrates it upon the events immediately before the mind. See also the suggestions at the close of the last chapter.

XXI. This is the first of the eleven consecutive chapters that deal with the Castle of Torquilstone. Observe how careful Scott is to explain the technical words he uses in describing it. Have you a sufficiently distinct picture of the castle in your mind to enable

you to draw a rough sketch of its main features ? Try
to do so. Compare Torquilstone with similar castles
in Scott's other novels (*The Betrothed*, *Old Mortality*,
Quentin Durward, etc.). Mark the sharp character-
contrast between Cedric and Athelstane. Do you think
the author's humorous insistence upon the latter's un-
failing gluttony is overdone ? What device, frequent
in romantic fiction, is used just at the close of the chapter to carry forward the reader's curiosity ?

XXII. Is Scott's portrayal of Front-de-Bœuf as a
" heavy villain " open to criticism at any point ? For
the mingling of paternal affection and avarice in Isaac's
nature, compare Marlowe's *Jew of Malta* and Shakespeare's *Merchant of Venice*.

XXIII. The scene between Rowena and De Bracy
is finely conceived, and affords an artistic contrast to
the still more admirable scene between Rebecca and
the Templar in the succeeding chapter. What qualities possessed by Rowena fit her to be the heroine of a
romantic tale ? Has she shown any defects, as a typical heroine, or as a woman, up to this point ? Are
the last four paragraphs — the inserted ones — in
keeping with the general tone of the story ? Do you
think the writer of a historical novel ought to bring
forward actual proofs of the manners and facts which
he uses in his narrative ?

XXIV. Notice the similarity in the construction of
the last four chapters. In each a scene involving two
persons (Cedric and Athelstane, Isaac and Front-de-
Bœuf, Rowena and De Bracy, Rebecca and the Templar) is interrupted by the " blowing of the horn " outside the castle. Do you think that this scheme of
following the fortunes of the different groups up to an

incident that affects them all could be bettered? Why is the scene between Rebecca and the Templar the climax of the four? By what means is the contrast in character between Rebecca and Rowena most effectively shown? In the Templar's story of his own life, do you find any traces of the conventional Byronic hero?

XXV. What details in this chapter seem to you most characteristic of Scott? What are some of the differences between conversation in novels and conversation in actual life?

XXVI. In this chapter, as in the preceding one, observe what is gained by shifting the emphasis so that it falls, for a while, upon the minor characters. Is Scott altogether consistent in the motives he assigns for Wamba's conduct? What means are used to heighten our respect for the moral qualities of Wamba, Cedric, and Athelstane, in turn? Notice how the disguises furnish a new set of interests and serve as an interlude between the more dramatic portions of the action.

XXVII. May this chapter fairly be criticised for its lack of unity? Is the delineation of Ulrica, and the story she tells, unnatural at any points? Compare her manner of talk with that of Mrs. Macgregor in *Rob Roy* and of Meg Merrilies in *Guy Mannering*. What speech of De Bracy, in this chapter, is most characteristic of him? In the discussion about the ransoms, study carefully the motives of each speaker. Do you think the haste and confusion of the latter part of the chapter enhance the effect of excitement and expectation?

XXVIII. Do you consider the opening sentence of this chapter a fortunate one? Can you recall instances, in the chapter, of purely conventional epithets, like Rebecca's "slender" fingers and "ruby" lips? Of sentences arranged in reverse order to give an archaic effect? Of sentences recalling the rhythm of the Scriptures, or that of blank verse? Note that De Bracy's "middle course between good and evil" is one that Scott frequently forces upon his heroes. An interesting parallel to Rebecca's conversation about Jews and Christians will be found in Lessing's *Nathan der Weise*.

XXIX. This chapter is one of the most famous in the whole range of English fiction, and is an admirable example of Scott's power of vigorous, impassioned description. The device of making the observer of the action relate it to another, who is unable to witness it, is at least as old as the story of Bluebeard. It has been skillfully employed in Rossetti's *Sister Helen*, Tennyson's *Harold* (act v.), and elsewhere.

XXX. In this death scene, and in similar passages elsewhere in Scott's novels, do you think the author lays himself open to the charge of confounding tragedy with melodrama?

XXXI. This admirable chapter, the final one of the eleven devoted to the siege of Torquilstone, contains obviously one of the main climaxes of the book. It will be well for the reader to review the characters of the story and the general plot-movement up to this point, with the aim of seeing exactly what has been accomplished and what still remains to be done by the author in satisfying the expectations that have been raised. The account of the capture of the castle will be most enjoyed by those readers who are able to form an exact picture of the building and its outworks. Compare the features of this siege with similar ones described in *Old Mortality*, *Quentin Durward*, *Woodstock*, *Peveril of the Peak*, and elsewhere. Is the manner of De Bracy's submission an adequate indication of the real personality of the Black Knight? Observe how Scott secures our sympathy for all of the personages in this chapter by assigning to each of them some brave or chivalrous action.

XXXII. The few sentences of landscape depiction, at the beginning of the chapter, may suggest a comparison between Scott's novels and his poems as regards the extent to which he avails himself, in the two arts, of landscape effects. Distinguish carefully chapters like the preceding, designed to give a picture of characters in a certain mood, from chapters containing situations or events that directly advance the plot. The freedom with which Scott makes his personages jest upon sacred subjects was sharply criticised by one reviewer at the time of *Ivanhoe's* first appearance. Do you think this chapter, and the following one, are really at fault in this respect?

XXXIII. In this continuation of the comic interlude, begun in the preceding chapter, note the ease and skill with which national and professional types of character are contrasted with each other. The humorous situation involved in making Isaac and the Prior fix each other's ransom is thoroughly characteristic of Scott. Mark his power of shifting sympathy from one side to the other, and of changing the tone of description toward the end of the chapter, as more serious interests again assert their claims upon the reader.

XXXIV. In the delineation of well known historical figures, like Richard and John, how far do you think the novelist is forced to adopt the popular conception of the figure? Is Scott's depiction of the natural treachery

of John in accordance with all we know of that prince ?
Compare Shakespeare's *King John.* In an historical
novel, is it better that some great historical personage
should be the leading figure, or may that place be better filled by a fictitious character ? Study Scott's varying methods in *The Abbot, The Talisman, Kenilworth,
Quentin Durward, Woodstock,* and elsewhere.

XXXV. This is the first of a group of chapters, the
scene of which is laid at Templestowe. What are some
of the obvious advantages of a change of scene in a
story of romantic adventure ? Observe how the reader's
attention, in this closing period of the story, is more
and more directed toward Rebecca. In the delineation of the Grand Master, notice how natural it is for
Scott to make his ecclesiastics either worldlings or
fanatics. The same thing is to be observed in *Peveril
of the Peak, Woodstock, Old Mortality,* and elsewhere.

XXXVI. In this finely dramatic situation, note the
precision of the character-drawing. The " scrap of paper " mentioned in the closing paragraph is one of the
link-devices used to hold this group of chapters together.
Do you find Scott superior or inferior to other novelists
of high rank in the art of calculating his effects and giving the reader hints of them a long time in advance ?
Does what you know of Scott's method of composition
throw any light upon this question ?

XXXVII. It was possibly Scott's own legal training
that made him delight in introducing trials into his
works of fiction. Particularly interesting analogies to
the one described in this chapter may be found in the
account of the " Vehmegericht " in *Anne of Geierstein*
and in canto ii. of *Marmion.* Rebecca's demand for a
champion gives the artistic " motive " for the remain-

ing chapters of the story.   Do you think any irony is intended in her last speech about England, " the hospitable, the generous, the free " ?

XXXVIII. Study the effective contrast between the mental processes of the cultivated Orientals and the unlettered English messenger.

XXXIX. Note what is called " tragic elevation " in the dialogue, i. e. a language removed, sublimated, from the speech of daily life.   Distinguish between scenes that test the moral fibre of a person when he is quite unconscious of any struggle (see almost every chapter of Scott) and scenes like the foregoing, embodying a conscious moral or spiritual struggle, which are comparatively rare in Scott.   Contrast him, in this regard, with George Eliot and Hawthorne.

XL. Note, as before, how the forest scene gives relief from the high tension of the previous chapter. The variety and unforced humor and dramatic situations in this chapter can scarcely be praised too highly. Review the successive hints that have been given as to the real personality of the Black Knight and Locksley. Do they enhance the reader's pleasure in the scene when the disguises are finally thrown off ?   Observe the skill with which the Robin Hood legends and the actual traits of Richard I. have here been mingled.

XLI. In Scott's analysis of Richard's nature, and especially in the words " the brilliant but useless character of a knight of romance," observe how his shrewd Scotch judgment offsets his sentiment.   It is in this capacity for alternate sympathy with both sides of a question that much of his power as a story-teller lies. See Julia Wedgwood's " Ethics and Literature " in the *Contemporary Review*, January, 1897.

XLII. Scott's note on the raising of Athelstane is the best possible comment upon his happy-go-lucky methods in arranging his plot. He said himself that he always "pushed for the pleasantest road towards the end of a story." As a whole, do you think he insists too much upon the gluttonous side of Athelstane's nature for even the best comic effect ?

XLIII. For a parallel to the by-play among the minor characters, at the outset of the chapter, recall the scene between Isaac and Wamba at the beginning of the tournament (chapter vii.). The Templar's last proposition to Rebecca provides the "moment of final suspense" which often occurs in fiction and the drama. In the Templar's death, notice how Scott gives a natural cause for an event which is designed to impress us, and does impress us, as an act of divine justice. Observe how simply, and yet how seriously and adequately, Scott deals with this great theme of the judgment of God.

XLIV. The withdrawal of the Templars furnishes one of the most purely picturesque incidents in the book. Do you think the final disposition of the characters exhibits poetic justice? Reflect carefully upon the last paragraph of Scott's Introduction, which bears upon this question. It is one of the noblest passages in all of Scott's works, and it was written at a time when he had had full experience of both good and evil fortune.

b. Hawthorne.

[Review questions based upon the eight tales reprinted in the Little Masterpieces Series, Doubleday & Page, N. Y.]

Dr. Heidegger's Experiment. How would you characterize Hawthorne's humor, as here exhibited ?

Compare this tale with any other writings of Hawthorne in which the same theme appears.

Do Dr. Heidegger's friends impress you as individuals or as types? Is the final paragraph effective?

The Birthmark. Explain how the opening paragraph establishes the theme of the story.

Do you find evidence here of a morbid imagination? Is there anything fantastic or exaggerated in the development of the plot or the characters?

What do you think of Aylmer as a representative of the scientific spirit?

What do you conceive to be the "moral" of the story?

Ethan Brand. This should be compared carefully with those portions of the *American Note-Books* that describe Hawthorne's sojourn in the Berkshire Hills in 1838.

Can you name any modern stories or poems in which the same conception of the Unpardonable Sin is found?

What are the most effective details in the setting of the story?

What are the most effective contrasts either in character or between scenery and character?

In what sense is *Ethan Brand* a fragment? Suggest a plan for expanding it into a more complete whole.

Wakefield. What are the most skillful touches in the delineation of Mr. Wakefield's character?

Comment upon the union of fancy and imagination in this tale.

Do you detect any irony in it? What are its chief points of suggestion to you?

Drowne's Wooden Image. Comment upon the purely poetical elements of the theme.

Can you describe in detail the carven figure-head?

Is the clearing up of the mystery at the close altogether satisfactory to the reader?

What part of the tale would give a story-teller the greatest difficulty in your opinion?

The Ambitious Guest. Point out the sentences, here and there in the story, that most plainly foreshadow the catastrophe.

By what means has the author secured unity of effect?

Comment upon this tale as an example of " local color " in fiction.

What seems to you its most admirable feature either in idea or workmanship?

The Great Stone Face. Does Hawthorne ever seem to you to err on the side of too great simplicity, as when we say that an idea is " childish " rather than " childlike " ?

What do you consider the most memorable sentence in the story?

Is its ethical teaching too sharply forced upon the reader?

The Gray Champion. What points of excellence in narrative does this tale exhibit?

How can the writer of such a sketch show imaginative power while keeping close to historical fact?

Is anything gained by hinting, rather than actually declaring, that the Gray Champion was one of the Regicides?

General Questions.

Which of these stories do you like or admire most, and why?

What are the most obvious characteristics of Hawthorne's style, as here exemplified?

Taking these tales as fairly representative, do you find Hawthorne's imagination too sombre?

Do you notice anything " bloodless " or " unsympathetic " or " dilettanteish " in his personality as a writer?

If you find these stories excelling most contemporary work in the same field, where does Hawthorne's superiority seem to lie?

c. Poe.

[Review questions based upon the seven tales reprinted in the Little Masterpieces Series. Doubleday & Page, N. Y.]

Fall of the House of Usher. How does the opening sentence strike the key of the story?

As the story advances, what details are most successful in securing a cumulative effect?

In what passages are the moods and forms of nature used to harmonize with human emotions?

Do you detect any intrusion of purely rhetorical devices?

Ligeia. Trace the correspondence in physical features between the Lady Ligeia and Robert Usher and the portraits of Poe himself.

Find instances of description by suggestion merely.

Do the mythological allusions add anything to the effect?

Distinguish between the sensational and the emotional impressions produced by the closing paragraphs of the story.

Do you find ground for Poe's opinion that this was the finest of all his tales?

The Cask of Amontillado. Point out the rhetorical means by which brevity and rapidity of movement are here secured. What is gained by the apparent reticence of the narrator?

How do you think his tone of cold hatred for Montresor is best exhibited ?

The Assignation. Do you find any trace here of the Byronic hero ?

How would you characterize Poe's taste as shown by the interior decoration of his houses ? Point out instances of Poe's fondness for allusions to far-away and mysterious places and objects.

Do you find any use of symbolism as distinguished from sensuous imagery ?

What is gained by keeping the secret of the plot until the final sentence ?

MS. found in a Bottle. Why is the opening page characteristic of Poe ?

What are the most effective details in the portrayal of the storm ?

Study the sequence of the details that are designed to indicate the antiquity of the doomed ship.

What elements of the story seem to you most genuinely romantic ?

The Black Cat. What are the dangers of an opening paragraph like the one here ?

What faults of taste do you discover ? Is too much stress laid upon physical rather than spiritual horrors ?

In what respects, if any, do you find this tale superior to the ordinary " penny dreadful " upon a similar theme ?

The Gold-Bug. What traces of Defoe's influence are manifest here ?

What are the elements that make this story more cheerful than the others in the volume ?

In the main plan of the story, what do you think is gained by first showing the success of Legrand's scheme, and then analyzing and explaining the method he followed?

General Questions.

Which of these tales do you admire most, and why?

Do you see evidence of Poe's lack of power to portray objectively a variety of types and situations?

Do you think there is justification for the remark that "Poe has a manner rather than a style"?

Do you find Poe deficient in humor, judging from these tales alone?

What do you think of his skill in fixing the tone or atmosphere of each tale?

How is Poe's gift of imagination most clearly shown?

Summarize briefly your own personal opinion of Poe's artistic weakness and strength.

d. Review questions upon George Eliot's Middlemarch.

How does the preface indicate the keynote of the book? Determine to what extent the words first spoken by each character are intended to be typical of the speaker. In what ways are the characters of Dorothea and Celia most effectively contrasted? How do Dorothea's strongest and weakest traits unite with each other to help forward the action of the story? Indicate the successive steps by which Dorothea's disillusion with regard to her husband was completed. Why do most of the attractive descriptions of Dorothea's personal appearance come after her marriage rather than before it? What are the commonplace traits in Lydgate? How far did he deserve his unpopularity in

Middlemarch? In the delineation of his professional ambitions and struggles, how much is due to the time in which the book is laid, and how much would always be true of a young doctor with similar aspirations? What are the forces that made him slacken his resolution? Why was his casting a ballot for Tike a crisis in his career? At what point after their marriage did Lydgate definitely surrender to the superior will power of Rosamond? Do you remember any other instances, in George Eliot's novels, of people crippling the lives of others by their egoism? Was Lydgate justified in taking money from Bulstrode? What were the causes of Mr. Casaubon's failure as a scholar? Does your discovery of the serious nature of his illness alter essentially your attitude toward him? What are the characteristic qualities of Mr. Brooke's conversation? Describe Will Ladislaw's personal appearance. Explain his liking for Rosamond's society. Describe Mr. Bulstrode's voice. What hints are given of his hypocrisy before we are actually told of it? Compare him with any other hypocrites in George Eliot's books. Was Mary Garth right in refusing old Featherstone's last request? Is the character of Featherstone overdone? Does Rosamond's alleged cleverness appear in her conversation? What trait in Rosamond is most irritating to the reader? What are the attractive features of Farebrother's love for Mary Garth? What are Farebrother's limitations, as George Eliot seems to have conceived them? What is the process by which Fred Vincy attains to strength of character? Are there any characters in the book whose talk reminds you of people in Dickens? Instance the stationary, as compared with the developing characters.

What group of characters do you consider most successful?

Determine to what extent the first action of each character is intended to be typical of the person. Give examples of very slight incidents which are nevertheless significant " moments " in the story. What situations do you think the strongest? Why? Can you recall any situations that are artistically ineffective? Do you think that the Dorothea-Casaubon plot is on the whole skillfully linked with the Lydgate-Rosamond plot? In what ways do any of the sub-plots affect the main plot? Is there justification for the author's own fear that in *Middlemarch* she had too much matter — too many " momenti " ? Do the plot-requirements of the story force any of the personages into actions that seem out of character? Do you think George Eliot successful in handling the Raffles episode? In general, do you think her gifts and training were such as to fit her for managing mystery as an element in plot? Is she apparently interested in action for its own sake? Does the plot of *Middlemarch*, in any of its details or as a whole, seem to you to fail either in intrinsic power or in its ability to hold the reader's attention?

In the setting of *Middlemarch*, what are the traces of the impressions made by the author's own early life? Why is there so little landscape depiction, when compared with some of her other books? Give instances, however, of landscape in harmony with the mood of a character; in contrast with the mood. What impression do you receive of George Eliot's ideas about the influence of village life upon character? Of provincial life in general? Of the power of environment in determining character? What pictures of Middle-

march life do you most definitely recall, as you look
backward to the book ? Can you think of anything in
this novel which is out of keeping with its general
atmosphere ?

How far are you reminded of George Eliot's own
personality in the account of Dorothea's girlhood ?
Does Dorothea's theory of life, as she gives expression
to it in the latter part of the story, correspond with
what we know of George Eliot herself ? How far
does she sympathize with Mr. Casaubon's scholarly
labors ? Does she betray sympathy or antipathy for
any particular character or groups of characters, or
would you say that her delineation was perfectly impartial ? What evidence is there in this book of her
own revolt against evangelicalism ? Comparing *Middlemarch* with her earlier novels, are you conscious of
any change in her philosophical attitude ? Does the
book show any evidence of the author's artistic instinct
and purely scientific interest working at cross purposes ?
In what features of the book is George Eliot's power
of imagination most clearly manifested ? Comparing
it with her earlier novels, do you discover any evidence
of flagging energy ?

Considering the book from the standpoint of style,
do you find anything awkward or cumbersome in it ?
Why does the theme need, for its adequate treatment,
a large canvas ? Are any of the minor characters
drawn with too much detail ? Is there any violation
of the principles of good narrative style ? What characteristics of the author's writing do you think most
admirable ? Indicate passages that betray through
their vocabulary George Eliot's scientific knowledge.
What do you think of her fondness for moral reflec-

tions ? What aphorisms in the book seem to you most striking ? Does the style impress you as being self-conscious ? Point out passages where the author, not satisfied with direct delineation of action, tries to make the action doubly plain by the addition of analysis and comment. To what extent does irony appear as an element of style ? Do you think the style is always in harmony with the subject-matter ?

Summing up the book, does it on the whole give weight to the belief, inculcated elsewhere by George Eliot, that "character is fate" ? That ordinary causes are more significant, in the conduct of life, than extraordinary causes ? How would you express, in the fewest possible words, what you conceive to be the "moral" of the story ?

INDEX

INDEX

9

𝕮𝖍𝖊 𝕽𝖎𝖛𝖊𝖗𝖘𝖎𝖉𝖊 𝕻𝖗𝖊𝖘𝖘

Electrotyped and printed by H. O. Houghton & Co.
Cambridge, Mass. U. S. A.